JAPANESE INDUSTRY IN THE AMERICAN SOUTH

JAPANESE INDUSTRY

IN THE

AMERICAN

SOUTH

Choong Soon Kim

ROUTLEDGE • NEW YORK AND LONDON

HD
9710.3
U53
T24
1995

Published in 1995 by

Routledge
29 West 35th Street
New York, NY 10001

Published in Great Britain in 1995 by

Routledge
11 New Fetter Lane
London EC4P 4EE

Library of Congress Cataloging-in-Publication Data
Kim, Choong Soon,
    Japanese industry in the American south / by Choong Soon Kim.
       p. cm.
    Includes bibliographical references.
    ISBN 0-415-91402-7 (hc.). —ISBN 0-415-91403-5 (pbk.)
    1. Automobile supplies industry—Tennessee—Management—Case studies. 2. Electronic
industries—Tennessee—Management—Case studies. 3. Corporations, Japanese—Tennessee—
Case studies. 4. Industrial management—Tennessee—Cross-cultural studies. 5. Intercultural
communication—Tennessee—Case studies. 6. Comparative management. I. Title.
HD9710.3.U53T24 1995   95-10266
338.88'7292'09768—dc20   CIP

TO MARGARET N. PERRY WITH GRATITUDE

CONTENTS

ILLUSTRATIONS

TABLES

ACKNOWLEDGMENTS

My desire to study Japanese industry in the American South, focusing on Tennessee, was reaffirmed during my stay in Japan in the fall of 1990, although the initial interest had started earlier. While writing a book on the culture of Korean industry,[1] I learned that in a multinational corporation a cross-cultural understanding among the employees could be as important as and sometimes more important than technical or professional competence. In the southern United States, Tennessee alone hosts 113 Japanese-owned firms whose investments total nearly $5 billion. I began to wonder: What are the major cultural obstacles, if any, to the Japanese business and industrial operations in the South?

But my initial effort (in January 1990) to obtain permission to study a prominent Japanese manufacturing firm was rejected, despite an unusual effort made by Lamar Alexander. Alexander was at the time the president of the University of Tennessee and had been instrumental in bringing that particular firm to Tennessee when he was governor. My research was halted temporarily.

Several months later in September 1990 at the reception dinner in honor of my Visiting Professorship at Hirosaki University, Hirosaki, Japan, a dean of Hirosaki University asked me, "How are the Japanese industries doing in Tennessee?" The dean, knowing that Tennessee hosts many Japanese manufacturing firms, no doubt anticipated a lively conversation at the dinner table. I was unable, however, to answer the dean's question. In order to avoid a momentary awkwardness, the dean commented, "When the Nissan workers defeated the United Auto Workers' (UAW's) attempt to form a union at their plant in Smyrna, Tennessee, by a two-to-one margin in 1989, they had a negative affect on the Japanese labor union movement in 1990. The 1990 shuntō (spring offensive) has been like 'stale beer.'"[2] I was keenly aware of the fact that the UAW's defeat at the Nissan plant had had a major impact on the UAW's organizational efforts in Japanese manufacturing firms in the United States, but I had been unaware of its impact on the Japanese labor movement at home.

In ruminating on the dean's question time and again during my stay in Japan, I decided to pursue my project vigorously upon my return to Tennessee. I am thankful for the financial support for my visiting professorship from Japan's Ministry of Education via Hirosaki University. This opportunity helped me to learn something about Japan and its culture before I undertook this project.

My plan to study the Japanese industrial plants in the American South could not have been accomplished on the basis of my interest and determination alone; it required numerous accommodations from the hosting industry that accepted me as a researcher. Despite my commitment, I had to endure more than twenty refusals from potential firms for the study before I secured permission from four. Such a refusal rate is not unusual, however. In fact, Robert Jackall reports that, before obtaining permission for his study on corporate managers, he had to cope with refusals by thirty-six corporations.[3] Considering such a hardship, I was rather fortunate.

Nevertheless, without the continuous efforts of administrators at the University of Tennessee, my good fortune would not have materialized. Former president Lamar Alexander wrote a personal letter on my behalf to an executive of a Japanese firm, as did his successor and current president of the university, Joseph E. Johnson. Our campus chancellor, Margaret N. Perry was highly instrumental in obtaining permission from the firms for this study. Not only did she induce the two university presidents to seek opportunities for my study, but she also wrote many letters and made many phone calls to convince others of the worth of my project. Former Commissioner of Education of Tennessee and current Chancellor of the State Board of Regents of Tennessee, Charles E. Smith, and state representative Roy E. Herron recommended me to Carl Johnson, Commissioner of Tennessee Economic and Community Development, hoping that Johnson might be able to persuade some Japanese firms to grant permission for my study. I am indebted to them.

Without understanding, support, and assistance from Mike Plumley, former chairman of our university development committee, this project never could have materialized. I am equally indebted to William Boozer, Nick Dunagan, John Gregory, Tsuneo Kakimi, Susan Leigh Lewis, Takao Okamoto, Clayburn Peeples, Bernie Sleadd, and Robert Sperry for their assistance in obtaining permission from the corporations that participated in this study.

After obtaining permission, my fieldwork in those firms was entirely dependent on the goodwill, hospitality, and cooperation of many Japanese and American executives, managers, and workers: Shinichi Chiba, Frank Dilianardo, Jim Holland, Masuhito Iinuma, Chikayuki Kakimi, Pris Lemons, Larry Moore, Masahiko Nishi, Esther Millon Seeman, Jim Winchester, and Hifumi Yasumatsu, to name just a few.

I would like to express my appreciation to Wilfrid C. Bailey, Roger L. Janelli, Larry T. McGehee, James L. Peacock, John Shelton Reed, Mile Richardson, and Clark W. Sorensen for encouraging me to undertake this project. The moral support offered by Albert Gore, Jr., Vice President of the United States, further galvanized me to work on the American South.

Whatever the weaknesses of this book, rest assured they would have been far greater without George Drew, John A. Eisterhold, Larry C. Ingram, and George Thomas, III, who took the time to read the early version of the manuscript and offered many invaluable suggestions. I owe many thanks to Phyllis A. Keller, who proofread the first draft of the manuscript, Bill Stapp, who assisted me in taking the photographs of a Japanese plant, and Vernon Matlock, who developed and reproduced the photographs.

I owe my special gratitude to my two friends, Carol Wallace Orr and Gail Ullman, who gave much editorial advice. I am indebted to Marlie Wasserman for inviting me to submit my project to Routledge. Routledge gave me enthusiastic support and an expeditious evaluation. Kimberly Herald has been a wonderful production editor, shepherding this book through the long process of production. I am thankful to Kathleen Silloway for meticulous copyediting. My appreciation also extends to the anonymous readers for their constructive criticism that has improved this book.

The fieldwork that ultimately led to the writing of this book was made possible by the University Faculty Research Grants from the University of Tennessee at Martin. I have benefited greatly from the strong support of the faculty and staff of the Department of Sociology and Anthropology, The University of Tennessee at Martin. The 1993 Alma and Hall Reagan Faculty Development Award freed me from classroom teaching in spring 1993 and allowed me to devote my time to writing. The Rockefeller Foundation's Scholar-in-Residence Award in spring 1993 provided me the uninterrupted time to complete the first draft of this book at the Bellagio Study and Conference Center, Bellagio, northern Italy, where I also had the privilege of drawing upon the wisdom of the other participating scholars: Donald H. Akenson, Jon H. Appleton, Donald Fanger, Henning Köhler, Gail Levin, Kenneth and Peggy McIntosh, Howard Shuman, and Esmé Thompson.

I was fortunate to have the opportunity to use the final version of the manuscript before its publication as text material in a graduate seminar on business and industrial anthropology at Yonsei University, Seoul, Korea, during my appointment as a 1993–94 Senior Fulbright Scholar. My colleagues in sociology tell me that books are always social products; nevertheless, I alone am responsible for any of this book's shortcomings.

My deepest debt of gratitude is owed to my family. To my parents, both of whom passed away during my stay in the American South, I owe an intellectual and emotional debt that can never be adequately expressed. My wife, Sang Boon, has offered constant encouragement and has been a full-time partner in my fieldwork and in the writing of this book. My two sons, John and Drew, have been my toughest critics. I have benefited from their comments and suggestions.

It is interesting to note that I became committed to this project when I was abroad, and then later also wrote the book abroad. Another noteworthy coincidence is that whenever I have been working on books about the South and southerners, southerners have run for and been elected as presidents of the United States: Jimmy Carter was elected when I published *An Asian Anthropologist in the South* in 1977[4]; and Bill Clinton was sworn in as I completed this project.

Choong Soon Kim
Villa Serbelloni, Bellagio, Italy

INTRODUCTION

In the early 1970s, after Japan took a major step forward economically and its industrial successes infused the consciousness of the American public, "quality control" of industrial products became a major issue of American industry and a household word in America. Actually, the concept of quality control of goods originated in the United States, but it has been publicized here as if it were a trademark of Japan.[1] Extravagant tales of quality, by Americans as well as by the Japanese themselves, have prompted many jokes. David Halberstam entertains with one that goes: "A Frenchman, an American, and a Japanese are captured by a hostile tribe. All three are to be killed but are granted one last wish. The Frenchman asks to sing the 'Marseillaise,' and the Japanese asks to give his lecture on quality control one last time. It is the American's turn. His request is to be shot before the Japanese, so he will not have to listen to any more Japanese lectures on quality."[2]

Japanese Industry in the American South is an ethnography ("thick description")[3] that delineates Japanese industrial operations in the American South. The ethnography describes the ability as well as the inability of Japanese expatriates to understand and adapt to foreign ways of thinking and acting in an alien cultural setting. It also deals with the struggles of the Japanese to remain competitive in the American South, requiring numerous concessions, compromises, and accommodations. It is, in fact, widely reported that the success or failure of an overseas industrial firm depends on how effectively its employees can exercise their skills as workers and also their sensitivity and responsiveness as human beings to the new cultural milieu.[4] In a multinational corporation, a cross-cultural understanding among the employees has proven to be as—if not more—important as technical or professional competence.[5]

With or without such a cross-cultural understanding, direct foreign investments in the United States have increased from $ 13.2 billion in 1970 to $403.7 billion in 1990, a more than thirtyfold increase in two decades.[6] In 1991, for example, Japanese industries in the United States hired 719,400 employees. The manufacturing sector alone hired 337,500 workers, mostly Americans, and paid more than $10 billion in wages and salaries in the same year.[7] More than a million Americans have Japanese colleagues and bosses. Nevertheless, there are very few empirical or longitudinal studies on Japanese industry in the United States. Furthermore, there are virtually no studies that deal with a concrete nexus of social relations in a particular business and/or industrial setting. By providing a detailed ethnographic account of Japanese industry in the American South, this book can contribute to our knowledge of industrial relations in multicultural settings.

During the course of my fieldwork, which focuses on Tennessee, I have searched for answers to questions such as: Why are Japanese industries coming to the American South? To what extent does Japanese industrial management in the American South replicate the industrial relations model used in the home plants in Japan? What are the reactions of Americans—southerners in particular, including workers, managers, and industrialists—toward the Japanese expatriates? At the same time, I look at the impact that the Japanese have had on Southerners—workers, managers, and the owners of industry alike. The impact goes above and beyond sheer economic factors: having to meet the challenges of the Japanese has led Americans to rediscover their own strengths and weaknesses. In essence, then, this book is also an ethnography of southern industrial workers who work for Japanese industry.

AN INDUSTRIAL ETHNOGRAPHY

My original research plan—to study ethnographic accounts of one Japanese manufacturing plant—would concur with the literal definition of industrial ethnography, that is, an "anthropological case study of whole industrial cultures found in a single business enterprise or permeating a given industry."[8] As James L. Peacock concedes, however, "ethnography is always more than describing....[It] is also a way of generalizing,"[9] so I decided to take a broader approach. I wanted to include more than one type of industry in case there could be some differences according to type and size.

Since an enlarged focus would allow more comparisons and some generalizations, I studied three Japanese and/or joint-venture manufacturing firms, one in each of the three divisions of Tennessee; as a frame of reference for comparison, I included one typical American manufacturing firm. Of the non-American firms, two are Japanese owned: one is a medium-sized firm, called pseudonymously Midtech, and the other is a large firm that I shall call Eastech. The third company, called Westech, is a small firm owned jointly by American and Japanese industrialists. The American manufacturing firm included in this study, assigned the pseudonym of Henry Companies, is medium sized.

Eastech, located in East Tennessee, began its operation in 1991 with an investment of $80 million. It is a subsidiary of one of the world's largest electronics firms and employs 320 people. Its parent company hires nearly 200,000 employees and has yearly sales of $37.8 billion. In 1991, Teikoku Databank gave Eastech's parent company a credit rating of A (96 on a scale of 100) and ranked it at the top in sales among 1,208 Japanese competitors.

Midtech, founded in 1990, has 184 workers and is located in Middle Tennessee. Capital investment for this subsidiary is moderate at $12 million; yet its parent company in Japan hires 1,500 employees and carries an investment of $20 million. Teikoku Databank's 1991 rating of Midtech's parent company in Japan was B (70 points), with a sales ranking of tenth among 624 competitive Japanese firms.

Westech, a fifty-fifty venture of an American firm and a Japanese company, is the smallest of the four. Established in West Tennessee in 1988, it employs 86 workers and has an investment of $8 million. Its Japanese parent company hires 580 workers, and its total capital is reported to be less than $10 million, with annual sales of $14 million. The credit rating of Westech's parent company in 1991, according to Teikoku Databank, was C (65 points), and its sales ranking was seventeenth out of 1,062 Japanese competitors.

Henry Companies, founded in 1967 and located in West Tennessee, employs over 1,200 employees, and its total assets are reported to be $39 million. Henry Companies, Midtech, and Westech manufacture auto parts; Eastech produces electronics.

Two of the plants in this study are in essence small- to medium-sized firms in terms of the number of employees in accordance with Komiya and Wakasugi's definition: "in manufacturing enterprises that have fewer than 300 employees or have a paid-in capital under ¥100 million [about $882,000 as of the April 1993 exchange rate]; in the wholesale sector, those having fewer than 100 employees or capital under ¥30 million [about $264,000]; in retail and service, those having fewer than 50 employees or capital under ¥10 million [about $88,200]."[10] Not only do the sizes of the plants make them ideal for anthropological fieldwork, but also their inclusion is important in understanding the core of Japanese industry. In Japan, small- and medium-sized firms are most active in foreign direct investment and are major players in all economic activities in Japan worthy of our attention.[11] Many Americans own some of these firms' products, which include components of various models of automobiles and consumer electronics.

Because this book does not, in my judgement, reveal any business secrets or embarrass the individuals whose stories are included in this book, I thought it unnecessary to use pseudonyms. In the course of my fieldwork, however, I learned that the Japanese prefer not to be identified by their real names or the names of their firms, and I have therefore agreed to conceal their identities. Also, most respondents felt uneasy during discussions in which a tape recorder was present. Some refused to talk with me until the tape recorder was no longer threatening. I therefore abandoned the use of any recording device.[12] All the conversations in this book are reconstructions from my fieldnotes, which were transcribed from my shorthand and memory at the end of the day; nevertheless, I have tried to preserve the original conversations as much as possible. I accept responsibility for any awkward transcriptions or misunderstandings.

Any overly anxious effort to model-build, to theorize, and to generalize the outcome of a single study on the basis of highly aggregated statistics and abstract economic analyses can be misleading and uninterpretable.[13] Perhaps it may lead to a "pebble" analogy, as Francis L.K. Hsu has warned: "Some of our scientific investigations are not unlike counting, classifying and 'computerizing' pebbles on the beach to determine the causes of rising and ebbing of tides."[14] Such a warning is equally applicable to this study. This book is an ethnography of industrial relations, of Japanese industries functioning in a particular setting, the American South, in particular Tennessee.

Despite its significance as the major building block for scientific inquiries, ethnography, particularly its capacity to document local realities, has not yet been fully recognized by some academicians. As Clifford Geertz has indicated, "In anthropology, anyway social anthropology, what the practitioners do is ethnography."[15] James W. Fernandez's testimony is quite convincing as he points out that the works of Bronislaw Malinowski, Ruth Benedict, E.E. Evans-Pritchard, Marcel Griaule, and Clyde Kluckhohn, for instance, are considered "major 'points de repère' in anthropology" not because of their theoretical contributions but because of their "skillful presentation of local point of view."[16] Fernandez relates that "they did not allow that essential academic interest to override local realities."[17] I too want to be an ethnographer first and ethnologist second.[18]

"BOOMERANG EFFECT"?

The research premises of western scholarship on Japan have often been influenced by the socioeconomic and political moods of any given time, despite researchers' efforts to be objective. Similarly, the general public's image of Japan has changed throughout history. Sheila K. Johnson points out in her book, *The Japanese Through American Eyes*, that

> Most middle-aged Americans have experienced during their lifetimes a whole range of attitudes toward Japan called forth in succession by

changing historical situations: rage and fear during World War II, pity and compassion during the occupation, admiration and curiosity during the late 1950s and 1960s, followed by a return to fear (this time of Japan's impact on American industries) mixed with appreciation for her products during the 1970s and 1980s. None of these feelings, moreover, entirely superseded the preceding ones; instead they overlie one another in the complex pattern we see today. Nor does any one individual or social group in America display the entire range of feelings toward Japan. An individual's feelings will be influenced by age, sex, political persuasion, education, and the nature of his or her contact with Japan.[19]

There are, indeed, many Japans in the minds of many Americans. Domination of the American marketplace by Japanese industrial products, especially automobiles and electronics, has changed the ethnocentric bias of Americans toward the Japanese and East Asia as a whole. Once the Japanese were thought to be alien, quaint, and mysterious,[20] as they were depicted in American films, television, and comic books.[21] Currently, some Americans consider that the Japanese way of doing business is rational and efficient, while the American way is inefficient and unproductive. Many western scholars praise the outstanding Japanese performance, even describing it as a "miracle" in works such as *Japanese as Number One*,[22] and *Taking Japan Seriously*,[23] to list just a few. Such beliefs about the Japanese have led in some circles to a "reverse ethnocentrism"—i.e., considering the culture of an other as superior to one's own—in the American imagination, and its new "bias is no less apparent" than that of the past.[24]

A recent trend of reverse ethnocentrism in the American imagination has even mythologized Japan's success, for which the list of reasons is plausible but lengthy. It includes virtually every feature of Japanese history and culture: the unique Japanese historical experiences and family system; its ethos, such as the willingness to accept a social order of horizontal hierarchy; the emphasis on groupism over individualism; the work ethic; high savings and literacy rates; an ethnically and racially homogeneous population; even discrimination against women and minority workers. Confucianism, once considered by the Weberian School to be a hindrance to the development of capitalism, is now thought to be a positive and functional element in Japan's success. The list lengthens when additional factors are included: the close ties between government and industry, the barriers to foreign penetration of the domestic market of Japan, and, most of all, the unique Japanese managerial practices—guaranteed lifetime employment, length-of-service wages and promotions, and enterprise unionism. It would seem that everything anybody can say about Japan's success is true.

Departing from these conventional views, new perspectives on Japanese industrial success have been introduced recently. David Friedman believes that Japan's economic success can be explained primarily as the result of a growing diffusion of *flexible* manufacturing strategies. "Flexible production is 'the effort to make an ever changing range of goods to appeal to specialized needs and tasks with tailored designs,' while mass production is 'the attempt to produce a single good at the highest possible volume to reduce costs through economies of scale.'"[25] Consumers appear to be willing to pay a premium for goods that are semitailored.

In a similar vein, a team of scholars at MIT, in a five-year and $5 million study of the automobile industry throughout the world, claims that the success of the Japanese auto industry (and other manufacturing industries) is largely based on *lean production* instead of mass production. The lean producer:

> combines the advantages of craft and mass production, while avoiding the high cost of the former and the rigidity of the latter. Toward this end, lean producers employ teams of multiskilled workers at all levels of the organization and use highly flexible, increasingly automated machines to produce volumes of products in enormous variety.[26]

Despite the fact that mass production has given American industry its leading position during the twentieth century, there is a growing trend among scholars to reevaluate its utilities, as indicated in "lean production" and "flexible production." Many Americans believe assembly-line or mass production was the invention of an American, Henry Ford. Known as "Fordism," mass production was expanded further by Alfred Sloan in a gigantic way in his General Motors operation. In fact, however, mass production was invented first in China, as early as the sixteenth century, in porcelain manufacturing plants that were supervised and operated by the imperial government. "In such plants, some workers specialized in making the base, some in glazing, others in painting a decorative figure, while still others specialized in coloring the edges. Every teapot, cup, or plate thus went through a number of specialized departments before its completion."[27] There is no way of knowing whether Fordism was an independent invention or a by-product of "stimulus diffusion" (that is, receiving the idea only) from China. It appears that the patent belongs to the Chinese, although the credit for innovation of the existing principle, by arranging and rearranging the ideas, should be given to Americans.

While western scholars' explanations for Japan's ascendancy are plausible, Japanese answers seem remarkably simple, if not naive. For example, Kazuo Ishikure, president of Bridgestone Tire U.S., which has its headquarters and a plant in La Vergne, Tennessee, maintains such a simple view:

"We learned what we know from American scholars and businessmen who came to Japan after the war to teach us and whom we have watched carefully in the United States. There is nothing Oriental or mysterious about it."[28] Ishikure's answer is not necessarily "Oriental humility," but it contains an element of truth.

Indeed, had American industrialists been humble enough to learn the concept of quality directly from W. Edwards Deming and applied it to their industry, they could have done just as well as the Japanese, maybe better. They would not have had to labor in learning a hard-to-pronounce Japanese word, *kaizen* [ky'zen], meaning a customer-driven strategy for quality improvement.[29] And if the Japanese had been too ingrown to learn from William R. Gorham, the American electrical engineer who is considered the founder of the Datsun (Nissan) motor company in terms of technology, Nissan might not be the success we see today.[30] Also, without American engineer Donald Stone's technological assistance, Nissan's small engine, which allowed the Japanese to challenge the West, might not have come into being so easily.[31] The "just-in-time" theory of manufacturing, in which parts arrive from suppliers just in time to be part of the final assembly, is widely publicized as Toyota's invention, yet it is an American creation. In fact, years before Toyota even learned about its logic, the principle was practiced at the Rouge, Ford complex in Detroit. "Toasting Philip Caldwell, the head of Ford who in 1982 was visiting Japan, Eiji Toyoda, of the Toyota company, said, 'There is no secret to how we learned to do what we do, Mr. Caldwell. We learned it at the Rouge.'"[32]

The impact on America of Japan's success is aptly described as a "boomerang effect," that is, like the action of a hunting weapon invented by the Australian aborigines: "It is hurled at a mark—such as a bird—and, if it misses, returns to the thrower."[33] American invention and technological knowledge went to Japan and, in returning to their origins, are now hitting America hard. Americans have been good teachers, but they have failed to be good students; Japanese have not been good teachers, yet they have been good students.

Returning to the subject of reverse ethnocentrism, it should be noted that Americans have conflicting perceptions of the Japanese. "Hard-working Japanese" is a familiar stereotype.[34] Akio Morita, the Sony chairman, urges his corporate colleagues "to ease up, work fewer hours, raise salaries and pay higher divdends. In short, they should act less like Japanese and more like Americans."[35]

On the contrary, a Japanese journalist, Shogo Imoto, depicts a different breed of contemporary Japanese who do not fit the existing Japanese stereotype:

> Japanese are supposed to be workaholics....But do Japanese really toil so hard? After observing people in a variety of occupations, I have my doubts....The average Japanese office looks busy, but appearances can be deceptive. People devote a lot of time to activities that are essentially

unproductive....Former French prime minister Edith Cresson and others have complained that competing with Japan is impossible because its people work like ants. She may have stumbled on the truth without realizing it. Ants have a reputation for being regimented, hard workers, but biologists say only about 20 percent of them actually live up to that image. The remaining 80 percent spend their time amusing themselves or simply loafing. The same goes for Japanese, even though statistics suggest we work longer than Americans and Europeans.[36]

There may be some elements of truth in these remarks. Perhaps the slowdown of Japanese workers is a result of their newly acquired affluence or the "penalty of taking the lead," as Thorstein Veblen has implied.[37] The lay term is "complacency." In fact, as the recession in Japan, which began in the early 1990s, becomes more severe, "many top Japanese executives and policymakers fear that Japan's competitiveness is threatened for the first time in years. Noboru Hatakeyama, a vice-minister at the Ministry for International Trade and Industry (MITI), has even been quoted as calling Japanese companies—which now carry more than a million surplus workers on their payrolls—'lazy,' a put-down once reserved for Americans."[38] Perhaps the problems of the American past are becoming contemporary problems for Japan. There is some indication that Japanese tend to emulate western practices: "Japan's industrial titans...are now doing what the nation has done so often before: borrowing Western practices to make [their] own economy work better. Companies are aping the West to downsize payrolls, merge, and streamline distribution."[39]

If American attitudes toward the Japanese undergo changes over time, so do Japanese attitudes toward Americans. Throughout most of the postwar period, Japanese feelings toward America and Americans were overwhelmingly favorable. The Japanese admired America for its military and technological prowess, respected the relatively benign nature of the occupation, and were grateful for U.S. aid in rebuilding the country. Recently, however, America's stature in the minds of many Japanese, particularly in elite circles, has been undeniably eroding, which has led to a new stereotype, another form of reverse ethnocentrism among Japanese toward Americans. Many Japanese view American industrial workers as lazy, greedy, and unself-disciplined. "America's problems derive, in the Japanese view, from too many vacations, too much greed, too little discipline—and, as only a few actually say but many seem to believe, too few Asians and too many blacks."[40] Former Prime Minister Yasuhiro Nakasone's racial remarks about Americans in 1983, and his notorious "low I.Q." comments in the fall of 1986, caused some dismay in America. A *Newsweek* poll conducted in 1990 gave a glimpse of the negative Japanese view of Americans.[41] A recent *TIME* survey indicated that for decades the Japanese suffered from an inferiority complex, but now it is America's turn.[42] During the *TIME* survey, Masao Kunihiro, an anthropologist and a member of the Diet's [congress's] Upper House, commented, "But many of us, rightly or wrongly, now feel that the U.S. is no longer turning out mousetraps which are better than ours. Sadly, there's been an erosion of the Puritan work ethic in America, a country which taught us so much."[43]

In January 1992, following President George Bush's visit to Japan, remarks about American workers by prominent Japanese politicians generated quite a commotion in the United States. Prime Minister Kiichi Miyazawa told the Japanese parliament that "American workers are lazy, greedy, and lack a work ethic."[44] An influential, elderly Diet member, Yoshino Sakurauchi, reiterated and reinforced the prime minister's statement by saying that "American workers are lazy, illiterate, inferior, and overpaid."[45] Indeed, many Americans fit right into the Japanese image, but others put in long hours of hard work. Nevertheless, Juliet Schor points out that the average employee in the United States puts in 163 more hours a year now than in 1970 and that Americans are laboring 320 hours longer a year than their counterparts in Germany and France. More than 7 million Americans hold two or three jobs to make ends meet. Japanese manufacturing workers put in six weeks' worth of hours more every year than their United States counterparts, but they do it by working six-day weeks and skipping most of their vacation time.[46]

Imprudent remarks by Japanese leaders, like those of Kiichi Miyazawa, have led to yet another alteration of Americans' view of the Japanese and have escalated the already pervasive Japan-bashing,[47] which has taken various forms. In December, 1991, Los Angeles County canceled a $121.8 million Japanese rail contract. In January, 1992, in Japan-battered Michigan, where antagonism ran deep among auto-workers, UAW Local 900 in Wayne pushed foreign cars to a back parking lot at a local Ford plant. In February 1992, a Japanese businessman was slain in Ventura County, California, and a Japanese university president was murdered in his hotel room in Boston; occurring at the height of Japan-bashing, these killings were widely believed to be hate crimes.[48] Not only Japanese and Japanese Americans but also many non-Japanese Asian Americans have been insulted, threatened, or discriminated against because of their morphological proximity to Japanese. Some inconsiderate presidential hopefuls used Japan-bashing on their campaign trails, and worsened the already bad situation.[49] In 1992, the U.S. Civil Rights Commission released a report documenting widespread cases of discrimination and hate crimes against Asian Americans and urged politicians to halt Japan-bashing, saying that the rhetoric inflames bigotry, even violence, against Asian Americans.[50] Eventually, such Japan-bashing led to the "buy America" movement. A senator from Michigan sponsored a bill to give a tax credit to people who buy American cars, as did a New York state legislator.[51] Although "buy America" sentiment appeals to many Americans, they are confused about company ownership and where the products are actually made. Even though Chrysler's Lee Iacocca is a champion of "buy America," his Dodge Stealth is built in Japan by Mitsubishi, then styled by Chrysler in the United States, and sold by the Dodge dealership.[52]

In the midst of such commotion and confusion, some American manufacturing firms, knowing that Japan-bashing is not an answer, are preparing to meet the Japanese challenge. The pseudonymous Henry Companies is one such firm. This book relates the competitive strategies of Henry Companies to overcome American weakness and promote American strength.

THE ACTOR-ORIENTED CONCEPT OF CULTURE

Reverse ethnocentrism may romanticize Japan's success as cultural.[53] Nevertheless, in the course of my fieldwork, it has been difficult, if not impossible, for me to deduce the cultural factors that *cause* Japan's success. Such difficulties stem from the ambiguous definition of the concept of culture itself and the different usages of the concept by different actors who are involved in the study. People included in this study—Japanese, Americans, informants, and even the anthropologist—speak about culture from their own frames of reference. The term culture is often used to explain and justify their experiences and behavior as they infer and imagine the experience and behavior of other people.

In fact, in surveying the anthropological definitions of culture, one can easily identify hundreds of them, ever since it has been defined as "the most complex whole" by Edward Tylor in 1871.[54] "Different schools and branches of anthropology differ in the emphasis they give to culture (for example, British social anthropology emphasizes more the social context of culture, whereas American cultural anthropology emphasizes culture itself)"[55] Peacock is correct when he points out that "anthropologists have promiscuously showered affection on the notion of culture, a notion so obvious in their experience and so central to their discipline. Yet they have never agreed on a single definition."[56] Geertz assesses the status of the concept of culture in anthropology similarly: "The term 'culture' has by now acquired a certain aura of ill-repute in social anthropological circles because of the multiplicity of its referents and the studied vagueness with which it has all too often been invoked."[57] Because of this, there is a continuing "debate within anthropology as to whether culture is 'subjective' or 'objective,' together with the mutual exchange of intellectual insults."[58]

For this reason, instead of verifying whether the concept of culture used by the actors and informants is anthropologically acceptable or not, in this study I employ the concept to interpret one another's actions. An effort is made to explain how the informants themselves employ the concept of culture to interpret one another's actions—in other words, an ethnography of speaking culture. This effort is necessary because this book is about actor-oriented descriptions: "Seeing things from the actor's point of view" in Geertz's words.[59] As Geertz indicates, "anthropological writings are themselves interpretations, and second and third order ones to boot. (By definition, only a 'native' makes first order ones: it's his culture.)"[60] In so doing, the actor's point of view can enhance our awareness of the reality and the various usages of the concept of culture in the real world—Japanese industry in the American South as in the case of the multinational corporations.

Magoroh Maruyama points out that native people are full of hypotheses of their own, which often cannot be dreamed up by outsiders.[61] A Japanese engineer at a Tennessee plant postulated such a native thesis to me: "Although western scholarship uses all sorts of jargon in explaining Japan's success in competing with Americans, I believe Japan's key strategy is application of the art of Judo." His remark was rather brief and casual, yet an interesting interpretation of how Japanese perceive their business strategy.

Judo is an unarmed combat sport where one gets an opponent off balance before throwing the person with maximum efficiency but minimum effort. Since the principal ploy of Judo is using the opponent's own power, strength, and weight against that person, the bigger, the stronger, and more powerful the opponent, the easier one can win—as long as one knows one's own strengths and weaknesses. Also, good Judo fighters must learn how to fall properly, for in their Judo careers they will themselves be thrown.

Like the Japanese engineer, Japanologist Ŏ-yŏng Yi made a similar observation on Japanese business strategy, using an analogy to Sumo wrestling.[62] Sumo, a form of popular wrestling native to Japan, dates back to hand–to–hand combat techniques of nearly twenty centuries ago. The idea is that one Sumo wrestler attempts to throw his opponent, who usually weighs more than 300 pounds, or to force the opponent out of the ring. Although it has more than seventy elaborate techniques, the principle of Sumo is the same as that of Judo: Use the power, strength, and body weight of the opponent against the opponent. Japanese call it "the national sport." The Japanese engineer and Yi seem like symbolic analysts in interpreting the meanings of a culture just as Geertz analyzes cockfights as a symbol of the Balinese view of social reality.[63]

Perhaps the Japanese are as good at figuring out their own strengths and weaknesses as they are at figuring out those of Americans. Yet thus far it appears that American scholarship has been zealous in learning Japan's strengths but less diligent in exploring America's strengths. There is an indication that some Americans are tending to be more like Japanese than like Americans. As James Fallows has pointed out, American success may not come from Americans becoming more like the Japanese but from becoming more like Americans.[64] Even if Americans can learn about Japanese strengths, unless they are sensitive to harnessing their own strengths and overcoming their own weaknesses, the American Judo game with Japan will be a mismatch.

The greatest American strength is ingenuity, which is deeply rooted in American culture. In addition to Deming, Ford, Gorham, and Stone, all mentioned previously, the list of American luminaries whose ingenuity has benefited humankind is long and includes Franklin, Edison, Bell, Salk, Dewey, Oppenheimer, and many others. More than one-third of the annual Nobel Prizes are awarded to citizens of the United States. No other single nation on earth can match the American records in scientific and technological inventions and innovations. Such accomplishments are possible in America because of the tradition and emphasis on diversity and pursuing individualism and creativity. Despite recent industrial accomplishments, Japan cannot match America's innovative and inventive technology. America, however, has given Japan full scope to refine and develop American inventions and discoveries—a Japanese strength.

No nation can easily surpass Japan's ability, for example, to transform American inventions adroitly into attractively compact and miniaturized consumer goods. The Japanese ability to manufacture fine-grained, quality products, especially in compact and miniaturized forms, and their flexible production techniques, are rooted in Japanese culture. As Mitsukuni Yoshida and his colleagues say in *The Compact Culture*:

> Flexibility, love of symbols, small size—these are all qualities that accompany the productivity towards compactness in Japanese culture. They developed and have been refined to an unusual level in Japan partly out of the necessity to use limited space economically, but these qualities also characterize the aesthetic preferences of the people....Over the centuries Japanese have devised innumerable ways to use space that are ingenious in their successful combination of pragmatism, harmony, and beauty. Folding, stacking, rolling, nesting, carrying, consolidating, miniaturizing, and transforming are some of the techniques for living that have created the compact culture."[65]

Characterizing the Japanese culture as one that is centered on miniaturization or compactness, Yi uses a railroad analogy: Japanese do not lay railways but use the laid rails for speedy driving.[66] In terms of science and technology, America laid the railways for Japan. The tape recorder is an invention of

Phillips, but Sony improved its usage in a compact form. The transistor radio is the invention of Bell Laboratories, but the Japanese miniaturized it as a "Walkman." It is as if American ingenuity plays the role of the birth parents of inventions; then the Japanese assume the role of adoptive parents, raising the American inventions properly and effectively. It is a Japanese strength to overcome their weakness as inventors by refining the inventions of others.

If the Japanese ability to manufacture compact and/or miniaturized industrial products is rooted in Japanese culture (as Yi, Yoshida, and others have indicated), another remarkable Japanese ability to borrow and adapt the foreign cultural traits can be attributed to the cultural patterns of Japanese "inclusiveness," that is "the act of incorporating or the attitude of wishing to be incorporated."[67] This inclusiveness is clearly evidenced in Japanese religious orientation. Harumi Befu draws the relation that:

> (1) The person may worship deities of different religions without any feeling of conflict. For example, a Japanese might pray at the Buddhist altar at home in the morning and go to a neighborhood Shinto shrine in the afternoon. (2) Moreover, there are religious edifices which enshrine deities of different religions. For instance, there may be a Buddhist temple on the premise of a Shinto shrine, or vice versa. (3) A Japanese religious concept of a deity may combine elements derived from different religions. (4) A priest of one religion may officiate at ceremonies of another religion."[68]

Such an inclusiveness is also presented in Japanese industrial relations: Japanese expatriates adopt the industrial relations of American industries, if necessary, while they retain some of their home practices. Because of this, any distinctive characteristics of Japanese industrial relations in the American South as compared with purely American characteristics are blurred. The inclusiveness allows Japanese expatriates to be flexible, adaptive, and borrowers of another culture.[69]

IN DIXIE

Japanese Industry in the American South is an extension and renewal of my earlier work on Dixie and its industrial workers in the late 1960s.[70] Since I was away from my study of the South for more than a decade while I worked on the industrial culture of East Asia, coming back again to work on the South allowed me to be "reflexive"[71] in viewing the region and southern industrial workers. Japanese investment in the South has had a profound impact on the economic, cultural, and even emotional life of southerners. Attitudes of southerners toward Asians, Japanese in particular, have changed immensely. The following two tales illustrate such a remarkable change.

On a hot and muggy afternoon in the summer of 1966, a Korean-born physician and friend of mine was mowing his spacious lawn in a small southern town. An onlooker who saw the Korean man mowing the lawn said to his friend: "The new folks who bought the vacant house yonder on Chestnuthill Street must be very rich." His friend asked, "How do you know?" The onlooker replied, "Because they hired an Oriental gardener. I saw an Oriental fellow was mowing the lawn." In fact, in the middle of the 1960s, there were hardly any East Asians in small southern towns other than a few "chicken sexers," people who travel from one poultry farm to another discerning the gender of chickens right after hatching in order to facilitate the extermination of the male chickens. As a Korean American, I drew remarkable attention from southerners while I was conducting my fieldwork in small southern towns in the late 1960s and even in the early 1970s. In contrast to 1966, on a lazy afternoon in the late spring of 1992, as I was waiting for my appointment with a Japanese executive in a wretched diner in a Tennessee town, a server asked me whether I was "Mr. Abe," an executive from Japan. Seeing an East Asian, she automatically assumed that I was the Japanese business executive to whom she was supposed to deliver a message. Certainly, Japan's recent economic ascendancy has altered the ethnocentric bias of Americans toward Japanese in particular and Asians in general.

Throughout this study, I have made an effort to answer the question: Why are Japanese manufacturing industries concentrated in the southern region of the United States? Is it for the so-called "southern hospitality"? The former governor of Tennessee, Lamar Alexander, who was active in "industrial hunting" for the state, averred that the Japanese chose Tennessee because of the remarkable cultural similarities between Japan and Tennessee.[72] In fact, John Shelton Reed commented: "Somebody once called Charlestonians [meaning Southerners] 'America's Japanese,' referring to their habits of eating rice and worshipping their ancestors, and the Southern concern with kin in general is indeed well-known—to the point of stereotype."[73] Many Americans assume that Japanese industrialists have figured out well in advance the advantages of the South, such as lower wage scales, and of Southerners who are white, rural, nonunion, eager to work hard, and unlikely ever to make any trouble.[74] I examine whether the Japanese corporations might possess knowledge about regional and cultural variations in the United States, and the culture of the American South in particular.

Nevertheless, the American public as well as industrialists may overestimate Japanese knowledge about American culture and the Japanese ability to be competitive with their American counterparts. Here again is the tendency of Americans to "over- and under-estimate" their own skills and virtues just as they do those of other cultures and nations.[75] In this case, it is an overestimation of the foresight and abilities of Japanese expatriates who work in industrial and business operations in the American South.

Americans tend to overlook the genesis of Japanese overseas direct investment and its short history. Compared with that of America and other western countries, Japan has a relatively short history of foreign direct investment. Consequently, Japanese industrialists are less prepared to deal with American culture than the American public might anticipate. Indeed, were the Japanese free from external pressure to curtail their ever-increasing exports, they would prefer to keep their manufacturing facilities at home.

The Japanese, like other Asians, have generally been centripetal or inward-looking. "Centripetal" is, in fact, an adjective that describes three Far Eastern countries: China, Japan, and Korea. The distribution of world population today bears witness to this characteristic. Hsu reports the case of China, which is equally applicable to Japan. Although Hsu's figures are outdated, they remain proportionally valid:

> The population of Europe minus Russia stands today at about 450 million. But the white population of the two Americas alone comes to over 500 million. In other words, there are at least as many whites outside of their home continent as within it. By contrast, only less than 3 percent of persons of Chinese origin are outside China today. The Chinese population in China today is about 750 million (conservative estimate) while the Chinese outside of China (including the South Seas, Caribbean, and the two Americas) comes to between 15 million and 19 million (estimates vary greatly).[76]

Many Japanese go abroad. In 1988, 8.5 million Japanese went abroad, 200,000 for extended periods of stay, 548,000 to live permanently, and 48,000 to become permanent foreign residents.[77] Considering the total Japanese population in Japan of 122.6 million in 1988, the ratio of total to overseas Japanese population is nowhere near that of the white European.[78] Because the Japanese have not been emigres to a large degree, they have not gained the experience and history in dealing with other cultures (except occupational forces) that westerners have.

Keeping these limitations in mind, this book delineates the Japanese efforts to learn to live with and do business with people whose cultural orientations are multifaceted. I chose the South for this study because Japanese manufacturing investment is concentrated heavily in the South. Suddenly, the South has become a "new industrial wonderland" of American industry. Industry observers theorized that GM (notorious for closing down American plants and opening new ones on foreign soil) put its Saturn plant in a small southern town in 1985 because Nissan and Toyota had done so well in the southern environment. Thus, the South provides a place where one can study the American competitive spirit in the manufac-turing sector. Also, I chose the South because I have acquired knowledge of the South from living, studying, and working in the region for the past three decades. Although focused on the South, however, the locus of study is not the object of study. "Anthropologists don't study villages," as Geertz indicates, "they study *in* villages," because they "can best study in confined localities."[79] Likewise, this book is the study of Japanese industrial operations in the South, not of the South.

A "DISTANT" NATIVE

During my residency at the Rockefeller Foundation's Bellagio Study Center, where I completed the first draft of this book, a fellow resident was amazed by my identity, and commented: "It is very difficult to conceive of a man who was born in Korea, trained at American educational institutions, lives in the United States, studied Japanese industry not in Japan but in Tennessee, and is writing about it in northern Italy!" I told her, "I'm as complicated as modern industrial products." The Ford Crown Victoria, for instance, is made from American, Japanese, Mexican, British, Spanish, and German parts, and is assembled in Canada.

In the first stage of my fieldwork, I was concerned about my identity as a fieldworker. Because my surname is a typical Korean name, the Japanese executives identified me as a Korean, not an American who happens to be of Korean ancestry. To them, Americans are either whites or blacks. To many Japanese, especially older generation Japanese, Koreans mean their former colonial subjects, and in Japan today, discrimination against Koreans per-sists.[80] As it happens, during World War II, I was educated in a Japanese–run school in Korea, learning Japanese language and culture and observing Shinto rituals. I was even expelled from the school during my grade school years be-cause of my refusal to collect brass bowls and chopsticks to make artillery shells for the Japanese imperial army. Since I personally have some negative feelings about Japan and the Japanese, it is conceivable that a Japanese might have similar feelings, either good or bad, toward me as a Korean. Whenever a Japanese executive asked me, "Can you speak Japanese?" I often answered "No," even though I could have carried on some rudimentary conversations. When the Japanese executives greeted me in their language, I found myself answering them in English. Perhaps this reaction is an unconscious residue of my unfortunate past as a colonial subject. Furthermore, I was taught throughout my boyhood that speaking Japanese in public and quasi-public places in the presence of Japanese is shameful, except when unavoidable.

As a fieldworker dealing with Americans who work for Japanese indus-tries, my initial experiences were different from my earlier fieldwork experiences with southern industrial workers in the late 1960s and the early 1970s. Then, "I was seen as a foreigner and because of that, was commonly assisted far beyond what I could expect. Southerners showed an eagerness to help me with my fieldwork. Even in a town known to have a tough racial perspective, I was treated very well. I was, however, excluded from most traditional customs. Commonly, there was a conditional acceptance relative to my remaining a foreigner and maintaining my foreign identity."[81] This time, many American workers in the Japanese industrial plants did not identify me as either an American whose origin happens to be an Asian or a Korean whose culture differs from that of the Japanese, even if I do share a morphological similarity with the Japanese. Rather, they saw me as yet "another" Japanese, or a "distant" relative to the Japanese. Also, because they had intensive and extensive contact with the Japanese and knew something, either good or bad, about them, they seldom displayed any curiosity about my presence or my "foreignness."

One year after the initial contact, however, as my fieldwork evolved into the second phase, most Americans in the Japanese plants realized that, even though I look Japanese, I am not Japanese after all. Even though I did not identify my nationality as American, they concluded that I am more like an American than a Japanese in my mannerisms, despite my look-like-Japanese appearance. (In fact, I have been in America longer than most of the American workers, who are under thirty years of age.) I came to realize as time went on that the attitudes of the American workers toward me had changed. They had become more open-minded and spoke more freely of their feelings about the Japanese and their management. A good many of them became sympathetic toward my effort and thus became cooperative. Some even became knowledgeable about Korea's long historical adversity under Japanese colonization.

At the same time, Japanese who had close contacts with me over the years began to understand my status as an Asian American in American society. They came to realize that there are more cultural similarities between Japan and Korea than between America and Japan. One told me, "I feel like you are one of us." Some even invited me to their homes on occasion, at which time, we were often able to communicate with each other without using any explicit language; body language alone was sufficient.

A real turning point in my establishing of rapport with the Japanese personnel came in January 1992, when Japan-bashing intensified. In fact, the bashing was not limited to Japan and the Japanese; it actually evolved into bashing all Asians and Asian Americans, since most Americans are not able to discern among Asians. Thus, Japanese executives saw that I was equally vulnerable to the American mood of Japan-bashing, and they started to tell me their honest views of Americans rather than their usual "diplomatic" expressions. They came to realize that I am after all a "distant" relative to them.

By and large, my identity as an Asian American of Korean ancestry was advantageous to my research for this book. Had I been a Japanese American, I might not have been able to approach the Americans as closely. Had I been a white or black American, I do not believe I could have established good rapport with the Japanese. In viewing American culture critically, the Japanese in the Tennessee plants always used Asian culture as their frame of reference when they talked to me, since it acknowledged the many similarities between Japanese and Korean cultures, especially their mutual orientation in Confucianism. I do not believe the Japanese identified me as one of themselves, but they did consider me to be very close to their category.

I was considered an "almost" although "not quite" to both Americans and Japanese during my fieldwork, and I remain a marginal person, which is to my advantage as a fieldworker. As a third party, neither a Japanese nor a white (or black) American, I may have written a book that is not biased toward or against either culture.

–1–

THE SOUTH AND SELLING OF THE SOUTH

Larry T. McGehee, an educator and syndicated columnist for southern newspapers, once referred to a southerner who was foiled in teaching the South to a northerner: "The effort of Quentin Compson, the young Harvard student narrator of William Faulkner's *Absalom, Absalom*, to make his Yankee roommate understand the South ended in frustration and in a commonplace declaration that 'You have to have grown up there to under-stand it.'"[1] William H. Nicholls has commented similarly; "Only a Southerner born and bred can fully appreciate the intensity of feeling with which most Southerners hunger for possessing the soil, love outdoor life, and appreciate leisure."[2] If that is the case, can I—as an emigré to the South 350 years later than the first families—understand the South? Truly, I may never be able to understand the South in the same way and with the same intensity as do native southerners.

Many scholars of southern studies date the progressive New South—economically at least—from the 1940s (especially post–World War II), mainly based on the South's sales pitch to recruit manufacturing industry from outside. In my assessment, however, the South's progressiveness began in the late 1960s and the early 1970s with the reduction, if not the elimination, of its commitment to white supremacy, the abolishment of overt racial barriers, the efforts to improve educational and training pro-grams, and the replacement of confrontational leaders with moderate ones. As a resident of the South since 1965, I have witnessed those changes, as has apparently the Knoxville Chamber of Commerce, which observed of the changing morality of the South in the 1960s; "What is morally right is economically sound."[3] The bonanza of the so-called "Sunbelt" movement in the 1970s further contributed to the progressive development of the New South.

Often southern writers have blamed the industrialized North for the Old South's economic dependency, labeling the southern economy as the "colonial economy." Henry Grady, a Georgia journalist, businessman, and prophet of the New South movement, reflected this southern sentiment eloquently and dramatically when he spoke to a Boston audience in 1889. Grady used as an example a poor fellow's funeral that he had attended in Pickens County, Georgia:

> They cut through the solid marble to make his grave, and yet a little tombstone they put above him was from Vermont. They buried him in the heart of a pine forest, and yet the pine coffin was imported from Cincinnati. They buried him within touch of an iron mine, and yet the nails in his coffin and the iron in the shovel that dug his grave were imported from Pittsburgh. They buried him by the side of the best sheep-grazing country on the earth and yet the wool in the coffin bands and the coffin bands themselves were brought from the North. They buried him in a New York coat and a Boston pair of shoes and a pair of breeches from Chicago and a shirt from Cincinnati. The South didn't furnish a thing on earth for that funeral but the corpse and the hole in the ground.[4]

If there was a colonial economy in the South, "southern blacks were the colonial economy's own colonial economy."[5] It is too familiar a story that does not require any further elaboration. Even today, despite progressive change, the term may be still applicable to blacks in the poverty-stricken rural South.

If my perspectives on the South and southerners are more sympathetic than those of some other observers, there may be two reasons. First, since I emigrated to the South thirty years ago, while the major attitudinal and political changes were taking place, I may have less prejudice against the South than do those who have known the region for a longer time. Second, like many other anthropologists, I have developed an affection for the region and the people I study. In fact, a northern intellectual who reviewed my earlier book on the South accused me of being a champion of the South.[6] I have no reason to either offend or defend the South. Nor do I have an urge to coerce anyone to "put your heart in Dixie, or get your ass out."[7] Even though my stay has been long, and I have two native southerners in my family (my sons, who were born and raised in the South), I do not consider myself a southerner who is fully integrated and wholly accepted by native Southerners. I am marginal. Even if I address southerners as "my people," as some anthropologists do the people they study, I doubt that southerners will ever consider me one of theirs.

Before I describe the history and characteristics of southern industry, some comments on the South as a region are necessary in order to understand the political economy of the region diachronically. Also, since I have used the terms "the South" and "Dixie" interchangeably without defining them, this is an appropriate place to make a distinction between the two terms.

1.1 • States of the South, with Dates of Statehood
Source: Lewis M. Killian, *White Southerners* (New York: Random House, 1970), 155

THE SOUTH VERSUS DIXIE

Where is Dixie, and where is the South? Am I talking about the same region, using two different names? A dictionary definition of Dixie is "the Southern States of the U.S. collectively."[8] Another reference traces two possible sources for the label of Dixie: "A Louisiana bank once printed $10 bills bearing the French word dix, which means ten. According to one story, people called Louisiana 'Dix's Land,' and then shortened it to Dixie. In time, Dixie came to mean the entire South. In another story, a slaveowner named Dixie, or Dixy, was kind to his slaves. 'Dixie's Land' became known as a happy, comfortable place to live. Gradually, the term came to refer to the South."[9] Whatever the origin, it seems to me that the word Dixie contains more than a designation of latitude.

What defines the South and what Dixie, then? Lewis M. Killian indicates that it is difficult even to define the South as a region.[10] Not every student of the southern United States seems to be in agreement as to how to draw the boundaries. George B. Tindall defines the South as Texas, Oklahoma, Missouri, West Virginia, Maryland, Delaware, the District of Columbia, and the eleven Confederate states.[11] Howard W. Odum identifies two southern regions: a Southeast, which includes the eleven ex-Confederate states plus Kentucky, and a Southwest, which links Texas and Oklahoma with New Mexico and Arizona. Some sociologists maintain that "among the various concepts of a 'region,' one is sociologically most adequate: 'the region is an area of which the inhabitants feel themselves a part.'"[12] Most often, references to the South imply the Old South, which comprises the Confederate states of Virginia, North Carolina, South Carolina, Kentucky, Tennessee, Georgia, Florida, Alabama, Mississippi, Louisiana, and Arkansas.[13] It is to this common definition, as shown in Illustration 1.1, to which I will adhere in this book.[14]

If defining the boundaries of the South itself is difficult, defining "Dixie" is equally hard. John Shelton Reed has made the following distinction between the South and Dixie:

> The fact that Dixie and the South are not altogether conterminous suggests an interesting line of speculation and requires that we consider further what it means when an entrepreneur names his business "Southern XYZ, Inc.," or the "Dixie ABC Company," and what it means when a city has a great many of one or the other or both....Some designate organizations that are, or aspire to be, regional in scope (Southern Bell, Southern Christian Leadership Conference, Southern Association of Agricultural Scientists); others, apparently, are named in a burst of regional patriotism (Southern Breezes Motel, Southern Fruit and News, Southern Comfort Massage Parlor.) The prevalence of the former indicates the extent of a city's integration into the region's economic and social structure; the latter can serve to indicate local businessmen's identification with the regional group—or, perhaps, their perception of such identification among their potential customers.[15]

He further elaborates:

> *Dixie,* on the other hand, seems to me to be a purer measure. A business or organization may use *Southern* in its name simply as a descriptive term, but *Dixie* is less likely to be used that way. The dual nature of the word *Southern* and the less ambiguous connotations of *Dixie* means that while *Southern* can usually be substituted for *Dixie,* the converse is not always true....*Dixie* is, as one journalist observed, "a meaner word" than *Southern.* If this line of reasoning is correct, it makes sense that Southern entries should be in large measure a matter of geographic location, of proximity to the region's commercial centers and major markets, but *Dixie,* one might say, has more to do with attitude than latitude.[16]

If these are the usages of, and distinctions between, the South and Dixie, there can be a New South, but no New Dixie. In a similar vein, I can be a southerner—someone who lives in the South—but I may not be a "Dixian" in my heart. In fact, I have never been sufficiently integrated, assimilated, and accepted to be a member of Dixie Land. Despite my effort to immerse myself in the culture of Dixie, coupled with a prolonged period of residency, intensive fieldwork, and formal schooling, I have found that I cannot achieve immersion by my own will and determination alone. I have come to agree with Rosalie H. Wax that "becoming a member of a society or culture of living people is always a joint process, involving numerous accommodations and adjustments by both the field worker and the people who accept him."[17]

SOUTHERN MYTH AND THE NEW SOUTH

Despite the nuances in meanings of the South and Dixie and the differences between them, in this book I use both terms interchangeably. To many, however, the American South is more than just a location in the southeastern United States. In the minds of many native southerners, "Southernness is an ingrained subconsciousness of a people's struggle over hardship, hurdles of poverty, despair, depression, and desperation. It is resistance to dispersal of family and family heirlooms in the aftermath of an inconclusive civil war. Acceptance of defeat has never come to the South; but awareness and understanding of what defeat is have been Southerners' schoolhouses and text-books."[18] To some others, the region seems as "sterile, artistically, intellectually, and culturally as the Sahara Desert."[19] Often it has been viewed as a "dark, mysterious land of prejudice, poverty, and decadence."[20] Still others pay homage to a mythical *Gone with the Wind* version of an antebellum society peopled by aristocratic beaux and belles living in elegant, white-columned mansions surrounded by fragrant magnolias under the pale moonlight.

In recognizing the American South as a distinctive cultural area, many journalists, historians, and social scientists have attempted to define the basic characteristics of the South.[21] Carole E. Hill has compiled the characteristics identified by various scholars and intellectuals.[22] They are localism, violence, religiosity, political conservatism, anti-Semitism, anti-Catholicism, antiunionism, poverty, racism, agrarianism, laziness, a fondness for rhetoric, romanticism, hedonism, a primitive mentality, simple-mindedness, and the dominance of the plantation system.[23]

These characteristics are interesting, and yet it is debatable that any or all of them are unique to the South or even particularly southern. In composition, the population of most southern cities and rural communities is no longer homogeneously black and white but heterogeneous. A vast region, the South contains many different life patterns and thus defies facile characterization. Indeed, almost anything anybody can say about the South is true. As Miles Richardson points out, in the South, there is on the one hand

James Earl Ray, the convicted assassin of Martin Luther King, Jr., and on the other, James Earl Carter, former president and civil rights advocate.[24]

Undoubtedly, there are many Souths, yet the idea of the South persists. When I was accepted by a southern university for my graduate work in the middle of the 1960s, I was hesitant to go to Atlanta because of its location in the Deep South. Fearing that I would be an object of southern racial prejudice and discrimination, my family suggested that I not enroll in the program. Generally speaking, foreigners believed that the American South epitomized White Anglo-Saxon Protestant (WASP) territory and that a non-WASP would be the subject of racism. Even a Korean who attended an American university outside the South told me then that "I've heard only two good things about the South during my stay in America: Beautiful ladies and fine weather." When I visited some Korean friends in San Francisco on my way to Atlanta, they rehearsed the negative images of the South and added some horror stories related to racial segregation. Their understanding of the South was similar to H.L. Mencken's in the 1920s, when he said that the South is ruled by poor whites, that its religion is usually "Baptist and Methodist barbarism," and that its education is close "to the Baptist seminary level."[25]

Fear of southern racial discrimination against the non-WASP, the perception of the South as a region to be backward, and ridicule of the South and Southerners are not limited to foreigners. When Killian, who was born, raised, and partly educated in Georgia, first came to the University of Massachusetts, he moved through a reception line for new faculty. "Ahead of him were several Europeans. Despite thick accents, they were greeted without comment. When he got to the head of the line and introduced himself, he was asked if he longed for home. At that point, he reports, he did."[26]

When I completed a book on the South nearly two decades ago, a scholar from Japan who studied history in a southern university and who was asked by my publisher to evaluate my manuscript wrote an interesting comment: "I went myself to the South as a graduate student of the American history in 1955. In my case there was a time when I heard from an American member of the American Embassy in Tokyo, 'why must you go to the South?' The author believes, as I do, that the South is unduly looked down [on] by other sections of America. The main reason of the South's being looked down by other sections is of course the prejudice of Northerners against the South." Such negative criticism about the South stems from various causes: Some southerners deserve the criticism; some outsiders writing about the South might be unfairly critical,[27] and northern-based mass media might exaggerate the situation.[28]

Even racial bigotry has been treated as if it were a unique southern trait. In a case of racial conflict in a small southern town, for instance, the national media are likely to generalize from the particular to the whole of the

South; but, in instances of racial strife in a western or northern city, the media are certain to specify the city and not generalize to the region. For example, one of the worst outbreaks of racial violence in recent U.S. history occurred in Los Angeles following the Rodney King police brutality verdict on April 29, 1992. The incident was reported specifically as racial violence in southcentral Los Angeles—not Los Angeles, not California, not the West coast. Note Killian's citing of a saying among white southerners that "Southerners love Negroes as individuals but dislike them as a group; Yankees love them as a group but hate them as individuals."[29]

According to my experience, the "present" South[30] is not as poor and backward as former Secretary of Labor Frances Perkins (during Franklin D. Roosevelt's presidency) implied when she stated: "Southerners needed to start wearing shoes."[31] Yet, the image of the Old South lingers in the minds of many. W.J. Cash, for one, made an astute remark regarding the change of the South: "The South, one might say, is a tree with many age rings, with its limbs and trunk bent and twisted by all the winds of the years, but with its tap root in the Old South."[32] Some people assert that regional cultural differences have existed and still exist, that they correspond at least roughly to Americans' perceptions of them, and that these differences are more substantial than are most differences thought to be important in the United States. For instance, Reed reports that some people think North-South differences are "differences in attachment to the local community, in attitudes toward the private use of force and violence, and in religious and quasi-religious beliefs and practice. There are differences which many observers have claimed exist."[33]

Whereas Cash saw only minor changes in the South of the 1930s and the early 1940s, Reed observes:

> And, to be fair, the changes of the past fifty years have indeed transformed more than the physical landscape of the South. For better or for worse, Atlanta *is* the model of the "New South" (a hackneyed phrase popularized by an Atlantan a century ago). The benefits of the South's development are clearly evident—in the pay envelopes of Southern workers, in public health reports, in the statistics of magazine and newspaper circulation, in state budgets for education and welfare, in nearly all of the eight hundred or so indicators of Southern deficiency that Howard W. Odum compiled in his 1936 book, *Southern Regions of the United States.*[34]

Indeed, the southern cities, like Atlanta and Birmingham, that historically had been insignificant before the 1860s are becoming great industrial and commercial cities. By now, most major U.S. companies and leading world firms are located in Atlanta. Atlanta, the capital of Dixie, has become the nerve center of the American transportation network. The William B.

Hartfield Airport in Atlanta is known to be the busiest airport in the United States, exceeding O'Hare in Chicago. There is a saying that "even if you're going to Hell, you have to go through the Atlanta airport."

In addition to its becoming a world transportation hub, Atlanta is commanding attention as a communications and world-event center. Especially during the 1991 Gulf War, Ted Turner's cable television network, CNN, put Atlanta—not New York, Washington, or London—on the map as the world center of news media. The scheduled 1996 Summer Olympic Games, which are already attracting global attention, will also expose the contemporary South to the rest of the world.

Politically, the South is achieving some prominence. For the first time in U.S. history, since 1828 when Andrew Jackson and John C. Calhoun went to Washington, the country's president and vice president both hail from the South. Unlike Jimmy Carter, Baptist peanut farmer from Georgia, Bill Clinton and Albert Gore, Jr., are Ivy League democrats and do not speak with heavy southern accents. Some call them "housebroken southerners" who were elected essentially by nonsoutherners. Yet, they have some "southernness" in their systems as reflected in Clinton's diet that includes not only the traditional chess pie but also "chili dogs," hamburgers, and other fast food. "The populist informality of much of the inaugural week" was also distinctively southern.[35] Clinton's preference to be identified as "Bill," as Carter's was to be identified as "Jimmy," is another southern trait. Whether Clinton and Gore are housebroken southerners or not, their triumph seems to indicate the gradual blurring of southern regional distinctiveness and/or acceptance of it.

THE SOUTHERN "COLONIAL ECONOMY" AND "INDUSTRIAL HUNTING"

Despite all its changes, the American South remains mystic, yet complex, and often contradictory. It is a mix of modern and ancient, traditional and futuristic: "East Texas, for example, is as Deep South in feeling as Savannah, Ga.; West Texas is truly western. Miami Beach is as much a suburb of New York—or Havana—as a Florida city. Yet there is much that knits this land and holds it together, with its own special character and flavor and language."[36]

It seems to me that some significant factors that knit the vast land of the South and its inhabitants together are its deprived economic position in the nation and its capacity for intellectual and cultural development. Southerners feel a relative deprivation in the national economy, a feeling that festers as bitterness, anger, and resentment. Following the Civil war, a lack of invested capital and the surplus wealth necessary to develop industry put southerners to work for the former enemy, the Yankee industrialists. The

South's courtship of competitive, low-wage, labor-intensive industries did not produce the accumulation of investment capital, consumer buying power, and skilled labor necessary for the region's economy to reach the "take-off" point of self-sustaining growth. Thus, since the 1970s, the South has made efforts to recruit foreign capital, using a curious blend of the old and the new. As a consequence of these efforts, Japanese and German investors have landed in Dixie. For many southerners, it is ironic to recognize that they have come to work for former enemies twice in their recent history: the Yankees after the Civil War, and the Germans and Japanese after World War II. Southerners are indeed cosmopolitan, if they do not have a short memory.

A brief description of how the South, under Yankee domination, strove to be a vital part of the nation may shed some light on current southern efforts to recruit foreign direct investment, especially Japanese industry, to the South.

COLONIAL ECONOMY

Indeed, southern history consists of a series of conjunctions leading up to the South's becoming an economic entity in colonial times. Some of these conjunctions were related to the South's ecological niche created by its geography, some were imposed upon the South by outsiders, and still others were created by the inhabitants of the region. Garvin Wright has summed them up:

> The tobacco, rice, and indigo regions of the eighteenth century were simply a few more elements among many others in the British colonial empire, with populations and economic structures midway between those of the sugar islands of the Caribbean and the grain-growing colonies of the North. They acquired some political separateness when they joined the American Revolution, and some economic distinctness when the northern states abolished slavery and the southern states did not. This political alignment was in place prior to the great antebellum cotton boon that crystallized the South as an economic entity unified by the market for slave labor.[37]

Failure of the secession effort of 1860–61 to secure slavery by creating an independent political unit within the nation eventually revolutionized the economic structure of the South. The slavery issue deeply wounded southern morality, and a defensive southern separateness lingers in many Southerners.

Nevertheless, because of its superabundance of natural resources, copious population, and rich cultural heritage, the South could have been a world center. As Rupert B. Vance acknowledged, "There may have been a day when the South was as well off as the rest of the nation. The aristocracy of Virginia and South Carolina, the traditions of New Orleans, the power and influence of the antebellum Cotton Kingdom attest to its early wealth and culture."[38] Yet, that day has long since passed. Instead, since the Civil War, the South has had the lowest incomes in the nation, and its people are the poorest, mainly due to deficiencies in capital, science, skills, technology, organization, and the wasteful economy.[39] Following the Civil War, the South had to make major decisions: To what should it turn for a livelihood, and how could it be best prepared for the future? Since exploitation of the land had been an integral part of the southern tradition, clearly agrarianism was a dominant theme in the economic life of the region. The land offered the highest promise of a livelihood for the future. The price of cotton was high, and most farmers no doubt believed that King Cotton would be back on his throne, stronger than ever.

Economic decline in southern towns and rural areas, however, was visible, especially in the Deep South. The combined factors of worn-out soil and soil erosion—stemming from the kind of crops (mainly cotton) Southerners raised and their method of farming—along with the invasion of the boll weevil undermined the cotton production and processing that were the mainstays of the southern economy. In 1929, for instance, it was estimated that every year more than 428 million tons of top soil were being washed into the Mississippi River alone, blocking navigation and increasing the danger of flood.[40] The effects of the boll weevil were so devastating that the Georgia legislature, for example, approved a measure allowing local tax exemptions for new industries.[41] Even before the invention of manufactured artificial fibers, the southern cotton crop was no longer a gold mine: as the cost of raising cotton went up, the price of cotton in the world market went down because foreign cotton was grown more cheaply than American cotton and sold for less.[42]

The Depression furthur weakened the infrastructure of the South's cotton economy. James C. Cobb depicts the situation:

> The decline of the tenancy system, accelerated by the Depression, was further encouraged by some of the proposed remedies for agriculture's ills, particularly the Agricultural Adjustment Act [AAA]. During the first seven years that AAA policies were in effect, the thirteen cotton states saw their sharecropping population decline by nearly one-third as the number of agricultural workers fell to below one-third of the work force.[43]

Cobb includes the impact of the New Deal as an additional factor that brought about modification of southern agriculture and called for an alternative—that is, industry:

> The New Deal's injection of cash into the southern cotton economy also accelerated the process of mechanization, allowing fewer farmers to cultivate more acres consolidated into a smaller number of farms. More machines naturally reduced the need for labor—either by cropper,

tenant, or wage hand....The suddenly superfluous agricultural worker faced the choice of out-migration or, if he could find it, employment in industry.[44]

Many Southerners realized that mere subsistence farming offered the promise of maintaining only a marginal life and economic status quo at best.[45] In fact, they found that even maintaining the status quo was a difficult task. They were forced to seek an alternative—perhaps industry.

There was a time, however, when some southern businesspeople had a vision that the South could use the industrial model of the Northeast. In 1898, the Richmond banker and railroad president John Skelton Williams, for one, was convinced that in the South there would be "many railroads and business institutions as great as the Pennsylvania Railroad, the Mutual Life Insurance Company, the Carnegie Steel Company or Standard Oil Company. It was assumed, of course, that as such corporations developed, southern counterparts of the Morgans, Carnegies, and Rockefellers would rise with them."[46] During the next few years, millions of dollars of New England capital went into southern plants and investments, mainly in South Carolina, Georgia, and Alabama.

Nevertheless, many discriminatory practices—such as a regional freight differential, a basing-point system, steel price differentials, patent control, and federal tariff schedules; along with several prejudicial acts, such as the Navigation Act, the Wool Act, the Iron Act, and the Hat Act—combined to hinder southern industrial growth.[47] In addition to discriminatory practices and acts, the detrimental factors that attributed to the industrial deficiencies of the South were "natural" economic difficulties:

The scarcity of liquid capital, technical ability, and skilled labor, for example, not to mention the handicap of a late start. In addition there were the chains of habit and custom and the deep groove of agrarian tradition that confined thought in ancient patterns. For the most part, however, these were transitory barriers, characteristic of any economy in the early phases of industrialization. The cotton-mill crusade demonstrated that none of them was insuperable and that the time had already passed when the lack of industrialization could be explained by them. Of the old "natural" handicaps that remained, there were none but were intensified by the new artificial restraints and barriers.[48]

As a consequence of these discriminations and deficiencies, the economic condition of the South was inferior to that of the North. C. Vann Woodward has shown statistical discrepancies between the South and the rest of the nation in per capita wealth and wages:

The estimated per capita wealth of the United States in 1900, for example, was $1,165 and that of the South, $509, or less than half. In 1912 the disparity was $1,950 to $993 in the South. Per capita wealth in the Middle Atlantic states in the latter year was $2,374. These figures do not accurately reflect true distribution of wealth, since they include valuations of all railroads, mines, mortgages, and other properties in the South owned by outside interests....More important for the mass of people was the South's celebrated wage differential, which in manufacturing industries was 12 percent in 1909: $452 per wage earner in the South as against the national average of $518. The differential in the extractive industries, where more than 60 percent of Southern wage earners were employed, was greater.[49]

Odum derived his term "colonial economy" from the fact that the southern region served as the supplier of raw material to other regions, which in turn processed the material and shipped it back as finished products.[50] Furthermore, southern railroads and other establishments in the modern sector were increasingly controlled by northern capital, and decisions affecting the economy of the South were made by men in northern boardrooms. Profits made in southern industries were drained off to the North, and the South remained in a colonial relationship to the North.

Such a colonial economy gave birth to a tributary pattern of Southern economy, according to Woodward, in that:

> Cut off from the better-paying jobs and the higher opportunities, the great majority of Southerners were confined to the worn grooves of a tributary economy. Some emigrated to other sections, but the mass of them stuck to farming, mining, forestry, or some low-wage industry, whether they liked it or not. The inevitable result was further intensification of the old problems of worn-out soil, cut-over timber lands, and worked-out mines.[51]

Under such deteriorating economic conditions, the conservative Nashville Agrarians manifested in their book, *I'll Take My Stand*, that the traditional element of the southern way of life could be preserved only by retaining agricultural society.[52]

INDUSTRIAL RECRUITMENT

Despite the cry of agrarians, many southerners, especially those in elite circles, were in favor of the New South movement led by Grady and the other New South leaders of the late nineteenth century. They attempted to persuade the southern masses that southern industrial growth could be achieved without disrupting traditional southern sociocultural values. This effort to encourage industrial expansion in thirteen southern states (the Confederate South plus Kentucky and Oklahoma) began with Mississippi.

During the Depression years, individual communities in the South granted subsidies and various concessions to attract commercial and industrial ventures. Yet the development efforts initiated by Mississippi in a 1936 program "lifted the curtain on an era of more competitive subsidization and broader state and local government involvement in industrial development efforts."[53] The theme of the Mississippi program was based on Balance Agriculture with Industry (BAWI) and offered various subsidies to attract commercial and industrial ventures to Mississippi. Subsequently, the Mississippi legislature enacted a law allowing five-year tax exemptions and permitting cities to finance through referenda the construction of new buildings to lure industries.[54]

In speaking to the legislature about passage of the original bill, Governor Hugh Lawson White of Mississippi echoed the voices of many southern politicians: "Our high percentage of native Anglo-Saxon citizenship, with an absence of the disturbing elements so common to large industrial centers, offers a great attraction for those looking for new fields in which to establish their factories."[55] White's speech served as an open invitation to employers in all regions of the country. Both southerners and the southern-based employers realized that the invitation was an offer of cheap labor with no labor unions attached.[56] Similar plans were adopted throughout most of the southern states, although the plans varied slightly.

Following the BAWI program in Mississippi, there was a full surge of industrial inducement programs in southern states. Industry-hungry communities in Tennessee, for example, engaged in extreme forms of industrial subsidization with little apparent regard for the state constitution's specific prohibition of such activities. "A 1937 survey of forty-one communities revealed that fifty-six plants built in the previous seven years had received some form of subsidy."[57] In the case of a garment factory in Manchester, Tennessee, workers were forced to pay for the plant at which they worked through 5 to 7 percent deductions from their salaries. A typical contract read: "I the undersigned hereby make application for employment at the garment factory erected by the town of Manchester, Tenn., that in the event of employment at the said town of Manchester, Tenn., securing employment for me with operator of said factory, I will pay to the said town of Manchester, Tenn., 6 percent of my weekly salary or wage to be paid as directed by the aforesaid town."[58] Employees of a Pennsylvania garment plant located in Dickson, Tennessee, and of the General Shoe Corporation in Lewisburg, Tennessee, agreed to similar payroll deductions for building funds.[59]

Subsidization was not exclusive to Tennessee. Douglasville, Georgia, provided a building for a garment plant, paid the employees' training wages, and granted the company a five-year tax exemption. Some cities in Arkansas purchased sites and made other grants available for municipal construction and industrial buildings. Counties in South Carolina provided free sites for textile mills. And a few communities in Alabama provided land and buildings for industrial plants.[60]

By and large, despite the effort, expenses, and publicity, "the industrial development promotions of the late 1930s were of modest scope and debatable effect."[61] Nevertheless, the movement brought in some industries to the region, even though they were low-paying industries. Southern wage earners were pragmatic and realistic and believed the common lamentation that a low wage is still better than no wage at all and that a wage from an industrial plant is still better than the whole family's subsistence-level farm income. The late 1930s BAWI program may be viewed as a meritorious prelude to southern growth since the 1940s, especially after World War II, and to the globalization effort of the 1970s, 1980s, and 1990s. The BAWI effort reduced regional parochialism in the South and strengthened the South's ability to recruit direct investment from abroad, especially from Japan. In the future, perhaps the BAWI will be credited with the ascendancy of the South over the other regions of the nation.

THE RESURGENCE OF "INDUSTRIAL-HUNTING"

The impact of the southern inducement to attract industries to the South was moderate in terms of any substantial change in the South's economy in the 1930s.[62] Yet the southern penchant for industry-hunting has continued and employs new as well as old methods. In the case of Tennessee, the advent in 1933 of the Tennessee Valley Authority (TVA),[63] which supplied a rather inexpensive and ample source of power, was a major attraction of industries to the state and also promoted technological improvements in agriculture.

Ralph McGill states that "it was not until the Second World War that the South made a substantial advance in absolute and relative income gains....During the five years from 1940 through 1944, Southern income payments rose from 12.5 billion dollars to 29.7 billion, an increase of one hundred fifteen percent."[64] When World War II began in Europe, the need for materials of war brought a few industries to Tennessee. The Oak Ridge National Laboratory and the Arnold Air Engineering Center at Tullahoma demonstrated the highly developed state of American science and technology, and they are still functioning.

The crusade for new industry started after World War II, mobilizing state and local governments, key public officials, growth-oriented business leaders, and influential private citizens. At the end of the 1940s the personnel of state planning and development boards included professionals. Some states, like Tennessee, preferred directors with training and experience in local and regional planning. Tennessee's Planning Commission employed twenty-eight persons in 1947, and its staff was trained in fields as diverse as history and geology.[65] Planning and strategy were called for, because southern industrial promoters were caught in an accelerating trend toward interregional and interstate competition for new plants. Governors responded to the escalated competition for industry by calling attention to the deficiencies of rival states.

In 1953, when the Tennessee Industrial and Agricultural Development Commission (TIADC) was established, primarily to develop new industry and to encourage the expansion of existing industries, it announced its plans to explain to all possible investors the advantages that Tennessee held for industrial location. Advertising in the *New York Times* and other newspapers of wide circulation began in 1953.[66] One advertisement selling Tennessee read:

> Pinpoint your growth opportunities in SCIENTIFIC TENNESSEE. If you're a science-oriented industry, you'll be right at home in Scientific Tennessee! The state is rich in technology with 24 research centers, 47 colleges and universities, Arnold Air Engineering Center, Oak Ridge National Laboratory, University of Tennessee Space Institute and many scientific companies. Shouldn't you see about Tennessee…now?[67]

The emphasis on science here is ironic, as Tindall noted, because almost exactly forty years earlier, the sovereign state of Tennessee essentially had outlawed the teaching of science! Tindall was referring, of course, to the prohibition against teaching the theory of evolution, the upshot of the well-publicized trial of John Scopes in Tennessee in 1927.

The efforts to recruit industry to Tennessee were not limited to newspaper advertisements. In 1954, a traveling representative made frequent trips to northern cities to depict the attraction of Tennessee to potential investors. State officials and prominent businessmen as well traveled often to northern and eastern industrial cities, including New York, Chicago, and Detroit. "In 1945–1946 the state had expended only $17,889 for industrial development; in the biennium of 1958–1959 it spent $233,803. Further, the staff of the Industrial Commission expanded from four in 1948 to twenty in 1959."[68] The efforts brought a remarkable result. "Of the states with 250,000 or more industrial jobs in 1955, Tennessee made the greatest industrial gains during the decade 1955–1965. Tennessee's 28 percent gain in manufacturing jobs compared with 25 percent in Florida, North Carolina, and South Carolina, and 21 percent in Texas."[69]

The courting of northern industry was not confined to Tennessee. By the mid 1950s, southern governors had begun to make frequent industry-hunting trips to the industrial-rich North. Such trips by governors engendered some resentment among northerners, who called the efforts "industrial piracy" and "raids."[70] One writer produced a facetious dialogue dealing with a southern governor's visit to a northern corporate headquarters. While the southern governor was waiting, the northern manager's secretary informed her boss of the governor's visit:

Secretary: There is a salesman here to see you.
Manager: Does he have an appointment?
Secretary: No.
Manager: What's he selling?
Secretary: A state.
Manager: A what? Who is he?
Secretary: He claims he's the governor.[71]

However humiliating the sales calls, and however hard the recruiting process, the southern effort brought substantial industry and concomitant economic gains to the South. By 1954 the South's goods-producing industry had an output value of $60 billion as compared with that of $11 billion in 1939. And between 1956 and 1959, almost 5,000 new industrial plants were located in the South.[72]

In its hunt for industry, the South's selling points were good climate, low taxes, cooperative government, and an abundance of eager, nonunion labor. The right-to-work laws in all eleven southern states, excluding Kentucky, were another selling point.[73] Some promotional advertisements emphasized "Anglo-Saxonism" and "a pool of labor drawn almost entirely from pure American stock." An advertisement lauding Louisville, Mississippi, carried a picture of a worker with the descriptive caption, "He speaks English!" and "Labor in Louisville doesn't require foremen who speak half a dozen different languages. Our workers are *Americans*. They talk and think American."[74] The hidden message, of course, emphasized the state's native-born population and revealed the bias against foreigners and their alleged propensity for joining labor unions. "Other advertisements stressed individualism, suspicion of outsiders, and willingness to give 'a day's work for a day's pay.'"[75]

Advertising to sell the South to new industries became aggressive in the 1960s. "The *New York Times* sold a total of $46,000 in state advertising space in 1949, but that amount had increased to $520,000 by 1961. The 295 state and local groups that responded to a Curtis Publishing Company Survey in 1961 anticipated a twelve-month investment in advertising of $3,287,330 with state appropriations representing approximately 79 percent of the figure."[76] For instance, "The 'Forward Atlanta' movement launched at the beginning of the 1960s aimed at making the Georgia capital more competitive with faster-growing southern rivals. The campaign raised about $1.6 million through private donations, approximately one-half of which went for advertising."[77] For 1964, the southern states averaged an annual budget for advertising that was more than 170 percent of the average for thirty-one states that reported their advertising budgets.

The manner and contents of the advertising had changed since Governor White's open invitation of the late 1930s. In the mid-sixties in Tennessee, for example:

> the Division for Industrial Development attempted to enlist both federal and state agencies in the promotional effort. The Tennessee Valley Authority had long been a boon to the state's development program. TVA's lakes supplied low-cost power, and its staff researchers provided information about raw materials, markets, and potential industrial sites. Such assistance facilitated the conversion of abandoned Stewart Air Force Base into an industrial center. In cooperation with TVA, the Division for Industrial Development asked that a new industry be supplied with water from Cave Lake State Park. In August, 1967, the chief geologist of the State Department of Conservation accompanied Industrial Development staffers on a trip to New Orleans to make a presentation to an industrial prospect.[78]

Tennessee even enlisted singer Eddy Arnold in the industrial-hunting brigade by naming him a member of the Tennessee Agricultural and Industrial Development Commission (TAIDC).[79]

By the end of the 1960s, as the region's economy began to reach the take-off point of rapid and self-sustaining growth, the South's sales pitch for the more sophisticated industries had begun. It was a blend of the old and the new: the familiar assurances of cheap, nonunion labor and low taxes, on the one hand, and new promises of tailor-made work forces, scientific knowledge and skills supplied by research facilities in the region, and a work force provided at state expense. At the same time, the South lacked high-skilled jobs. As McGill notes:

> For generations the South has watched many of her best young men and women leave—along with the poorly prepared—for cities in the East and West where there was more opportunity. Georgia's excellent Georgia Institute of Technology annually is made proud of the fact that the nation's large corporations snap up its graduates. But there is a frustration in the fact that a heavy majority of the positions are outside the South. The tide has not yet turned—but the flow of it has slowed.[80]

But by the 1970s, the tide had certainly turned. The exodus of skilled labor had become an influx. A new southern attitude developed: "In the past the Yankees came down to the South to see the South, but now they are coming down to live for good."[81]

The effort to recruit sophisticated and skill-intensive industries rather than low-wage and labor-intensive ones brought about a fruitful result in

North Carolina at the Research Triangle Park, which was conceived in the mid-1950s. As part of its plan to attract sophisticated industries to the region, it was located near three excellent universities: Duke in Durham, North Carolina State in Raleigh, and the University of North Carolina in Chapel Hill. By the mid-1960s, such newly emerging centers in the South won government research dollars, thereby expanding research for private firms and recruiting sophisticated industries to the region. The triangle region experienced a 28 percent increase in population, and per capita income rose significantly. By 1977, there were over twenty research facilities in the park, including IBM, which alone employed over 3,000 people. The park became a mecca for federal research offices, including the Environmental Protection Agency's main research center and the National Center for Health Statistics. The park's success significantly altered the demographics of the region by attracting highly educated, well-paid professionals. "By the mid-1970s the local population included more Ph.D.s per 100,000 people than any other metropolitan area in the country."[82]

Oak Ridge, Tennessee, with its National Laboratory and Atomic Energy Center, located near the University of Tennessee, also contains a high density of Ph.D.s. Currently, Oak Ridge and Knoxville together, within a stone's throw of each other, host more than 2,000 Ph.D.s. The Research Triangle concept spread in the South to include, among others: The Virginia Science Center; the Virginia Association Research Center, sponsored jointly by the University of Virginia, the College of William and Mary, and the Virginia Polytechnic Institute; and the University of Georgia's Research Park.

The growth of the South since the 1970s has been faster than that of the nation as a whole. In-migration beginning around 1970 gave the region a net gain over out-migration of 2.9 million people between 1970 and 1976. "Per capita incomes increased by 500 percent between 1955 and 1975, as opposed to only a 300 percent rise nationwide. Median family income rose by 50 percent between 1965 and 1975, while the national increase was only 33 percent....By the mid-seventies financial experts perdicted that between 1975 and 1986 half as many jobs would be created in the South as in the North or West."[83] The South no longer remained an isolated regional economy; it had become an integrated part of the national economy. The problems the South has been facing are no longer just problems of the South but problems of the nation.

THE "PRIVILEGE OF BACKWARDNESS"

The phenomenal growth of the South from the 1970s through the 1990s has not been solely the result of aggressive promotion and industrial recruitment. The South matured industrially by taking advantage of and building from its inherent weaknesses. There were several important factors in the process.

First, the concept of the "privilege of backwardness," used by Leon Trotsky, Alexander Gershenkron, Marshall D. Sahlins, and Elman R. Service to explain the rapid growth of some regions that were late to industrialize, is applicable to the South.[84] Since the South is less industrialized than the North, the South has more potential to grow than the North and to learn and borrow the North's technology quickly and inexpensively. Indeed, southern potential has been enormous, while the North has been suffering the "penalty of taking the lead," as Veblen concluded about Germany.[85] Most of the time, a less developed region has more potential to grow in terms of evolutionary potential, as Sahlins and Service have implied,[86] but the rapid growth of the South is relative, since average per capita income in every southern state has continued to be below the national average.[87]

Second, the South's efforts to improve education and provide training programs increased the market value of the South to outside industrialists. Historically, southern educational programs lagged far behind the rest of the nation's, a regrettable condition in a region that was attempting to attract skilled workers. The region had the highest dropout rate and lowest per-pupil expenditures for public schools. In the 1940s, per-pupil expenditure in southern systems was only 50 percent of the national average. This figure had climbed to 70 percent in 1950, but rose only 1 percent in the next decade. By 1968, average per pupil expenditures in the South stood at 78 percent of the national mean.[88] Southern industrial promoters came to realize that more rapid educational development was closely aligned to the region's economic progress. Cobb relates that:

> As the focus shifted in the late 1950s and early 1960s to more sophisticated, better-paying industries, it appeared that the quality of local schools might be a critical determinant of a community's overall attractiveness to new industry. Citing the importance of good schools, one corporate spokesman remarked: "There are all sorts of places that look like good sites in the boondocks of such states as Louisiana. They have water, sulphur, gas—everything we need. But you can't get anyone to go there to work."[89]

Many industrial firms that were considering moves pointed to a site's educational facilities as an important factor. Most firms, such as General Motors, Minnesota Mining and Manufacturing, and the Celanese Corporation (to name just a few), claimed to give special consideration to areas served by universities or junior colleges. As a case in point, after a $17 million industrial plant pointed out that Union City, Tennessee, had the worst school system among its eight potential locations, the city constructed a new high school.[90] "By the end of the 1960s, much of the South's educational system was involved in direct or indirect support of the most sophisticated industries in the region. Cooperation between educators and development leaders was yet another example of the extent to which the Southern states committed their public resources and relevant institutions to the crusade for industrial progress."[91]

In addition to improved education, southern recruiters of new industries saw the need for vocational training in order to supply adequate numbers of well-trained workers. Encouraged by the success of a Florida program that began in the mid-1950s, all of the southern states in the 1960s offered vocational training programs (as well as postsecondary preparation) at the secondary level. Also, during the 1960s, southern legislators cooperatively approved expenditures designated to place regional vocational-technical education centers within reasonable driving distance of every citizen. Tennessee, for example, had twenty-nine training facilities across the state, and the state made use of colleges and universities in its training programs, as did other southern states. The impact of available vocational-technical education has been documented in the case of South Carolina: between 1967 and 1971, manufacturers who had opened plants in South Carolina ranked the state's training program as the fifth most important factor influencing their location decisions.[92] Its impact was no doubt similar in other southern states.

By the mid-1980s, efforts toward improving educational systems were more visible in the South than in other regions, although a reform movement in America's schools became a national agenda beginning in April 1991. Yet if the South looks to go above and beyond the other regions of the nation to meet the demands of the twenty-first century, improving the region's educational and training systems remains a challenge as well as a burden. Early in 1991, the governor of Tennessee, Ned Ray McWherter, proposed education reforms that would cost $628 million and require the institution of a state income tax; he failed to obtain support from the state legislature. The educational programs in the South have a long way to go.

The third factor whereby the South capitalized on a weakness was the improvement of race relations. Gradual and painful though it may have been, the improvement not only bettered the image of the South but also contributed to the recruitment of new industries to the South. As civil rights concerns increased in the late 1950s and early 1960s, most image-conscious, nationally known firms shied away from areas where racial discrimination still officially prevailed and uprisings threatened. There were indeed some ugly scenes of southern racial strife, such as the blocking of integration at Little Rock's Central High School in 1957; the desegregation crisis in New Orleans in 1960; racial violence in Birmingham in 1961, in Oxford in 1962, and at the University of Alabama in 1963; and the slaying of civil rights workers in Philadelphia, Mississippi, in 1964, to name just a few. After the three civil rights workers were killed in Mississippi, one small factory moved across the state line of Mississippi into Louisiana in order to avoid having a Mississippi mailing address.[93]

Some southern media warned that racial turmoil would slow industrial growth. A survey conducted by the Atlanta *Constitution* revealed that 17.1 percent of key industrial and university personnel would leave Georgia if public schools were closed because of racial strife.[94] Because of a relative lack of racial strife, however, the population of Atlanta grew by 40 percent between 1950 and 1960, while the growth of Birmingham was only 14 percent in the same period, due to the city's negative reputation.[95] Cobb notes that "a look at states with reputations for slightly more moderation finds Georgia making significant gains after 1960 (and the Atlanta and University of Georgia integration decision in 1961). Texas, North Carolina, and Tennessee remained near the top in absolute growth in manufacturing employment throughout the period."[96]

It is difficult to evaluate directly the impact of racial strife on the recruiting of industry. Yet,

> judging from the number of cases cited wherein racial troubles in various southern states were said to have caused certain communities to lose prospective industries, it seems reasonable to suppose that those states that made the most peaceful transitions to desegregated facilities would also be those that attracted the most industry during the Civil Rights era. On the other hand, states where well-publicized defiance flared into violence could be expected to have enjoyed little success in attracting new plants.[97]

The *Chronicle* of Augusta, Georgia, came to the same opinion when it asserted that new industry would be scared away if Augusta could not solve school desegregation.[98]

Due to the growing moral soul-searching regarding racial justice by southerners themselves as well as by outsiders, and due to the passage of the 1964 Civil Rights Act, the South's previous commitment to white supremacy has changed significantly, and overt racial barriers have been abolished. In fact, while an estimated 6.5 million blacks fled northward between 1910 and 1970, since the 1970s the number of blacks returning to the South has exceeded the number moving out. In January 1990, *TIME* reported that "for the first time in more than a century the proportion of black Americans living in the South had taken an upward climb: 56% lived in the region in 1988, up from 52% in 1980."[99] Under the title of "You Can Go Home Again," *TIME* reported the stories of repatriated blacks who found the South more hospitable than the urban North.[100]

The fourth factor was the "Sunbelt" movement that began in the late 1960s and the early 1970s and that was another bonanza for southern industrial development. The old manufacturing belt, where the bulk of American heavy industry had grown to maturity for well over a century, became stagnant by the end of the 1960s; the warm, less-developed states of the Sunbelt were logical choices for new industrial sites. There were the familiar assurances of cheap, nonunion labor, low taxes, tailor-made work forces, and research assistance provided at state expense. Relaxed life styles, lower living costs, and an easing of racial tension were added inducements for an increasing number of Americans, including industrialists, to move southward.

"Sunbelt" originally referred to the states of Arizona, California, Florida, and Texas, but occasionally individual cities or areas in Georgia, New Mexico, and even Tennessee were included as part of this new quasi-region.[101] Instead of the Sunbelt, Kirkpatrick Sale called the area the "Southern rim" and included the lower third of the nation below the 37th parallel, where average annual temperatures exceed 60 degrees and the sun shines 250 to 350 days a year. The southern rim is wide enough to contain all the Confederate states, excluding Virginia.[102] Roger W. Schmenner defined the Sunbelt as South Atlantic, East South Central, West South Central, and Mountain.[103] In the 1970s, however, both terms—Sunbelt or Southern rim—became "increasingly interchangeable with the South."[104] Among southern states, the cornerstone of the Sunbelt was Florida, but most of the neighboring southern states did their best to grab some of the spin-offs from Florida, and southern promoters have attempted to capitalize on the bandwagon effect of the Sunbelt movement.

By the 1970s, southerners were no longer regarded as the backward people of the nation. Northern media started to report a positive side to the South, referring to a "New America." Southerners themselves began to have more self-respect; as one writer has written, "We Ain't Trash No More."[105] Political leadership of the South opened a new chapter: the region moved away from the confrontational politics of George Wallace and Lester Maddox to the moderate progressivism of Reubin Askew and Jimmy Carter. Carter's winning bid for the presidency in 1976 was based on his abiding religious faith and sincere concern for his fellow human beings, both black and white. William Lee Miller calls Carter the "Yankee from Georgia."[106] During the presidential campaign in 1992, with two southern sons on the ticket, "southern identities" were seldom an issue.

Foreign direct investment in the South kept pace with the region's progress. The early 1970s saw foreign industrial investment come to the South, and by the end of 1972, foreign firms had invested more than $5 billion. By 1978, many southern states, led by South Carolina, North Carolina, and Virginia, were attracting as much as $1 billion annually. Georgia and other southern states followed suit, with Georgia, for instance, quickly opening its outposts in Brussels, Sao Paulo, Toronto, and Tokyo.[107] Southern governors were heading for Tokyo as their predecessors had once gone to the industrial states of the North.

– 2 –

SOUTHERN INCENTIVES AND JAPANESE INVESTMENT

As Gunnar Myrdal has observed, "'the southern gentleman,' 'southern lady,' and 'southern hospitality' are proverbial, even if stereotyped."[1] Whether they are proverbial or not, such designations of the South and southerners are unique, for there are no equivalencies such as "western gentleman," "midwestern lady," or "northern hospitality." Nevertheless, just as there are many "Souths," there are many forms of southern hospitality. At times, the southern hospitality displayed to foreigners is so generous that some become suspicious about its underlying motives. Some overly sensitive foreigners might interpret the egregious benevolence to be a backhanded form of southern prejudice. Others might unwittingly abuse southern hospitality. I, for one, certainly have taken advantage of southern hospitality in my fieldwork. If southerners are hospitable to foreign guests in general, surely they are particularly hospitable to the Japanese who bring their capital with them and create jobs for southerners.

Cobb relates that southern hospitality toward foreign industrialists has taken the forms of "red-carpet" and "kid-glove" treatment.[2] South Carolina provides several examples. When some foreign executives inquired about tax rates in South Carolina, they suddenly found themselves in the office of the state tax commissioner sipping Coke and getting answers. Cooperative customs officials in Charleston helped South Carolina's Michelin Tire Corporation get equipment unloaded and inspected less than forty-eight hours after a freighter docked, although the same work would have taken from two to three weeks to accomplish in France. Governor John C. West of South Carolina provided a state plane for an English executive's visit to Charleston. When a French investor was jailed by the Jamestown police for reckless driving, an aide suggested that the governor call the investor following his return to France to express regrets about the incident. South Carolina lawmakers pleased their state's European executives by lifting the limit on tax-free liquor imports so that the industrialists could keep a good supply of their favorite wines without paying extra taxes on them. Such accommodation is not limited to South Carolina.

Although foreign industrialists acknowledge the hospitality of the South, their expressed reason for locating there is that southern labor is good and inexpensive. A Japanese consul explained, "The South has the only reserve of good labor left in the U.S. Southern labor is in fact cheaper to us than Japanese labor."[3] Many foreign employers have found that the southern attitude toward work is more like their. Others liken southern employees to "first generation, off-the-land workers" whose attitudes seemed to say, "I'm doing a job. I believe in God."[4] Many Japanese executives with whom I have had contact did not openly comment on "cheap labor," but they praised the reliability of southern labor. They said, "Southerners are fundamentally good people, trainable, and most of all reliable." Because of the attractive labor in the South, foreign investment in manufacturing fields there is rapidly increasing. Thus far, the state of Tennessee, for instance, has attracted over $8 billion of combined European and Japanese investment.[5]

JAPANESE MANUFACTURING INVESTMENT IN THE SOUTH

Although the Japanese developed export markets, mainly in developing countries, as early as the 1950s and the 1960s, Japanese direct investment in the United States did not begin until the late 1970s, intensifying in the 1980s and thereafter. In fact, of the 113 Japanese firms (both manufacturing/assembly and sale/distribution) currently in operation in Tennessee as of November 1994, 103 (91 percent) of them were established since 1980.[6] When the U.S. trade deficit with Japan became embarrassing to both countries in the 1970s, President Jimmy Carter urged the U.S. governors: "Governors: go to Japan. Persuade them to make in the United States what they sell in the United States. Bring their plants and those jobs to our states. And while you're there, persuade those Japanese to buy more of what we sell."[7]

FROM CENTRIPETAL TO OUTWARD DEPENDENCY

President Carter's mandate combined with several other factors to force Japanese enterprises to seek manufacturing outposts. Beginning in the mid-1970s, many countries in North America and Western Europe established trade barriers against unlimited Japanese exports by imposing import restrictions, antidumping duties, and voluntary export restraints. The Japanese foresaw the introduction of further restrictions, especially a trade diversion by the European Community (EC) (which did occur in the 1990s). In order to skirt existing trade barriers and to head off anticipated barriers against products such as color TVs, videotape recorders, passenger cars, machine tools, and copying machines, Japanese enterprises established production plants in host countries, especially in North America, Europe, and the newly developing Asian and Southeast Asian countries.[8]

Appreciation of the *yen* was yet another factor in the Japanese industrial expansion abroad. The extensive and quick strengthening of the *yen* brought about a sharp and widespread decline in the cost of initial investment and of production in the host countries, particularly in North America and Western Europe. The strength of the *yen* reduced the initial cost of investment in the United States by nearly half. It became an advantage for Japanese companies to establish production bases in the United States as well as in other countries.[9]

In addition to those external factors, there were some internal causes for Japan's overseas development, internal competition being one of them. Because of the competitive struggle in the Japanese domestic market, some enterprises, such as manufacturers of cars and electrical goods, transferred overseas. For Matsushita, Sony, and Honda, for example, the domestic market was too tight and going abroad was an opportunity they could not refuse.[10]

The Japanese government's inducements for foreign direct investment (FDI) contributed another compelling factor. In the early 1960s and the 1970s, "even before the revision of the exchange laws in December, 1980, Japanese enterprises in manufacturing, commerce, and services were generally free to undertake FDI. After the revision of the laws, financial and insurance firms became free to invest abroad."[11] Inducement policies included the low-interest loans provided by the Japan Export-Import Bank and other credit institutions, and special tax provisions for FDI by small- and medium-sized enterprises. As a result, between 1976 and 1980, before the revision of the exchange laws, 37.9 percent of all Japanese small- and medium-sized firms participated in FDI. In 1986–87, the percentage increased to 46.9 (1,662 of a total of 3,545 small- and medium-sized firms).[12]

Efforts to recruit Japanese enterprises were not on the mind of President Carter alone but also on the minds of many governors and state planners. After learning from a brief wire story in 1976, datelined Tokyo, that an unnamed Japanese auto company was conducting a study to determine the feasibility of building a plant in the United States, Ohio Governor James Rhodes and his development director hurriedly arranged a trip to Tokyo the very next day.[13] As it turned out, Rhodes was successful in recruiting Honda to Ohio. Similarly, Kentucky Governor Martha Layne Collins made eight trips to Japan before she finally succeeded in recruiting Toyota to Kentucky. Consequently, not only did Toyota invest $1.1 billion and commit to 3,500 jobs while Collins was governor, but several dozen Japanese auto-parts companies later built plants in her state.[14] Tennessee Governor Alexander recalls that when he was on his recruiting trip to Japan; "Twenty-three states had sent plant-hunting delegations to Japan during 1979; twenty-eight were already signed up for 1980."[15] It sounds as if the airstreams between the United States and Japan were as heavily traveled as the Oregon wagon trails.

Supplementing the states' recruiting efforts, the major Japanese manufacturers (such as Honda, Nissan, Toyota, and other big firms that had started to build their plants in America) attracted many small- and medium-sized part suppliers. For instance, since Nissan announced its Smyrna, Tennessee, plant in 1980, some thirty Japanese auto-parts suppliers and related firms have established their plants in Tennessee. In fact, one-third of Japanese business and industrial firms in Tennessee are related to the auto industry, mainly due to the presence of Nissan.

THE VISIBILITY OF JAPANESE INVESTMENT

Recent Japanese investment in highly visible real estate and other fields has generated for many Americans fears of a "Japanese takeover" or a "buyout of America." While publicity about Japanese investment is extensive, one seldom hears about European investment. According to the U.S. Department of Commerce data published in 1994, as shown in Table 2.1, Japan as a single country has the largest number of manufacturing affiliates (729) among seven major nations investing in the United States, and has the third largest assets ($69,998 million).[16] However, looking at total number of branches (including property, plant, and equipment) located in various states reveals that those of the United Kingdom outnumber those of Japan 2,894 to 1,975. A combined total of European and Canadian investments in manufacturing, including those of the United Kingdom, Germany, Canada, France, Switzerland, and the Netherlands, far exceeds that of Japan: While there are 729 Japanese manufacturing affiliates (a business concern owned or controlled in whole or in part by another concern) in the United States, there are 1,453 European and Canadian affiliates. Japan's share of the total foreign investment in the United States is 33.4 percent. While there are 8,463 European and Canadian affiliates and their branches in various states, there are 1,975 Japanese affiliates and branches. Japan's share is about 18.2 percent of that of those countries.[17]

Of the 729 Japanese manufacturing affiliates in the United States, almost 63 percent are located in eleven southern states, although their branches or U.S. headquarters are elsewhere. Indeed, Japanese manufacturing investment is concentrated heavily in the South, where affiliates hire 87,600 southerners (26 percent of the employees hired by all the Japanese manufacturing firms in the United States). Ranked distribution of Japanese manufacturing firms in the southern states and the number of employees hired by them, along with each state's proportion of the southern population, are shown in Table 2.2.

Of the eleven southern states, Georgia hosts the largest number of Japanese firms (102), followed by North Carolina (67) and Tennessee (60).

Table 2.1 • Distribution of Foreign Manufacturing Affiliates in the United States

Country	No. of Affiliates[a]	Total No. of Branches[b]	Total Assets (S Million)
Japan	729	1,975	69,998
United Kingdom	385	2,894	100,811
Germany	381	1,729	43,667
Canada	273	1,416	71,334
France	173	1,004	48,033
Switzerland	165	959	33,887
The Netherlands	76	461	20,673
Total	2,182	438	388,403

SOURCE: U.S. Department of Commerce, *Foreign Direct Investment in the United States: Operations of U.S. Affiliates of Foreign Companies*. Revised 1991 Estimates (Washington, DC: U.S. Department of Commerce, 1994), tables B-6 and F-22.
[a] A given affiliate is counted once in the all–U.S. total. It may have several branches located in various states.
[b] The branch is counted once in each state in which it has property, plant, and equipment. Because an affiliate may have property, plant, and equipment in more than one state, the sum across states exceeds the all–U.S. total.

Table 2.2 • Distribution of Japanese Manufacturing Industries in the Eleven Southern States

State	No. of Manufacturers[a]	Rank	Employees[b]	Rank	Proportion of Population in the South [c] (%)
Georgia	102	1	13,700	3	11
North Carolina	67	2	9,400	5	12
Tennessee	60	3	16,000	2	8
Florida	50	4	2,800	9	23
Kentucky	47	5	17,400	1	6
Virginia	36	6	4,700	7	11
South Carolina	25	7	11,000	4	6
Alabama	24	8	6,300	6	7
Louisiana	18	9	1,000	11	7
Mississippi	16	10	1,400	10	4
Arkansas	14	11	3,900	8	4
Total	459	d	87,600		99%

SOURCES: [a] U.S. Department of Commerxe, *Foreign Direct Investment in the U.S.* (1994), table F-22.
[b] Ibid., Table F-14.
[c] Bureau of the Census, *1990 Census of Summary Population and Housing Characteristics* (Washington, D.C.: U.S. Department of Commerce), 1-3.
[d] Since a given affiliate is counted more than once if it is located in more than one state, the total numbers do not correspond with the total number of affiliates in the United States.

The firms in Kentucky hire the largest number of employees working for Japanese manufacturing industries (17,400 employees), followed by Tennessee (16,000), and Georgia (13,700). Georgia, North Carolina, Tennessee, and Kentucky have a larger share of Japanese manufacturing industries proportionate to their population share. Florida has the fourth largest number of Japanese manufacturing firms among the eleven southern states, but the number of employees is remarkably fewer than its neighboring states. Considering their small proportion of the southern population, Tennessee and Kentucky are doing remarkably well.

These statistical figures on Japanese investment in the United States and the South are based on the 1994 edition of *Foreign Direct Investment in the United States* published by the U.S. Department of Commerce. However, the figures are based on 1991 data, which lag three years behind. Therefore, all the figures and analyses of the data pertaining to Japanese industry in Tennessee hereafter are based on the Tennessee Department of Economic and Community Development data as of November 1994.

WHY TENNESSEE?

Most of the tales about the U.S. governors' industry-hunting trips to Japan have been informally circulated. Tennessee governor Alexander, however, published a book that documents his experiences. Alexander admits that he was ill-prepared to deal with the Japanese and their culture on his first trip to Japan in 1979: "My own idea of Japan then was a picture-postcard stereotype: hot springs, Mt. Fuji, and Madam Butterfly, somewhere on the other side of the World."[18] He found that the Japanese knew very little about Tennessee other than Brenda Lee, the Tennessee Waltz, and Jack Daniels. Alexander relates his first lesson on Japan, afforded him by his own state economic development chief, Jim Cothan:

"Take a map," Jim urged.
"Of Tokyo?" I asked.
"Of the United States."
"Why the United States?"
"Because," explained Jim, "at the end of my seventh visit, after I had made my best pitch, my Japanese business prospect smiled politely and, through his interpreter, said:
'Thank you, Mr. Cotham. Now, please tell me, just what *is* a Tennessee?'[19]

It was the governor's task to convince potential Japanese businesspeople that Tennessee would be an ideal site for Japanese investment. The endeavor must have been enormous and difficult. Alexander was determined to recruit Nissan to his state of Tennessee. He "charged a task force of thirty people with doing whatever it took to make Tennessee the logical choice."[20] The governor knew there would be keen competition from the neighboring state of Georgia, where Donough and Cartersville were the two other alternate sites. Alexander recalls that:

> We worked very hard to persuade Nissan to come to Tennessee. In fact, our state development officials and I devoted almost all our energy on overseas job hunting to Japan. During my first twenty-four months as governor, I spent eight working weeks solely on Japan-Tennessee relations—three weeks in Japan, the rest with an endless stream of visiting Japanese....I noticed that while we talked, our visitors listened. While we worked, they watched. While we luxuriated in translation, they struggled to speak English....More and more of our visitors were coming from Nissan. First came the planners, then the engineers, then the policy makers, all requesting mountains of information, often the same information. Masahiko Zaitsu, from Nissan's Los Angeles office, was a guest at the Governor's Residence eleven times in 1979 and 1980. Our children began to think of him as some sort of Japanese uncle.[21]

By February 1980, even before Nissan made its final decision, the Nissan representatives found an ideal tract of land south of Nashville: a 433-acre dairy farm. Even though the land was not for sale, Alexander acquired from the owners of the land an option to buy. This left the governor and state leaders debating the issue of investing public funds of some $20 million to accommodate Nissan, including building a road and providing job training.[22]

The governor invited the entire leadership of Rutherford County, which includes Smyrna, to the governor's mansion for a briefing. The governor told them, "Tennessee is still at the back of the line economically, Nissan pays high wages, is environmentally clean. This is the kind of plant that will encourage Tennesseans to come back home again, be a magnet for other industry. That's the deal, guys, he told them. It's an opportunity that may never come again. What I need to know is: Do you want it or not want it? I can't wait to find out. I need to know right now."[23] The governor promptly received their approval.

Although the state had to invest a large amount of public funds to facilitate Japanese industry, the state leaders finally convinced themselves that, if the state built a road to accommodate Japanese industry, the road would be for Tennessee workers to drive to and from work; that an investment in training eventually would benefit Tennessee workers; and, most of all, that the state would do the same for an American company. It was a progressive decision at a time when the benefits of foreign direct investment in the

United States were not yet well evaluated. (In 1985, the state would spend $51 million when Saturn came to Spring Hill.[24] In 1990, the political economist Robert B. Reich, who became secretary of labor under President Clinton, would advocate just such a decision: "The typical argument suggests that a foreign-owned company might withdraw for either profit or foreign policy motives. But either way, the bricks and mortar would still be here. So would the equipment. So too would be the accumulated learning among American workers....After all, the American government and the American people maintain jurisdiction—political control—over assets within the United States."[25])

Although Alexander recalls the negotiations were complex, frustrating at times for both parties, and seemingly interminable, Nissan announced its intentions to come to Tennessee on October 30, 1980, six days before Republican Ronald Reagan's landslide victory over Democrat President Jimmy Carter. Alexander recalls, "I finally got a call from Marvin Runyon, the ex-Ford executive who was hired to run the Nissan plant. 'Lamar,' he said, 'We're coming to Tennessee.' My smile was a foot wide. It was the biggest news in our state in a long time. That afternoon, I went to the airport to welcome Runyon and Nissan President Takashi Ishihara. Zaitsu was there, wearing a big Tennessee T-shirt under his suitcoat."[26] Certainly, Lamar Alexander, as governor of Tennessee, can claim credit for the successful recruitment of Nissan. Said he, rightly so,

> We're obviously doing something right. After we made business history with the Nissan decision, Matsushita moved to Knoxville in 1981, Bridgestone rescued a thousand workers by buying a failing Firestone plant in La Vergne in 1982, and in 1985 Komatsu selected a site in Chattanooga to make construction equipment. Between 1980 and 1985, the number of Japanese companies in Tennessee more than doubled, from fourteen to thirty-two. The amount of Japanese investment in Tennessee jumped ten times, to about $1.2 billion. The number of Tennesseans directly employed at those Japanese enterprises grew from one thousand to nearly eight thousand; construction, purchases of parts and supplies, and the turnover of an annual $154 million in Japanese payrolls creates three to four times more jobs than that.[27]

TENNESSEE INCENTIVES

Without much doubt, Japanese industries apply hard-nosed business reasoning to decide where to locate their plants, and Tennessee has made every effort to accommodate the needs of the Japanese in order to attract their business. Industrial incentives offered by Tennessee are not unique; they are basically the same as those offered by neighboring states and include pre-employment job training, infrastructure improvement, tax credits or exemptions, bond financing, and enterprise zones (although the zones are unfunded in Tennessee).

The state Department of Economic and Community Development (ECD), created by the Tennessee General Assembly in 1972, is Tennessee's industrial recruiting arm. ECD provides clients with current lists of available manufacturing and distribution facilities and of available industrial properties, and with complete research and technical data on transportation, labor, taxes, demographics, financial assistance, licensing, and other services. While some southern states have foreign or out-of-state trade offices,[28] Tennessee has none, and thus ECD's marketing specialists fan out overseas. They also work at recruiting in the home office. A senior specialist in the Marketing Division, who was a cooperative and valuable informant for this project, was busy entertaining visiting Japanese dignitaries in addition to carrying out his formal duties.

Specifically, the Tennessee incentive package includes:

Taxes

Excise tax (6 percent, similar to corporate income tax):
  Credit: 1 percent of purchase price of industrial machinery
  No operating loss carry-forward for fifteen years

Sales tax (6 percent state, plus local tax of up to 2.75 percent):
  —Industrial machinery or repairs exempt
  —Raw material exempt
  —Pollution control equipment exempt
  —Reduced rate for manufacturer's use of fuel and water

Franchise tax (similar to property tax):
  Property under construction exempt

Local property tax:
  Goods in process exempt
  Finished goods inventories exempt
  Goods-in-transit exempt

Other:
  Target-job tax credit of up to $2,400 per employee
  No state personal income tax on earned income

Job Training

State provides free employment screening and training of workers for incoming industry.

Infrastructure Financing

State grants made to communities to support new or expanding industries

Grants (for)

Improving water and sewer systems and extending utility lines to industry
Access roads, rail spurs, ports, airport improvements
  Site improvement (grading, drainage, etc) for plant

Board Financing

Local industrial development boards can issue tax-free bonds to finance capital costs of a new or expanding industr; boards retain ownership of facilities and lease them to industry for amount to repay bonds
Property exempt from property tax; local governments negotiate payments in lieu of property taxes
Portion of federal Community Development Block Grant money for grants and loans to assist industries in locating or expanding in state

Intangibles

Tennessee markets itself as:
—near the geographical and distribution center of eastern U.S.
—a right-to-work (open shop) state
—having a strong work ethic

Lamar Alexander notes that Tennessee has been successful in recruiting Japanese as well as American industry for several reasons. One incentive specific to Tennessee is that the state is located in the center of the U.S. population: because three-fourths of the U.S. population resides within five hundred miles of Tennessee, transportation costs are minimized, as shown in Illustration 2.1. Alexander cites the example of Federal Express, which is headquartered in Memphis and hires 93,394 employees worldwide who deliver 1.7 million packages daily throughout the United States and in 180 countries.

Low taxes and right-to-work laws are additional reasons for Tennessee's success. Although some Japanese firms in Tennessee have unions, most do not. (In this context, note the Nissan plant employees' rejection by 1,622 to 711 of the effort by the United Auto Workers Union to organize Nissan in July 1989.[29])

Another incentive that Alexander notes is that Tennesseans, like the Japanese, still hold to "yesterday's value" of a work ethic. According to Alexander, Tennesseans neither despise nor dislike work. "In both Japan and Tennessee there is the same homogeneity which causes people to grow independent, self-sufficient, and skeptical of strangers."[30] Along the same line, the farm-oriented Tennessee workers are more likely to be docile and

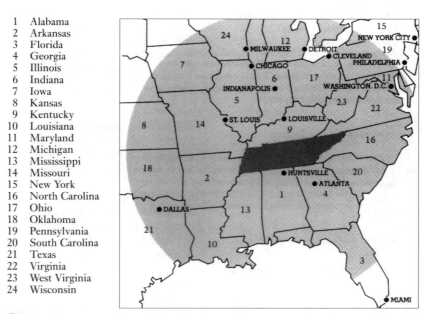

1	Alabama
2	Arkansas
3	Florida
4	Georgia
5	Illinois
6	Indiana
7	Iowa
8	Kansas
9	Kentucky
10	Louisiana
11	Maryland
12	Michigan
13	Mississippi
14	Missouri
15	New York
16	North Carolina
17	Ohio
18	Oklahoma
19	Pennsylvania
20	South Carolina
21	Texas
22	Virginia
23	West Virginia
24	Wisconsin

States that Fall Within a 500–Mile Radius of Tennessee

2.1 • States that Fall within a 500-Mile Radius of Tennessee
Source: Tennessee Department of Economic and Community Development

responsible, as agricultural societies are apt to stress obedience and responsibility in their socialization.[31] Japanese industrial firms at home and abroad seek workers who hold "yesterday's value" and whose backgrounds are rural, hoping that they bring their rural work ethic to the factories.[32]

JAPANESE VIEWS OF TENNESSEE AND TENNESSEANS

The list of Japanese industrialists' reasons for Tennessee as their choice for investment is not short, and for the most part it coincides with Tennessee's incentives. In addition to the state's central location vis-a-vis the U.S. population, the Japanese mention a sound infrastructure, especially the good state and interstate highways, including I-40 (east/west), I-65 (north/south), I-75 (north/south), I-24 (northeast/southwest), I-81 (north/south), I-55 (north/south), I-59 (north/south), I-155 (west/northeast), I-181 (north/south), and beltways such as I-240. The favorable business and work climate created by the state and local governments is another positive factor, as is the favorable regional climate (four distinctive annual seasons, with a mild winter). The mild climatic conditions facilitate cost-effective shipment of materials and products and make "just-in-time" delivery possible. The availability of land allows industries to expand their facilities whenever necessary. Inexpensive yet abundant utilities are readily available.

Another important factor is the "personality of the people," as one Japanese executive expressed what is often termed the "quality of worker and the virtue of hardworking ethic." The Japanese like the friendly, polite, and agreeable nature of Tennesseans, which originated with the agrarian-oriented work ethic. Reed reports, "'Southerners,' someone once remarked, 'will be polite until they're angry enough to kill you.'"[33] The executive points out that Tennessee workers are likeable, which does not mean to say that all Tennessee workers are skilled, well-trained, and as competent as they should be in accordance with the level of their educational attainment. According to the Japanese expatriates, the average Tennessee worker's dexterity is rough, and the pace of work is slow, but because Tennessee workers are personable, reliable, and dependable, the Japanese believe they can train them. Most of all, the Japanese employers consider the wage scale of Tennesseans, ranging from $6.00 to $11.50 per hour for nonskilled, starting workers, to be reasonable.

For the Japanese, having universities and colleges nearby is as important as other factors, since institutions of higher education are believed to influence the qualities of the public school systems. Finally, the Japanese cite quality-of-life factors, especially the spacious land and clean air of Tennessee and its natural beauty, which make Japanese feel at home.

The former president of Midtech commented on the quality-of-life factor in Tennessee:

Look at the green scenery, unlimited space, clean and crispy air! [He apparently was unaware of the humidity of Tennessee summers.] Anywhere and everywhere can be a park. Anybody who likes to golf can walk in, without making an advance reservation, and play. Can you believe the fee! I don't think you can find such a nice golf course with such inexpensive admission anywhere in the world other than the U.S. and Tennessee in particular. Perhaps most Americans take their landscape for granted, but for most Japanese it is precious. I've lived here in Tennessee over three years, and I feel like I am getting younger. Some Japanese executives are reluctant to take overseas assignments, but once they come to Tennessee, they soon become immersed in the beauty of Tennessee.

One of the Japanese executives concurred with his president's remarks. The executive had been to Midtech three times previously during the installation of machines when the firm established its plant in Tennessee. He was so attracted by the natural beauty of Tennessee and the friendliness of the people that this time he volunteered to come to Tennessee, leaving his wife and seventeen-year-old son in Japan. He regrets that his family cannot join him because of his son's schooling: he is preparing for his college entrance examination in Japan. He said, "I didn't have to come, but I like it here, and the experiences I am having here are a tremendous asset, although a bachelor's life here is difficult at times." His English is good enough for him to be involved in many activities, and he seems to enjoy his life in Tennessee.

The vice president of Westech, a joint venture with an American firm, told me that his wife loves Tennessee so much that he has ended up staying in Tennessee longer than he had originally anticipated. His wife is the oldest daughter of the sonless family of the owner of the Japanese parent company of the joint venture. If she disliked Tennessee, she could ask her father to let them return to Japan any time she wishes. She takes English lessons from a private tutor and is actively involved in community life.

Eastech is located in a most desirable scenic area in Tennessee in terms of natural beauty and the quality of life. It lies in the foothills of the Great Smoky Mountains, overlooking the Little Tennessee River that leads to Tellico Dam. The building resembles a resort hotel or a library, not at all fitting the stereotype of an industrial zone, with smokestack, polluted air, and worn-out factories. Not only the Japanese but everyone who works in the plant seem to delight in the aesthetic beauty of the site.

It is no wonder that the Meiji Gakuin High School of Japan decided to locate a site at Sweetwater, a small East Tennessee town in the foothills of the Smoky Mountains.[34] The principal told me that:

2.2 • A Rural Scene of East Tennessee, Foothill of the Great Smoky Mountains
(Courtesy of University Relations, the University of Tennessee)

2.3 • Tennessee Valley Authority's (TVA's) Norris Dam Created the First of the "Great Lakes of the South"
(Courtesy of University Relations, the University of Tennessee)

There had been several alternative sites, including New York, Chicago, and other major U.S. cities. But the final decision was based on the safety of the students and the aesthetic beauty of the locale. Japanese have images of the major U.S. cities as places where violent crimes are common. [He was almost apologetic to make this remark, although it is not untrue.] Even when I try to recruit teachers from Japan, their initial inquiry is about their safety. They would like to make sure that Sweetwater is not as same as New York, Chicago, and other major crime-pervading U.S. cities. As you know, Sweetwater is far from those cities. Sweetwater provides safety and security for our faculty and students, and has the rare beauty of the Great Smoky Mountains.

Each of the three firms may also have a specific reason or reasons for preferring Tennessee. Some speculate that, were Nissan not in Tennessee, it is doubtful whether Midtech, which is mainly an auto-part supplier, would have come there. The same is true for Westech, which is a joint venture with an American auto-parts supplier. Eastech, however, came to East Tennessee because one of its sister plants (part of the same conglomerate) came to East Tennessee seven years earlier. Eastech people already knew something about Tennessee in general and East Tennessee in particular.

Specific reasons aside, the three industries made every effort to study the site before making their final decisions.[35] The president of Midtech, in his capacity as executive managing director of the parent company in Japan, came to the United States ten times in 1986 and another ten in 1987 before making the final decision. He studied nineteen alternate sites in the United States before choosing Middle Tennessee. This indicates that even though the company is an auto-parts supplier, chiefly to Nissan, its site decision was not based solely on geographic proximity to Nissan's location. Neither did Westech come to Tennessee to become a major supplier to Nissan. The company's main customers are located outside Tennessee, including auto plants in Illinois, Michigan, and even Canada.

Interestingly enough, Japanese firms—at least the three firms included in this study—are concerned less about low taxes, right-to-work laws, and other incentives; and more about infrastructures, especially highway systems for transportation, and "quality-of-life" factors (such as climate and landscape), the quality of workers, and work ethics. There are some speculations that the "right-to-work" law is a key player in recruiting foreign manufacturing firms, including those of the Japanese, since all southern states, except Kentucky, have right-to-work laws. As reflected in Table 2.3, twenty-four states that have right-to-work laws share 5,075 (38.6 percent) of the 13,153 foreign firms and their branches in the United States; at the same time, those twenty-four states have 37 percent (92,187,513) of the total U.S. population of 248,709,873. Thus, the proportion of foreign manufacturing firms there is slightly larger than that of the population. The percentage figures are insignificant, the right-to-work law is more important than other factors. Table 2.3 supports the findings of Woodward and Glickman that:

> foreign investors did not merely follow the spatial adjustment pattern of domestic firms. Foreign investors were market driven, but primarily to regions where existing manufacturing activity was low in relation to demand. Although domestic manufacturing penetrated these regions too, the range of variables that affected domestic firms was greater. The reason may be that the range of organizational types and the stages of the industry life cycle are more diverse. For instance, the variables that influence firms with products in late stages of the industry life cycle— low wages and lower technology—affected only domestic, not foreign, firms. At the same time, *foreign firms no longer appear strongly influenced by right-to-work laws*, evidence that the previous perception that northern labor is inflexible is no longer the case.[36] [italics mine]

In choosing a region, foreign manufacturers consider the presence of right-to-work laws important but not as important as a location where manufacturing activity is low.[37] Honda went to the heart of the union state of Ohio, and Toyota selected Kentucky, which is the only southern state that does not have right-to-work laws. Since manufacturing industry is sparser in the South than in the Great Lakes and Mideast regions, where manufacturing is concentrated, foreign firms come to the South. The commitments and assurances made by the local governments to induce Japanese companies to come to their communities also appear to be more important than the existence of right-to-work laws.

As noted above, infrastructure seems extremely important for the Japanese industrialists. Perhaps the Tennessee Industrial Infrastructure Program (TIIP) that was initiated in 1987 by Governor McWherter recognized its importance. The TIIP provides grants to communities to provide utility services and facilities for industries locating or expanding in the area and creating job opportunities for Tennesseans. Grants for up to $100,000 for site preparation are available to all ninety-five counties of Tennessee. Thus far, rather than offering other incentives, Tennessee is more interested in focusing its resources on investing in infrastructure, training for the labor force, and educating young people. Tennessee maintains that it is wrong to give the state tax base away in order to try to recruit industry. Tennessee's neighboring state of Georgia agrees and offers very few tax incentives. However, Tennessee now faces tough competition from its northern neighbor, Kentucky. For the people of Kentucky, it was a great loss when GM's Saturn moved south to Tennessee. In order for the state to recover, Governor Martha Layne Collins made many trips to Tokyo, offering all sorts of incentives to Toyota.[38] As a result, Toyota went to Kentucky.

About half of Kentucky's 120 counties are economically so distressed with high unemployment rates that the Kentucky legislature created the Kentucky Rural Economic Development Authority (KREDA) in 1988 to spur growth. KREDA became the prime industrial recruiter, offering incentives such as corporate income tax credits and even diversion of employee personal income taxes from the state to the businesses that

Table 2.3 • Distribution of Foreign Manufacturers in and Population of States that Have Right-to-Work Laws

States with Right-to-Work Laws	No. of Foreign Manufacturers[a]	State Population[b]
Alabama	239	4,040,587
Arizona	227	3,665,228
Arkansas	134	2,350,725
Colorado	224	3,294,394
Florida	447	12,937,926
Georgia	532	6,478,216
Idaho	66	1,006,749
Iowa	156	2,776,755
Kansas	170	2,477,574
Louisiana	191	4,219,973
Mississippi	139	2,573,216
Montana	49	799,065
Nebraska	98	1,578,385
Nevada	75	1,201,833
New Hampshire	144	1,109,252
North Carolina	442	6,628,637
North Dakota	48	638,800
South Carolina	252	3,486,703
South Dakota	38	696,004
Tennessee	331	4,877,185
Texas	617	16,986,510
Utah	121	1,722,850
Virginia	305	6,187,358
Wyoming	30	453,588
Total	5,075	92,187,513

Source: [a]Foreign Direct Investment in the United States (1994), table F-22.
[b]1990 Census of Summary Population and Housing Characteristics, 1-3.

employ them. Kentucky's tax abatements are so generous that industries can locate in counties with above average jobless rates and negotiate virtually all of their state corporate income tax liability. Consequently, Kentucky's incentive program has propelled the closure of thirty–five transactions thus far, and has enticed some firms to locate in Kentucky rather than in Tennessee—firms such as the International Paper and James River Corporation, which, with an annual payroll of $14 million in Kentucky, employed 100 workers in 1993 and expects to employ 300 more by 1995. Should Tennessee and other states try to match Kentucky's tax-abatement incentives? Debate was vigorous in Tennessee. A special business-tax study committee of the Tennessee legislature examined the issue, and chamber of commerce executives statewide pushed for tax abatement incentives. Kentucky's neighbor Ohio has responded to the Kentucky program with its own package of tax abatements.[39] Tennessee did not replicate Kentucky's incentive program. But, in 1994, the Tennessee General Assembly enacted the "Jobs Tax Credit Program," that is a credit against a qualified business enterprise's franchise tax liability of two thousand ($2,000) for each new full-time employee job created during a fiscal year and in existence at the end of the year.

Despite such inducements, none of the Japanese firms located in Tennessee relocated to Kentucky. So far, the industries that have chosen Kentucky over Tennessee are domestic. When I asked a Japanese executive about the possibility of his company's relocating to Kentucky because of the tax abatement program, he smiled and said, almost reluctantly, "I don't think so. Because, whatever the contents of the tax abatement program are, when you drive from Tennessee to Kentucky, you don't have to see the state boundary sign to know you're in Kentucky. Suddenly, the highway becomes bumpy, narrower, and rough-riding." To him at least, infrastructure—well-developed, well-paved, well-kept highways—is more important than the other incentives.

THE STATES' DILEMMA

As the U.S. economy remains distressed and the unemployment rate a major concern, the interstate struggles to compete in an economic war to recruit industries is bound to escalate. Tennessee poured $21.2 million into recruiting Nissan, $29.3 million into building the Saturn Parkway (an interstate-style connector between the Saturn plant and I-65), and $21.7 million into training Saturn workers for their jobs. The most recent figure, in 1992, of $150 million in South Carolina's incentive package to recruit BMW's first U.S. auto plant is a stunning expenditure of public funds.[40] An increasing number of states are mortgaging their future with inducement packages to recruit industries their way.

No one can be certain about the boost to economy by luring industries and jobs with tax abatements and land giveaway. Woodward and Glickman have pointed out a dilemma:

> While mayors and governors attempt to recruit foreign-based multinationals, critics question this new international boosterism. The incentives—granting substantial tax abatements, conducting expensive job training programs, providing foreign firms with infrastructure and other forms of support—may waste public resources. In some instances, foreign-owned branch plants compete directly with local enterprise, creating jobs in one area and displacing them in others.[41]

Despite such criticism, there is an increasing demand from local recruiters and job-seekers to attract foreign investment. It remains to be seen whether Tennessee's TIIP will be altered in response to Kentucky's new tax abatements program. Tennessee insists logically that the state cannot give its tax base away for the recruitment of industry. Kentucky is obviously willing to give up some revenue in order to succeed against other states in the competition to recruit industries to Kentucky. By recruiting industries, Kentucky hopes that people will acquire jobs.

Both Tennessee's and Kentucky's arguments have some merit, but the wasted recruitment efforts of an excessive competition, even what some call a war, between and among the states, could end up with all as losers. Japanese has a word for it, *tomodaore*, meaning drowning together or mutual destruction. Each state has to make its own decision about what is best for the state in the long run. Some state industrial recruiters are very eager to offer more incentives, recognizing that Japanese investment in the manufacturing sector has been relatively inactive since the early 1990s. Such a slowdown of new Japanese investment in Tennessee and elsewhere, however, has little to do with the lack of state incentive programs; rather, it results from Japan's recession. Also, most of the Japanese firms who were interested in coming to the United States have already come. An effort needs to be made to study what measures would stimulate expansion of the already existing firms in the state and what actions, besides recruiting new firms, would increase employment.

JAPANESE INVESTMENT IN TENNESSEE AND ITS DISTRIBUTION PATTERNS

Before discussing the distribution patterns of Japanese firms in terms of the socioeconomic and demographic characteristics of the three parts of Tennessee, an explanation of Tennessee's "three grand divisions" is essential.

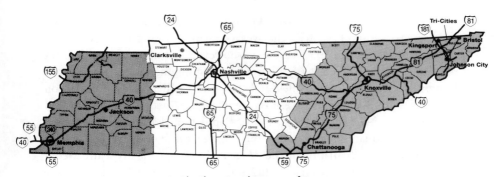

2.4 • The Three Grand Divisions of Tennessee

THE THREE GRAND DIVISIONS OF TENNESSEE

The state's constitution delineates "three grand divisions"—East Tennessee, Middle Tennessee, and West Tennessee—and legislators subsequently defined these divisions. For Tennesseans, the three geographic divisions have "determined the economic, social, and political life [of the residents]. Those who settled in the fertile Mississippi Valley, for example, found a daily existence different from that of their parents who lived in the Cumberland Basin and their grandparents who established homes in the Mountains of East Tennessee and western North Carolina."[42] The three divisions of Tennessee are shown in Illustration 2.4.

In East Tennessee are the mountains—primarily the Great Smokies, the Ridge and Valley, and the Cumberland Plateau. Cherokee Indians inhabited these mountains for hundreds of years prior to the arrival of the Europeans. During the 1790s, frontier people settled in the generous valleys and along the rivers. In the early 1800s, others followed, some moving westward from coastal regions and others southwestward from Pennsylvania. The immigrants were mainly Scotch-Irish and Germans, but they included non-English-speaking nationalities as well. The geographic isolation of the settlers tended to perpetuate their folk cultures and differences in their speech.[43] East Tennesseeans have always had a fondness for music referred to as "hillbilly," inspired by the music of their European ancestors.[44] Historically, the Southern Appalachians have been a hindrance to east-west movement. Major roads were nonexistent prior to 1928, but highway construction in the 1930s and 1940s led to a large outmigration from the region. Since 1950, outmigration has tapered off, despite the recent completion of highways, including Interstate 40, which helped to prevent further decline of the population. The region is a well-known national park and vaction center.

The Ridge and Valley region of East Tennessee (which extends from Tennessee's northern border with Kentucky and Virginia southwest 150

miles to the southern border with Georgia and Alabama) has had historically an agricultural base, with the average farmer owning 135 acres (higher than the state average). These days, however, manufacturing industries
in this region produce everything from aluminum, chemicals, electric
heaters, nuclear reactors, saddles, and stoves, to wooden items. This region
includes two major cities, Knoxville (165,025 people in 1990) and
Chattanooga (147,574 people in 1990). Population density of the region,
with 136 per square mile, is higher than that of the state average of 95 per
square mile. The population of the Ridge and Valley is mostly white except
for Hamilton County (which includes Chattanooga and has a nonwhite
population of 19.1 percent). Since its establishment in 1933, the TVA has
provided an ample source of inexpensive electricity in the region. Oak
Ridge (24,605 people in 1990)—known as the "Atomic Bomb City," a center that developed and produced materials for the atomic bomb during
World War II under the Manhattan Project—has drawn many well-trained
scientists. Because the Ridge and Valley region has been blessed with a
moderate climate, abundant water resources, and a vigorous people, it
should continue its industrial growth so long as manufacturing and service
industries increase. The region boasts major interstate highways I-40, I-75,
and I-24. It is no accident that some Japanese manufacturing industries are
coming to this region.

The Cumberland Plateau, situated between East and Middle Tennessee,
is isolated from the other regions by widespread dissection of the plateau
surface. The people who live in this region are predominantly rural whites
who earn a livelihood by part-time farming and off-the-farm employment
of family members in factories, mines, and forest industries. Population
density is less than a third of the average for the entire state, with no urban
concentrations. This region ranks low economically, educationally, and in
health services, with some localities fitting the popular image of
"Appalachia."

Middle Tennessee consists of the Highland Rim and the Central (or
Nashville) Basin. Pasture land is widespread in this region. The Highland
Rim in most places sits 200 feet to more than 300 feet higher than adjoin-
ing portions of the Basin. The small plains of the Highland Rim support
only local trade centers, with no sizable urban centers. Although the
Highland Rim is an integral part of Middle Tennessee, it is overwhelmed
by the Central Basin, better known as the Nashville Basin, after the name
of its largest city and the state capital (510,784 persons in metropolitan
Nashville in 1990). The regional economy has been agricultural, producing
a variety of crops, such as wheat, soybeans, tobacco, corn, and cotton. In
addition, 90 percent of country music recordings and 50 percent of the
world's single records have been recorded in Nashville, known as "Music

City USA." The music industry provides employment for over 5,000 persons, and the "Grand Ole Opry" attracts nearly 800,000 visitors annually, generating hundreds of millions of dollars from tourists.

Aided by the state government, in recent years the Central Basin has become one of the state's most rapidly growing industrial centers. DuPont, employing over 3,000 workers in Davidson County, and General Electric Company, employing nearly 2,000 people in Murfreesboro, Rutherford County, are major industries. Recently, many Japanese manufacturing industries, including Nissan, have moved into Middle Tennessee counties along with GM's Saturn. All of a sudden, traditional farming towns in Middle Tennessee have become the "New Detroit," collectively an automobile capital.

Compared to the rest of the state, West Tennessee is historically young. This region was known as the Western District and belonged to the Chickasaw Indians until 1819. After 1819, the area was carved into counties. The rivers of West Tennessee, mostly tributaries of the Mississippi River, are generally slow-flowing and sluggish. Five counties of West Tennessee have direct access to the Mississippi River and four to the Tennessee River, which makes a natural border between West and Middle Tennessee. In the past, these tributary streams were used to some extent for commercial transportation, but, except for the Mississippi River, they are no longer of importance in this respect. West Tennessee's topograph consists primarily of hills, valleys, some swamps, and low plains rich in plant nutrients. The surface of the plains generally coincides with the high water level of the Mississippi River. Because of a humid, subtropical climate, with relatively mild winters, hot summers, and abundant precipitation, West Tennessee is truly the agricultural heart of Tennessee, raising crops such as soybeans, wheat, corn, and especially cotton. It is indeed a cotton-growing region of the country.

Shelby County, which includes Memphis,[45] is the largest metropolis in Tennessee, with a population of 759,253 in 1990. Nearly 46 percent of its population is black, whereas the state as a whole is slightly less than 16 percent black. Memphis is one of the world's largest spot cotton markets, with cotton having been shipped from the port as early as 1826. Although manufacturing occupies a prime position in the economy of Memphis, the city is situated in the heart of a great agricultural region. In addition to being one of the world's largest cottonseed products centers, Memphis is the second largest meat processing city and the third largest food processor in the United States. The progress of Memphis has been aided by eight railways, three interstates (I-40, I-240, and I-55), and eight U.S. highways. The city is served by almost all U.S. commercial airlines and is a hub of Northwest Airlines. Also, there is a federal barge line and several private carrying companies serving the Mississippi River system. Japanese manufacturing industry is sparsely represented in West Tennessee, compared to Middle and East Tennessee, with the exception of Memphis and vicinity.

The "three grand divisions" of the 41,328 square miles of Tennessee land are unevenly divided: 32.2 percent of the land is in East Tennessee; 41.9 percent in Middle Tennessee, and 25.8 percent in West Tennessee. As shown in Table 2.4, in virtually every category the figures for West Tennessee are less favorable than for the other two divisions. West Tennessee has a slightly higher population density than Middle Tennessee, a slightly higher percent in the labor force than East Tennessee, and slightly less unemployment than East Tennessee. The most distinctive difference between West Tennessee and the other two divisions lies in racial composition, with West Tennessee having a higher percentage of the black population.

DISTRIBUTION OF JAPANESE INDUSTRY IN TENNESSEE

In the distribution of Japanese firms in Tennessee, two patterns emerge. First, when major Japanese manufacturing firms locate their plants in a particular locale, such as Nissan in Middle Tennessee, their suppliers usually follow and locate not far from them. Second, the firms tend to cluster geographically, overwhelmingly in East and Middle Tennessee and close to transportation and communication centers.

SALES AND DISTRIBUTION FIRMS

As shown in Illustration 2.5, the forty-seven Japanese sales and distribution centers are located either in or near the three major cities of Knoxville, Nashville, and Memphis. Davidson County, which includes Nashville, hosts twenty-three Japanese sales and distribution firms, and Shelby County, which includes Memphis, is the home of eleven Japanese sales and distribution firms. Rutherford County, a suburb of Nashville, hosts the Nissan plant and also seven Japanese sales and distribution firms. Mount Pleasant of Muary County, Ripley of Lauderdale County, Rogersville of Hawkins County, Loudon of Loudon County, Jackson of Madison County, and Maryville of Blount County (a suburb of Knoxville), each host one Japanese sales and distribution firm. The only pattern here appears to be that the sites are near metropolitan areas, affording the firms excellent transportation and communication facilities.

MANUFACTURING AND ASSEMBLY FIRMS

According to figures from the Tennessee Department of Economic and Community Development (ECD), as of November 1994, sixty-nine Japanese manufacturing and assembly plants are dispersed among thirty-

Table 2.4 • Socioeconomic and Demographic Characteristics of Tennessee by the Three Grand Divisions

	Three Grand Divisions		
Characteristics	East Tennessee	Middle Tennessee	West Tennessee
No. of Japanese Manufacturing Firms	21	33	15
No. of Counties	33	41	21
Percent of Land Area	32.2	41.9	25.8
Population (%)	1,832,138 (37.6)	1,685,822 (34.6)	1,359,225 (27.9)
Population Density	136.1	87.1	102.7
White Population (% of State)	1,703,433 (42.1)	1,464,142 (36.2)	880,491 (21.8)
Black Population (% of State)	112,697 (14.5)	200,345 (25.8)	464,993 (59.8)
Total Civilian Labor Force (% of State)	894,364 (37.2)	857,061 (36.5)	653,662 (27.2)
Percent in Labor Force	58.9	62.6	59.4
Unemployment Rate	7.6	6.2	7.3
% High School Graduate or Higher among 25 Years and Over	57.7	58.1	57.3
Per Capita GNP	10,098	10,584	9,924

Source: U.S. Bureau of the Census, *1990 Census of Population and Housing: Summary Social, Economic, and Housing Characteristics Tennessee* (Washington, D.C.: U.S. Department of Commerce, 1992), 1-24, 26-44, 45-71, 90-108; U.S. Bureau of the Census, *1990 Census of Population and Housing: Summary Population and Housing Characteristics Tennessee* (Washington, D.C.: U.S. Department of Commerce, 1992), 1-25, 26-50; Tennessee Department of Economic and Community Development, November 1994.
Note: An average of each of the three divisions is calculated by adding all the averages of the counties included in each division and then dividing by the numbers of counties included in each division; thus the outcome of the average of three divisions will differ from the state average.

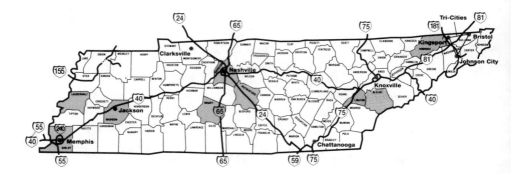

2.5 • Location of Japanese Sales and Distribution Firms in Tennessee

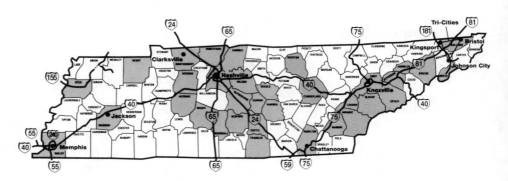

2.6 • Location of Japanese Manufacturing Firms in Tennessee

Table 2.5 • Distribution of Japanese Manufacturing/Assembly Firms among the Three Grand Divisions

Three Grand Divisions

	East Tennessee	Middle Tennessee	West Tennessee
No. of Counties (%)	13 (39.4)	16 (48.4)	4 (12.1)
No. of Firms (%)	21 (30.4)	33 (47.8)	15 (21.7)

Source: Tennessee Department of Economic and Community Development, November 1994.

three Tennessee counties. Looking at Illustration 2.4 and Table 2.5, among these counties, a great majority (78.3 percent of 69 firms) are located in either Middle Tennessee (48.4 percent of thirty-three counties) or in East Tennessee (39.4 percent of thirty-three counties). As also shown in Illustration 2.4, most Japanese manufacturing and assembly plants are located along the interstate highway system. None of the Japanese manufacturing and assembly plants is located in a county where there is no major interstate highway system or that is not at least within 10 miles of the county boundary line, with one exception. A plant in Henry County, a joint venture in West Tennessee, is located next to the headquarters of the American parent company.

An official of Eastech stated: "Since our products have nothing to do with the auto industry, which is concentrated in Middle Tennessee, we decided to come to East Tennessee, to be away from the auto-related industry." "Why not in West Tennessee, then?" I asked. The Eastech official answered, "Because we like East Tennessee. Our sister company has been in East Tennessee since 1982, and it is doing very well. We learned about East Tennessee, and we like it here thus far."

Here again, it seems that quality of life rather than practical matters may strongly influence the Japanese's decisions about where to locate their industries on foreign soil. But to test this impression, I have attempted to deduce some possible answers as to why some Tennessee counties host several Japanese firms and others none by examining selected socioeconomic and demographic data drawn from the 1990 U.S. Census. I pondered: What are the differences among the counties that host Japanese manufacturing and assembly plants and those that do not? What are the differences among the Three Grand Divisions of Tennessee? Are racial factors involved in location choices?

Recent biased remarks made by Japanese politicians about the minority population of the United States, an increase in Japan-bashing, and a rising tide of "Buy American" sentiment, have contributed to accusations that Japanese industrialists in the United States are averse to certain minorities. Accordingly, there is a growing body of literature that deals with the effects of racial aversion on industrial recruitment and economic growth patterns.[46] While studies indicate that industrialization did not by pass predominantly black counties, there are some significant findings related to racial composition. The findings of Stuart A. Rosenfeld and his associates indicate: *"Among poor counties only, those with a relatively smaller black population (less than 33.3 percent) grew 50 percent faster than poor counties with relatively more blacks (more than 33.3 percent)"*[italics original].[47] Glenna Colclough analyzed census data from counties in Alabama, Georgia, Mississippi, and South Carolina, and concluded that "manufacturing gains are more likely in predominantly rural, white counties, and deindustrialization is more likely in predominantly black counties."[48] The study of Michael Timberlake and his associates is of particular interest here, since their work focused on the Mid-South that embraces the South-Central stretch of the Mississippi River, including West Tennessee, west of the Tennessee River. Their conclusion concurred with the findings of Colclough: "There are clearly fewer manufacturing enterprises to be found in nonmetropolitan Mid South counties in which 30% or more of the population is Black than one would expect on the basis of the level of education, urbanization, and poverty."[49]

What about the Japanese manufacturing firms, then? Do they conform to the American industrial location patterns revealed in these studies? Since fifty-four (78.3 percent) of the Japanese manufacturing and assembly firms are located either in East or Middle Tennessee, and the black population in those two divisions is only 8.9 percent (313,042) of the total population of the two divisions (3,517,960), the aggregate statistics shown in Table 2.4 might lead us to conclude that Japanese industrialists avoid establishing their plants in counties with large black populations.

As Hamilton and Orru have warned us, however, aggregated and abstracted data can be misleading and often uninterpretable.[50] Indeed, Table 2.4 could lead us to conclude that Japanese industrial firms tend to discriminate against blacks. But when the same census information is arranged in a different way (see Table 2.6), the counties that have Japanese manufacturing and assembly plants have a higher black population by 1.7 percent on the average than do the counties that do not host Japanese manufacturing and assembly plants. By the same token, on the average, the counties that do not host Japanese firms have a higher white population by 2 percent than do the counties that host Japanese manufacturing and assembly plants. Thinking again about Hamilton and Orru's warning, however, how significant are these small differences in racial composition between the counties that host Japanese firms and the counties that do not? According to Table 2.6, the more significant differences are in the size of the civilian labor force, the percent of the population in the labor force, the unemployment rate, the percentage of people twenty-five years old or older with high school educations or more, and the per capita GNP. These factors are more favorable in the counties that host Japanese firms. As shown in Table 2.7, the factors found on the county level apply equally to towns and cities where there are Japanese manufacturing and assembly plants.

The county statistics in Table 2.8 and Table 2.9 offer further evidence against racial bias by Japanese manufacturing firms in Tennessee. Six Tennessee counties that have black populations of more than ten percent host twenty-one Japanese firms, while fourteen Tennessee counties that have black populations of less than one percent host only two Japanese

Table 2.6 • Socioeconomic and Demographic Characteristics of an Average Tennessee County by Presence or Absence of Japanese Manufacturing/Assembly Firms

Characteristics	County Hosting Japanese Manuf./ Assembly Firms	County not Hosting Japanese Manuf./ Assembly Firms	State Average
No. of Counties	33	62	—
Population Size	103,172	23,750	—
Percent of White Population	90.7	92.7	83.0
Percent of Black Population	8.5	6.8	16.0
Size of Civilian Labor Force	51,869	11,184	25,317
Percent in Labor Force	68.9	59.1	64.0
Unemployment Rate	6.5	7.3	6.4
Percent of High School Graduates or Higher among 25 Years and Over	63.3	54.8	67.1
Per Capita GNP	11,470	9,630	12,255

SOURCES: U.S. Bureau of the Census, 1990 *Census of Population and Housing: Summary Social, Economic and Housing Characteristics Tennessee* (Washington, DC: U.S. Department of Commerce, 1992), 1–24, 26–44, 45–71, 90–108; U.S. Bureaus of Census, *1990 Census of Population and Housing: Summary Population and Housing Characteristics Tennessee* (Washington, DC: U.S. Department of Commerce, 1992), 1–25, 26–50; Tennessee Department of Economic and Community Development, November 1994.
NOTE: An average of county in each category is calculated by adding the total counties' averages and then dividing by the numbers of counties included in each category; thus the outcome of the average of two categories will differ from the state average.

Table 2.7 • Socioeconomic and Demographic Characteristics of an Average Tennessee Town/City and County that Host Japanese Manufacturing/Assembly Firms

Characteristics	Town/City That Hosts Japanese Firm	County That Hosts Japanese Firm
Percent of White Population	86.3	90.7
Percent of Black Population	12.6	8.5
Percent in Labor Force	61.7	68.9
Unemployment Rate	7.3	6.5
Median Age	34.7	34.7
Percent High School Graduate or Higher among 25 Years and Over	63.5	63.3
Per capita GNP	11,527	11,470

SOURCES: U.S. Bureau of the Census, 1990 Census of Population and Housing: Summary Social, Economic and Housing Characteristics Tennessee (Washington, DC: U.S. Department of Commerce, 1992), 1–24, 26–44, 45–71, 90–108; U.S. Bureau of the Census, 1990 *Census of Population and Housing:* Summary Population and Housing Characteristics Tennessee (Washington, DC: U.S. Department of Commerce 1992), 1–25, 26–50; Tennessee Department of Economic and Community Development, November 1994.

firms. The two tables seem to indicate that, except in Madison County, the higher the percent of black population in the county, the more Japanese firms tend to be located there. The black composition of Shelby County, which includes Memphis, for instance, is 43.6 percent, and the black population of the city of Memphis is 54.8 percent; Shelby has the most Japanese manufacturing and assembly plants (eleven firms) for one county in the state. Rosenfeld and his associates' generalization does not appear to apply in the case of Japanese manufacturing and assembly, at least in Tennessee.

If a predominantly white population were the biggest single factor in industrial site selection for the Japanese, then Polk and Pickett counties, neither of which has one single black person, according to the 1990 U.S. Census, should host many Japanese manufacturing and assembly plants. Yet, neither county has attracted any Japanese investment thus far. These two counties are sparsely populated (population density is 90.4 in Polk County and 90.4 in Pickett County, while the state average is 118.3), have median ages is older than the state median age of 33.6 (Polk is 36.3 and Pickett is 37.7), and the percentage of people 25 years and older who have at least a high school education is 51.3 in Polk and 45.8 in Pickett County, much lower than the state average of 67.1 percent. Because of these factors, the percent of people in the work force in both counties cannot reach 60 percent, while the state average is 64.0 percent. Consequently, per capita GNP in these two counties is below $10,000 ($9,311 for Polk County and $9,564 for Pickett County), less than half that of the U.S. average. These figures may reveal the fact that poverty in rural southern counties is not necessarily associated with blacks.

To summarize, putting the available socioeconomic and demographic characteristics together with my own observations indicates that the presence or absence of Japanese manufacturing firms in Tennessee counties, cities, and/or towns is unrelated to the racial composition of the area. There are, of course, many unknown variables regarding manufacturing site decisions, yet the primary determinants are the availability of a well-educated labor force, a sound infrastructure, and a well-developed interstate highway system that runs in every direction. Consequently, since quite a few West Tennessee counties, especially in the northwest, are far from the interstate highways, Japanese firms are not established there. Avoidance of the West Tennessee counties by Japanese industry is probably not related to the fact that West Tennessee counties have larger black populations than do the East and Middle Tennessee counties.

The quality-of-life factor as a Japanese industrial location determinant is hard to quantify. But a number of Japanese executives whose firms are located in East and Middle Tennessee told me that their preference is based

Table 2.8 • Distribution of Japanese Manufacturing/Assembly Firms by Tennessee Counties with 10 or More Percent Black Population

County	Percent of Black Population[a]	Division of Tennessee	Number of Japanese Firms[b]
Davidson	23.4	Middle	5
Hamilton	19.1	East	3
Henry	10.1	West	1
Madison	31.0	West	2
Robertson	11.0	Middle	1
Shelby	43.6	West	11

SOURCES: [a]U.S. Bureau of the Census, 1990 *Census of Population and Housing: Summary Social, Economic and Housing Characteristics Tennessee* (Washington DC: U.S. Department of Commerce, 1992), 1–24.
[b]Tennessee Department of Economic and Community Development, November 1994.

Table 2.9 • Distribution of Japanese Manufacturing/Assembly Firms by Tennessee Counties with Less than 1 Percent Black Population

County	Total Population	No. of Blacks	Percent Black	No. of Japanese Firm[a]
Campbell	35,079	130	0.4	0
Cumberland	34,736	42	0.1	1
Fentress	14,669	2	0.0	0
Grainger	17,095	102	0.6	0
Jackson	9,279	7	0.0	0
Johnson	13,766	61	0.4	0
Macon	15,906	44	0.3	0
Pickett	4,548	0	0.0	0
Polk	13,643	0	0.0	0
Scott	18,353	5	0.0	0
Sequatchie	8,863	2	0.0	0
Unicoi	16,549	3	0.0	1
Union	13,694	3	0.0	0
Van Buren	4,846	5	0.1	0

SOURCE: U.S. Bureau of the Census, *1990 Census of Population and Housing: Summary of Social, Economic and Housing Characteristics Tennessee* (Washington, DC: U.S. Department of Commerce, 1992). 1-4.
[a]Tennessee Department of Economic and Community Development, November 1994.

on the similarity between the physical characteristics of East and Middle Tennessee and those of Japan. East and Middle Tennessee, with mountains, valleys, and rivers, are more like home to the Japanese than the featureless landscapes of West Tennessee.

Deciding on a location for an industrial firm is a complicated process that involves innumerable considerations. It is understandable why many companies list an array of reasons as to why they came to a specific site and tell us the reasons are equally influential.

_3_

MYTH AND REALITY OF JAPANESE INDUSTRY IN THE SOUTH

JAPANESE KNOWLEDGE OF THE SOUTH

There is a general belief that before the Japanese establish their factories overseas they prepare well to deal with the natives and the local culture. Such a myth is reinforced when one learns that, in preparation for their overseas assignments, Japanese managers read a Chinese classic, Sun Tzu's *On War*, as if they were soldiers preparing for a major battle.[1] The school brochure of the Tennessee Meiji Gakuin High School in Sweetwater, Tennessee, even states that the mission of the school is "to educate children of the overseas Japanese *kigyou senshi*," meaning literally "combat soldiers in business enterprises." It sounds as if Japanese industrialists prepare to do battle rather than business in Tennessee.

General belief and military imagery notwithstanding, most Japanese expatriates in Tennessee are amazingly ill-prepared to deal with the people of the region and their culture. All Japanese expatriates know in the abstract that the United States is gigantic in size and that its population is ethnically and racially complex. Few of them, nonetheless, have a real comprehension of the actual size and complexity of the United States, for their frame of reference is always their homeland, and Japan is a relatively small country with a homogeneous population. Except for Japanese executives and managers at Eastech, which has a long history of foreign business operations (including one in an English-speaking country), most Japanese expatriates have undergone virtually no preparation other than taking intensive English lessons for a few weeks or a few months before moving to the United States.

Japanese expatriates assigned to work alongside southern workers are unaware of the history and culture of the American South. When the newly opened Tennessee Meiji Gakuin School was menaced by a "cross-burning,"[2] for instance, the principal of the school seemed unaware of the seriousness of the incident. In my interview with him, I received the impression that he thought the cross-burning was the townspeople's way of

71

celebrating. According to the principal, the *New York Times* reported the incident and then a leading Japanese newspaper quoted the *Times*, after which he had to answer many phone calls from students' parents who were concerned about the safety of their children. In addition to the school principal, almost no other Japanese with whom I talked during my fieldwork knew that the Ku Klux Klan (KKK) was first organized in Pulaski, Tennessee, some seventy miles south of Nashville. I was unable to find any Japanese in Tennessee who understand the symbolic meaning of the Confederate flag and the reason why most blacks hate the Rebel-flag waving at the University of Mississippi football games.[3]

Although many Japanese and many Americans have visited each other's countries, and although cultural exchange between the two countries has been extensive, the gap between the cultures remains wide, and misunderstandings are common. In fall 1992, a Japanese high-school exchange student in Baton Rouge, Louisiana, was shot to death after he knocked on a resident's front door wearing a Halloween costume. Confronted by a gun, the student continued to walk toward the man even after being warned by the command, "Freeze!" He did not know what the word meant. Frankly, before the word "freeze" became an issue in the tragedy via mass media, I too was unaware of the word. The tragic killing is a classic case of the misunderstandings and miscommunications that result from language barriers.

Even if the Japanese "combat soldiers in business enterprises" know something about the cultural heritage of Dixie, that knowledge has not yet filtered down to the "field commanders'" levels. Perhaps the Japanese industrialists in Japan assume that Asians are immune to, or at least less subject to, racial discrimination in the South, since the traditional racial strife has been between blacks and whites.[4]

There is yet another myth held by the general public: that the culture of Japanese industry in the South is uniquely Japanese. People believe that, since the Japanese have been so successful in industrial management, they must replicate their unique managerial practices in their plants in the American South. The American mass media have publicized some of the positive aspects of Japanese industrial relations, particularly job security, decent wages, and good working conditions; thus, southern workers have shown an unusual interest in and enthusiasm about working for Japanese firms. In fact, when Toyota established its plant in Georgetown, Kentucky, 130,000 workers applied for some 4,100 openings.[5] And, when Nissan was adding a second passenger car line at its Smyrna plant in 1989, the plant hired 150 workers out of a pool of 20,000 applicants.[6] A great many southern workers believed that they would find lifetime employment in the Japanese firms. The reality of Japanese industry in the South is quite different.

3.1 • A View of Eastech.

THE PHYSICAL SETTINGS OF JAPANESE INDUSTRY

The three firms, Eastech, Midtech, and Westech, are no strangers to foreign direct investment in an alien land. Westech, a joint venture, is relatively small in scale and capital compared with some Japanese international giants. Yet the parent company in Japan has over seventy years of history and extensive experience. From October 1978, the company has been offering technical know-how to a Korean rubber company. Founded some eighty years ago, the parent company of Midtech is much larger than that of Westech both in capital and in the total number of employees in its four major plants in Japan. In addition to its plant in Tennessee, Midtech has subsidiaries in Thailand that give technical assistance to firms in England and Indonesia. Founded more than seventy-five years ago, the parent company of Eastech and its conglomerate form the biggest of the three and one of the world's largest electronic giants. One of its subsidiaries, located in Singapore since 1972, exports to twenty-two countries around the world. Of the three firms, Eastech's parent has the most extensive experience in international business operations.

A common characteristic among these three plants, despite many variations, is that they are newly built, so that their physical appearances are attractive. They all look as if they were office complexes of trading or business firms. One finds in them no nonpolluting, high-rising smokestacks or other stereotypical features of manufacturing plants and run-down factories. The offices of white-collar employees and managers are adjacent to the production floor, so production workers have easy access to managers.

The managerial practices of Japanese firms in Tennessee vary from firm to firm and from location to location. A visitor to a Japanese industrial firm in the United States, however, would be surprised by the absence of "Japan-ness," at least on the surface. Based on the company name and its

3.2 • A Japanese Engineer with an American Operator in the Eastech Plant

logo, one would have trouble identifying whether it is Japanese. Most of the time, the Japanese firms use an abbreviated version of the name of the company or an American name. No Japanese flags are hung; as in domestic firms, the flags of the United States, of the state, and of the company are flown. Upon entering the reception area, one is greeted by Americans.

The physical layout of the offices of white-collar workers in Japan differs from that of most U.S. domestic firms. For privacy-conscious Americans, almost every manager in a domestic firm has his or her own private office. Even some low-echelon clerks have their own offices, or at least partitions reaching almost to the ceiling in order to provide semi-privacy. In most Japanese firms in Japan, except for a few top executives, Japanese white-collar workers work in large open offices, grouped by sections or departments. The lowest-ranking employee sits next to the entrance door. Usually a deputy sits at the left or right side of the back, facing the subordinates, side view, so that he (almost always he, rarely she) can keep in close contact with the people he supervises and observe their activities. The desk of the head of the section or department is not in a separate room but at the back or center of the office—right next to a tea table, several comfortable chairs, and a couch—where the head calls up his subordinates for small group meetings or where he receives visitors.

The physical layout of most Japanese firms in Tennessee does not copy the Japanese practice but rather is a hybrid or a combination of Japanese and American arrangements. There are more private or semi-private offices for the middle managers and, in large rooms, more partitions to facilitate semi-privacy. An interesting phenomenon is the height of the partitions. In the firms that are owned solely by Japanese, partitions are very low, to allow a supervisor oversight of the entire section or department. In the joint venture firms, however, such as Westech, the partitions are higher than in the average Japanese-owned firm in Tennessee yet much lower than in most domestic firms that have adapted the Japanese practice of partitioning. Perhaps the height of the partition represents a societal value placed on privacy or serves as an indicator of acculturation.

In Midtech, when I began my fieldwork, the physical setting of the firm had numerous, small, private and semi-private offices for middle- and upper-echelon managers and executives. For the general clerks, there was a large, open office space without any partitions. However, when the newly appointed Japanese president remodeled the main office building, he made fundamental structural changes in the plant. Except for a private office for the president, he eliminated all private and semi-private offices in order to create a large open space for all white-collar employees and to provide conference rooms—one large and several small—for various meetings. My informant told me that the new president believed that the new arrangement would enhance work efficiency and facilitate cooperation among white-collar workers. The informant added that the new president was expected to generate some profits by 1993, and that every employee of Midtech wore a button for the campaign "93," the target year for profit making.

My early impression of the remodeling on Midtech's business, was that it seemed to have affected the morale of the employees. Whenever I visited the firm before the remodeling, most employees seemed to be in an upbeat mood, and some even cracked jokes with me. After the remodeling, most of them became formal and reserved, probably because everyone could see us when we carried on conversations and everyone could hear what we were talking about. No one wanted to talk about anything private. It appears that the remodeling created some stress in most workers, both Japanese and Americans, except for the president who initiated the change.

In addition to affecting employee morale, the new physical setting caused some inconveniences and discomforts. The director of human resources, for example, who is responsible for administration, personnel, safety, training, and other mundane matters, was, after the remodeling seated in the corner of the hallway between two receptionists and the main office, with no partition. A person wanting to take a grievance to the director would be reluctant to do so, because the remodeling physically made it easy to identify and overhear conversations by anyone approaching the director. I sat in the reception area and observed the way the new system works. When a visitor, perhaps a salesman or a buyer, comes in, one of two receptionists calls the appropriate person, who then escorts the visitor to a vacant meeting room to discuss business; the worker does not have a private office. Some American employees of Midtech still display resentment over the lack of privacy resulting from the remodeling. The director of human resources who manifested his dissatisfaction with the new physical layout resigned from the company in 1994. Regardless of such complaints, however, the new Japanese president accomplished his goal (escaping the red and eliminating revenue loss) by the target year of 1993. Midtech thrives toward generating profits. Since January 1995, every Midtech employee has worn a button displaying the slogan, "Sun Shine," for profit making.

The setting and physical arrangement of Eastech differs from that of both Midtech and Westech. Perhaps due to their long experience in overseas business operation, Eastech has seen to it that a visitor cannot approach the main office without first clearing security at the front gate. A security guard inquires of a visitor the nature of the visit, time of appointment, and with whom the appointment has been made. When the security officer is satisfied with all the information, he or she issues a parking pass and instructs the visitor where to park. I often took advantage of being Asian. The guard automatically assumed that I was a Japanese businessman or even someone associated with the parent company in Japan. Because of my Asian features, my entrance at the front gate was always smooth; the guard never checked with the person with whom I had an appointment. (In my earlier visits, even some Japanese engineers thought that I was Japanese.)

After an Eastech visitor clears security and enters the main building, a receptionist arranges for the visitor to go to the appropriate section or department. In my case, my informant always came out to greet me, and we usually took a seat in the company's cafeteria or went directly inside the plant. When visiting Westech or Midtech, one has to fill out the company's visitation log indicating hours of visit, name of the visitor, person to visit, reason for the visit, and citizenship of the visitor. After one supplies all the information, the receptionist issues a visitor's tag or badge to be worn during the entire visit. Eastech, however, does not require visitors to enter data into a log. As I identified myself, the receptionist always issued a visitor's badge. Considering the tight security system at the front gate, the procedure in the reception area appears to be simpler than that of the other two firms. Perhaps the receptionist in Eastech trusts that the front gate has already screened the visitor, so that she does not need further verification.

In spring 1993, the subsidiaries of major Japanese corporations began to feel fiscal restraints resulting from a prolonged recession in Japan. Eastech, for instance, abolished its receptionist position and instead made security guards at the front gate responsible for screening visitors and issuing visitor's tags. The guard now calls and informs the appropriate person of the visitor, and the employee greets the visitor in the reception area. It is indeed a lean operation.

PARKING

In the parking lots of most of the Japanese-owned firms, one sees clearly marked spots for the physically handicapped, but there are no reserved parking spaces for the company president or any other executive. All employees have equal access to available parking spaces.[7] In comparison, in an overseas Korean manufacturing firm in the Midwest, with an industrial culture similar to that of the Japanese companies in Tennessee, I noticed that a special parking space was marked and reserved for the chairman. It would seem that the Japanese are more conscientious than the Koreans about upholding the egalitarian values that appeal to their American employees.

UNIFORMS

In most Japanese-owned firms, everyone, including the company president and executives, wears the same uniform, with a name tag above the right breast pocket carrying only the first name. No rank and title are specified anywhere, either on the uniforms or the hard hats. Anyone who has been in Japan knows that wearing a uniform there is common practice. Street sweepers wear uniforms; so do school children and office workers. Although businesspeople in Japan are not required to wear uniforms *per se*, they commonly wear uniform-like clothing, mostly dark blue, dark gray, or black suits with ties.

At Eastech, a dozen engineers, because they are on temporary assignment from the parent company in Japan, wear a different color uniform from that of the regular employees in the firm. In so doing, the Japanese engineers are easily identifiable to the American workers who may need their assistance. In contrast, employees of the joint venture of Westech do not wear uniforms. As in any ordinary American industrial firm, the working clothes of Westech employees range from jeans to more formal, but comfortable, clothing.

UPHOLDING AMERICAN EGALITARIAN VALUES

As an effort to court America workers' good graces (or to win American workers' favor), some Japanese industries in the United States have introduced several programs. The programs are based on upholding American egalitarian values that the Japanese consider an American strength. The programs are: euphemeizing job titles and Americanizing Japanese names.

EUPHEMIZING JOB TITLES

The origin and function of the Japanese way of referring to their industrial workers as "associates," "engineers," or "technicians," are unknown.
Some speculate that such a designation is a deliberate attempt to elevate the
stereotypical image of the blue-collar worker to some sort of professional
status. Bridgestone addresses its employees as "engineers," and Nissan calls
its employees "technicians."

Euphemizing job titles is a fashion in Far Eastern countries. When I was
in Korea prior to the mid-1960s, a chauffeur was addressed as *unjŏn'su*,
meaning "a person who operates automobiles." When I visited Korea in the
early 1980s, I unintentionally offended a chauffeur by using the old term. I
should have addressed him as *unjŏn'gisa* or simply *kisa*, meaning literally
"an *engineer*" who operates automobiles. I wondered whether such a change
in term of address really brought about any change in one's social status
and/or functional relationship to others in the society.

In this context, I asked the president of Midtech about job titles in his
firm, particularly about the term "engineer." He bluntly criticized the practice adopted by some Japanese firms as a "deception." In his firm, everyone
is addressed as "employee." He told me, "How can I call a general laborer
and unskilled employee in my firm an engineer? He or she knows, and I
know, that it is not true. Perhaps I might end up insulting a real engineer.
The title should be earned, not simply given by others. I myself am an engineer. I worked very hard to earn the title." When I asked the same question
of an American worker, he said: "I don't really care what they call me. As
long as I do my job and they pay me an honest wage for my day's work, I'm
fine." The Japanese practice of addressing their employees with professional or semi-professional labels may not go over well with all of their
American workers, who may be less impressionable than the Japanese
expect them to be.

When Japanese firms call their employees "associate," they believe they
are adopting the American value of egalitarianism. By addressing everyone
as associate, from the chairman of the board to rank-and-file workers, those
firms intend to issue a strong message: "We are all equal in the company,
although job assignments are different." Certainly, a good many Japanese
firms employ "associates," but among the three firms included in this
study, only Westech uses the term "associates" for its employees.

AMERICANIZING JAPANESE NAMES

The most consistent, congruent, and uniform rule of Japanese industrial
culture in Tennessee is the extensive use of first names. As noted above,
even the name tag on an employee's uniform carries only a first name.

Every Japanese working in a Japanese-owned firm in Tennessee has adopted a common American-style first name, such as Mark, Sue, or Mike, or a simplified version of her or his Japanese name that can be pronounced easily by Americans, such as Tag or Chik. These nicknames are printed on business cards and uniform name tags. The Japanese encourage American employees to address them by their reinvented first names, regardless of their ranks, ages, and other classifications. Since it is indeed difficult for most Americans to pronounce multisyllabic Japanese names, they no doubt welcome the simplified nomenclature, whether or not they recognize the practice as a Japanese appeal to the egalitarian values of the American work force.

It is amazing how flexible and adaptive the Japanese are as compared with other Asians, particularly Koreans. In Korean firms located in the United States, most Korean personnel have kept their traditional Korean names, which are difficult for the average American to pronounce. For historical reasons, Koreans are adamant about not altering their names or not having them altered. As the Japanese colonial rule over the Korean peninsula was intensified during World War II, the Japanese required the Koreans to adopt Japanese patterns of names as an attempt to annex the Korean culture to their own. (In order to enter a public school that was run by the Japanese colonial government, I had to change my traditional three-syllable Korean name to a Japanese name with six syllables.)

I wondered how the Japanese respect for old age and seniority could be compatible with the informality of using just names. How would an elderly Japanese executive feel when an American worker young enough to be his grandchild addressed him by his first name? The elderly Japanese executive to whom I put this question smiled and said, "Oh, yes, my name is 'Tony,'" and commented:

> In Japan, it would be unacceptable for a rank-and-file worker who is young enough to be my grandson to address me without prefixing my name with an honorific, such as *san* (Mr.) or *sensei* (teacher). In Japan, it is absolutely impossible for a youngster to call me "Tony." But, here I don't mind because I asked them to call me as such. It's supposed to be the American way—friendly, intimate, relaxed, and informal. It doesn't really bother me who calls me "Tony." The simple truth is "Tony" is not my name anyway, so I don't have any particular feeling about it. Even if they called me by an obscenity, I don't believe I'd care. Because I try to learn English by memorizing each word, I don't have the same feelings as the natives would have. If identifying me as "Tony" is easy for American workers, it's okay with me.

Despite the Japanese's insistence that their employees address everyone by first names, in reality not many young American rank-and-file workers address their senior Japanese executives this way. Referring to the president of the company, who is just about to retire, a young American worker told me, "I just call him 'Mr. K' because I can't pronounce his full name. Also, I don't want to call him by his American first name. You know, he's too darn old for that." "K" is the initial of the retiring president's long last name, which is hard to pronounce and takes several aspirations.

INTERCULTURAL UNDERSTANDING IN JAPANESE INDUSTRY

By now, the importance of cultural understanding in international business and industry is a textbook case. Gary P. Ferraro asserts; "The success or failure of a company abroad depends on how effectively its employees can exercise their skills in a new location. That ability will depend on both their job-related expertise *and* the individual's sensitivity and responsiveness to the new cultural environment."[8] Various studies indicate that failures in overseas business settings often result from an inability to understand and adapt to foreign ways of thinking and acting rather than from technical or professional incompetence.[9] In the early 1990s, the mass media began to report on the important role that business and industrial anthropology could play in enhancing cross-cultural understanding or obviating misunderstanding in international business and industry.[10] However, anthropological work, which moves slowly and proceeds cautiously, cannot catch up to the rapid pace of international business and industrial expansions. Hence, businesspeople and industrial workers who are assigned to foreign cultural milieux face all sorts of "culture shock," from which the Japanese expatriates in the American South, Tennessee in particular, are not exempt.

CULTURE SHOCK

According to anthropologist Kalervo Oberg, who popularized the term, *culture shock* is:

> precipitated by the anxiety that results from losing all our familiar signs and symbols of social intercourse. These signs or cues include the thousand and one ways in which we orient ourselves to the situations of daily life: when to shake hands and what to say when we meet people, when and how to give tips, how to give orders to servants, how to make purchases, when to accept and when to refuse invitations, when to take statements seriously and when not. Now these cues which may be words, gestures, facial expressions, customs, or norms are acquired by all of us in the course of growing up and are as much a part of our culture

as the language we speak or the beliefs we accept. All of us depend for our peace of mind and our efficiency on hundreds of these cues, most of which we do not carry on the level of conscious awareness.[11]

Culture shock is "the psychological disorientation experienced by people who suddenly find themselves living and working in radically different cultural environments....Cultural shock ranges from mild irritation to a deep-seated psychological panic or crisis."[12]

Whenever one goes into an alien society and culture, regardless of how well one has prepared emotionally and intellectually to cope with the "foreignness," it is impossible to escape from culture shock. Japanese expatriates in the United States have felt culture shock, either good or bad, possibly both. In fact, some Japanese have had a rather shocking introduction to a negative aspect of American culture. T.R. Reid has reported a tale of some ugly Americans:

> The well-dressed Japanese businessman was walking down a busy sidewalk in New York when he accidently bumped into a young man. The impact caused the American to drop a bag he was carrying, and a bottle of wine smashed to the sidewalk. "You idiot! You smashed my Lafite-Rothschild!" the American shouted angrily. "That's a $200 bottle of wine—and you broke it!" Stunned, embarrassed and fearful, the Japanese pulled out $200 and paid on the spot for the lost wine. In fact, according to Hiroko Kazama, who recently taught a seminar here on travel to the United States, that sidewalk collision was no accident, and the broken wine bottle was really just $2.99 rotgut.[13]

Culture shock goes both ways. A former trainee who had been in Japan told me bluntly, "It was shocking, all right." An American floor manager told me about his observations during his training in Japan:

> Persons like me, who had some college experience, were a bit more curious about other cultures, and made deliberate efforts to learn about Japanese culture. Perhaps I might have experienced less cultural shock than some others. I tried to eat all kinds of Japanese food. But some of our guys couldn't eat any Japanese food; they were not interested in adventuring in Japanese culture. Even though the Japanese provided sandwiches for lunch, it wasn't the same as our guys had in mind. Some of those guys wanted to eat McDonald's hamburgers because it reminded them of home. One fellow ate nothing but McDonald's hamburgers all the time during our full month's stay. You can imagine what kind of shape he had when we were ready to come home....It was shocking to observe Japanese supervisors yelling and shouting at their workers in front of everyone, even in the presence of foreigners like us. It was a

sheer humiliation, and a genuine cultural shock to us....You can read our report and you will find a consistent suggestion that, before the company sends us to Japan for training, either our company or the hosting Japanese company must provide a rather detailed orientation to Japanese culture. We need to know what to expect from Japan, so we can at least prepare for it mentally.

Koji Taira commented on the training of American workers in Japan: "Japanese firms operating in foreign countries regularly send their host-country employees to Japan for training and indoctrination. In Japan, not only do they acquire work skills, but they pick up a taste for Japanese-style living and habits."[14] Taira's assessment of the results of training American workers in Japan is not exactly the same as that of the floor manager.

It is true that the history of Japanese overseas direct investment is relatively short as compared with that of the United States and Western European nations,[15] and that the Japanese are often hesitant and even reluctant to invest overseas.[16] As a major player in foreign direct investment, however, the Japanese have developed a cultural awareness program for overseas personnel, but it is not yet adequate for the intensity of their overseas investment, even though they are concerned about possible frictions and negative responses from the host country. As Tetsuo Abo indicated, "culture is not simply a residual after we take out the 'rational' factors, but an understandable factor which exerts a regular influence on certain functional levels of an economy."[17] If this is the case, orientation to the culture of the host country or region for the Japanese managers who are assigned to their overseas firms could be very helpful.

An official in the Japan Center in Murfreesboro, Tennessee,[18] told me that the center answers more inquiries from Americans and American companies about the Japanese and their culture than the reverse. (The center has even introduced experts—usually of Japanese origin—on Japan and Japanese culture to the American firms.) If this trend continues, Tennesseans may acquire more knowledge about Japanese culture than the Japanese will have about America, the American South, and Tennessee in particular.

Although the Japanese occasionally socialize with Americans after work and on weekends, more often they tend to get together with their own countrymen on the golf course on weekends and at other gatherings. Japanese are gregarious among themselves but not among Americans or other outsiders. None of the three firms included in this study has any institutionalized program to provide knowledge about American culture. Some wives of the Japanese personnel working in the Tennessee firms have managed to learn English via tutorial services, but no formal or organized classes or other activities are available for Japanese emigrants.

AMERICAN PERSONNEL IN JAPANESE FIRMS

Some reports and statistics are available on the chief executive officers in Japanese firms overseas and American firms in Japan. "A survey done [in 1983] by the Japan Overseas Enterprises Association reports that of all Japanese subsidiaries located in advanced countries, in only 16.2 percent have local people been appointed to executive positions. Also, interestingly, in as many as 79.5 percent of the cases, the respondents predicted that in the future the president would [continue to] be a Japanese."[19] Figures comparing the practice of American business enterprises and those of Japanese are interesting. Hideki Yoshihara states:

> In Japan, presidents of many foreign companies are Japanese. Of 1,052 companies for which data are available, 699 (66.4 per cent) have Japanese presidents. Three-fourths of the 611 American companies (450 companies) have a president who is Japanese. These data are in sharp contrast with the small number of foreign nationals being appointed presidents of Japanese overseas subsidiaries. The general tendency is to appoint Japanese presidents in foreign subsidiaries lo-cated in Japan, while there are but few cases of foreigners being appointed presidents of Japanese subsidiaries abroad.[20]

Another report presents a slightly different figure but basically points out the same reality: "Official Japanese figures show that 85 percent of Japanese firms in the United States have a Japanese chief executive. Only 20 percent of American firms in Japan have an American in charge."[21] There are no known statistics regarding managers other than the chief executives. Some scholars such as Yoshihara assume that Japanese domination of managerial positions might be similar to that of the top executives.[22]

The chief executives of the firms included in this study include both Japanese and Americans, regardless of the aggregate statistics on executive appointments in overseas Japanese firms. The chairman, chief executive officer (CEO), and president of the joint venture of Westech are all Americans. Eastech has a Japanese CEO. Midtech has a Japanese president and CEO. Since these firms were not selected randomly and do not represent a large enough sample on which to generalize, I looked at the CEOs of sixty Japanese manufacturing and assembly firms in Tennessee and found that ten (17 percent) of them are Americans and thirty-six (60 percent) are Japanese nationals; Data were unavailable on the other fourteen (23 percent). These figures are similar to those in the reports mentioned previously.

The overwhelming number of CEOs in Japanese firms overseas are indeed Japanese nationals. Japanese scholars have been critical of this parochial worldview and management of Japanese overseas operations. A comment made by Yoshihara is worth noting here:

> There are many Japanese companies which may be characterised as multinational enterprises. Their business activities are spread over the globe, with bases in almost every country of the world. What are the genuine advantages of multinational enterprises compared with domestic companies? One important advantage is that multinational enterprises can recruit excellent foreign talent and utilize their capabilities. However, in the case of Japanese multinationals, many local managers and engineers feel frustrated and cannot display their capabilities to the fullest. Also, there are few local nationals who reach the position of company president, and few graduates from top schools are recruited. Thus, Japanese multinational companies are not capitalising on the genuine advantage of multinational corporations, that is, the opportunity for utilising human resources in every country they operate in.[23]

If the Japanese are working toward building firms of global scale, they will need to hire the most talented people, regardless of their origins and nationalities.

There are a couple of factors that impel many Japanese firms to appoint only Japanese nationals as CEOs. Some Japanese industrialists believe that in order to maintain a competitive advantage over others they have to apply the production system created at home;[24] and that to transplant the system properly, they must use their own personnel.[25] An informant in Midtech told me that a strong Japanese identity in the firm is of the utmost importance. Japanese Americans are not so welcome, because they usually lack that strong identity, or "Japan-ness."

Another factor dictating the appointments of Japanese nationals as CEOs is beyond the industrialists' control. Many overseas Japanese firms, especially small-scale suppliers to the major manufacturing industries, are too small to afford the salaries commanded by competent American executives. Midtech falls into this category. Although some Japanese firms in Tennessee employ several thousands of people, others hire fewer than fifty employees, with the median number 140. The average size of a Japanese firm in Tennessee is indeed very small.

Westech, as a joint venture, is small, yet it has an American chair and a president who are locals. The highest-ranking Japanese is vice president in charge of sales—an irony, because overseas Japanese firms commonly hire as sales managers local persons familiar with the local markets.[26] For Westech, however, since it manufactures auto parts, a person familiar with "local markets" is a Japanese whose local markets are the Japanese auto plants in the United States and Canada.

Any charge or criticism that some Japanese firms in the United States, and in Tennessee in particular, do not employ American executives and managers is not always applicable to giant Japanese firms. Nissan, for instance, has an American president, and Eastech also has an American COO and several American middle managers. Since Eastech is a subsidiary of one of the world's largest electronics makers and is also experienced in overseas direct investment, the firm can afford to recruit highly capable American executives. Thus, the style and manner of operation at Eastech are almost the same as those of world-ranking American and European corporations, which is an indication that the major criteria for employing American executives in Japanese firms in the United States, at least in the case of Tennessee, are the firm's size, scale of operations, amount of capital investment, and history of overseas operations. Such big firms are usually well known to the American public and capable of attracting qualified American executives and meeting their expectations, including a high salary. This observation warrants a discussion of the difficulties overseas Japanese firms often experience in recruiting highly qualified Americans.

DIFFICULTIES FINDING QUALIFIED AMERICANS

Even if most overseas Japanese firms were willing to fill middle- and upper-managerial positions with Americans and to promote them, not many well-qualified, ambitious young Americans want to work for the Japanese. The reasons for their reluctance are well-documented and widely reported; Yoshihara relates an episode that explains. Once he asked a question of C.A. Bartlett, professor of International Business and Economics at Harvard Business School, "Assuming that you graduated from Harvard Business School, would you want to work for a Japanese company in the USA? 'No,' was his answer."[27] Then, Bartlett summarized from his perspective some reasons why graduates from Ivy League and other first class American business schools would not want to work for a Japanese company:

> First, the initial salary is low....Furthermore, after joining the company, the pace of salary increases and promotions is slow. This is because of the seniority system....The second reason is the lack of sufficient opportunities for promotion. Most of the presidents of these companies in the USA are Japanese nationals....Even if one is promoted, the idea of reaching, at best, the post of vice-president will not be attractive....The third reason is the Japanese language. Since the company is a subsidiary, communication with the Japanese parent company is inevitable. Often such communication can be carried out only in Japanese: communicating in Japanese is difficult for Americans....A fourth reason is the lack of opportunities for participation. Important decisions are handed down by Japanese, while Americans cannot take part in the mainstream decision-making process. Final decisions are made at meetings, but these meetings are no more than simple formalities.

Important decisions are handed down by Japanese after 5 P.M., communicating with the Japanese parent company.[28]

Disinclination to work for overseas Japanese firms is not limited to Americans. Yoshihara points out that the reluctance is common among Europeans as well as many nationals from the newly industrialized Asian countries. To summarize their sentiments: The methods for performing the various jobs are not always easy to understand; the foreign subsidiary has insufficient strategic autonomy; the Japanese factory's organizational climate is egalitarian, so that managers and engineers are deprived of the special treatment and rights they enjoy in their current jobs; and, Japanese companies overseas are not attractive due to their low profiles.[29] Indeed, not many Americans can even make a distinction between Mitsubishi and Matsushita.

Most of the points included in Yoshihara's list may be valid for white-collar workers having elite business school degrees. Since my fieldwork in Japanese firms was among employees rather than potential employees, I cannot assess the attitudes of the latter toward the Japanese firms. Whenever I met job seekers, they were mostly blue-collar workers who were eager to work. It is my impression that Japanese firms are very popular among blue-collar workers and that the Japanese work better with blue-collar workers than with white-collar workers and business school graduates.[30] Japanese and American blue-collar workers enjoy a well-developed mutual affinity and admiration. An American blue-collar worker told me, "I don't really care whatever the name of the company I'm working for. As long as it offers me a good job, I'm fine. IBM, GE, or any other big names wouldn't offer me a job anyway." Certainly they are pragmatic rather than concerned about the reputation of the company, as the business school graduates might be.

White-collar, especially managerial, positions are, however, different from blue-collar jobs. One of my informants, who held an MBA degree and was director of human resources in a Japanese firm, suddenly resigned from his position. This action surprised everyone in the company, because he was the first Tennessean hired by the firm when it was established. Even though he denies that his resignation had anything to do with job dissatisfaction or with working for and dealing with the Japanese, he had apparently become considerably frustrated. He saw the limit of his growth opportunity in that firm. Several of the factors in Yoshihara's list apply to this man's resignation.

One middle manager told me of his frustration. As an energetic, dynamic, and straightforward person, he was irritated and thwarted by the Japanese's chronically hesitant, notoriously slow, and often inscrutable decision making. He told me:

You've lived in this country long enough, so you understand American culture, right? If you are straightforward in America, as long as you're not rude to others, your opinion can be valued. But, if you're like that in Japanese company, they think you're rude and crass. That's okay. I don't have to express my feelings directly. But, boy, it drives me crazy when they don't tell me what they think and actually mean. You know what I mean?...Most of all, I'm tired of the many meetings. People who are not directly related to the topics at hand are also requested to attend these meetings....You've heard the talk about decision making by consensus. I'm not so sure whether I'm included in this process.

It appeared to me that the frustrated manager was ready to move whenever he could find a job elsewhere that would pay him better or at least the same. From listening to his frustration, I could understand why "50% of American managers either resign or are fired within 18 months of foreign takeover."[31] This is indeed a high rate of turnover, much higher than that of rank-and-file workers, whose average turnover rate is about 5 percent (in the case of Eastech).

During my fieldwork, I met a former vice president of one of the major Japanese auto makers. An MBA degree holder from an elite business school, he could have stayed with the Japanese company if he had wanted to, but he resigned and became president of Henry Companies. The size and scale of Henry Companies, an American manufacturing firm included in this study, is nowhere near that of his previous firm. He did not move solely because of the frustrations involved in working in a foreign-owned firm, but because he wanted to be involved actively in decision-making. He told me in an informal gathering at the home of a Japanese executive, "In my whole business career, I have always worked for gigantic corporations. My own ideas and initiative have often been buried in a large bureaucratic organization. At this stage of my professional career, instead of following instructions from others, I really would like to implement my own ideas in actual business operations. The company I represent now is small enough to implement my ideas." He was very careful not to directly criticize his former employer, yet there were enough allusions to indicate that his ideas were not implemented and his voice was seldom heard in that Japanese auto giant. Most of all, as a graduate of one of the best business schools in the country, he would not have been happy to remain as "vice-something" for the rest of his career. He is no longer "vice-something."

THE DILEMMA OF JAPANESE PERSONNEL IN THE JAPANESE FIRMS

Working in Japanese firms is not easy for Americans because of cultural differences. At the same time, Japanese managers, especially middle managers, who work in overseas Japanese firms are not free from difficulties and frustration. Unlike the chief executives, middle managers play the role of "double boiler:" they must take enormous pressure from the bottom, ranging from communication problems to other culture-bound problems of the rank-and-file American workers; yet they do not know exactly what is "cooking upstairs," at the top executive level. A Japanese middle manager observed to me:

> Democratically oriented Americans tend to misunderstand the basic nature of the corporations. A corporation cannot be run always democratically. It's almost like a military organization—chain of command, spans of control, job classifications, divisions of division heads, and standard operating procedures to guide every decision. Often a direct order comes from Tokyo....Many American employees, including managers, think that we Japanese get together in the evening after all the Americans go home, and make a lot of serious business decisions. They feel that they are cut off from those meetings, thus feel very alienated....First of all, we are not wining and dining together all the time. Sometimes, even if we are having a gathering, I myself do not feel so comfortable associating with top executives either. We have a very rigid hierarchy in terms of rank as well as age grade....About certain decisions that have been made or changed overnight, I myself was not aware of it. I don't think even the president anticipated such a new order until we got a fax or phone call from Japan. See, we are 14 or 15 hours behind Tokyo time, depending upon whether the summer daylight savings time is in effect or not. When the Tokyo office opens in the morning at 9 A.M., our time here in Tennessee is evening, after American managers and employees have gone home. When we receive a new order or instruction, we cannot inform the American managers right away. You know how fast they are in their homeward rush after work. We have to wait until the next morning. Then, we may have to change it, if necessary. As they hear about such changes and new instructions, Americans think we changed it ourselves in the evening after they left for home. On many occasions, we are falsely charged with alienating the Americans....I must admit, though, we are not doing a good job of explaining the time difference. Even if we do, for many who do not have experience in dealing with different time zones, it would be very difficult to really get a feel for it. Also, many Americans think we are working too long after quitting time, especially top executives. More often than not, although we like to be punctual in quitting as much as Americans do, some of us have to wait to see any urgent messages coming from the headquarters in Japan as they open their office at 9:00 A.M. in the morning.

By talking to other Japanese middle managers, I have learned that the problems and the frustrations they face in Tennessee are not any easier to take than those of the Americans and are possibly harder. In fact, except for a few who volunteered, most of them came to Tennessee not by choice but because they were assigned by the firms.

Such problems and frustrations are common in other foreign industries located in the United States. An angry Korean vice president for engineering in a Korean firm in the Midwest once called up all Korean engineers in the plant to chastise them for their tardiness and told them, "If you perform the way you are doing now, I'm going to send you back home!" After the meeting, one engineer told me, "Wouldn't it be good if he would do that. I really want to go home. I'm tired of staying here, leaving my family back home. Actually, I'm staying longer here than the company promised me. I wish he meant to."

Except for locally hired people of Japanese origin, who mostly serve as bilingual translators, typists, and clerks, the employment status of most Japanese working in the subsidiaries in Tennessee is dual. Dispatched from Japan, they are regular, permanent members of the firms in Japan and have their careers in their parent companies. Thus, their job security is believed to be the same as for those who stay at the parent companies, if the companies have institutionalized lifetime employment. Despite the common belief to the contrary, however, not every business firm in Japan has institutionalized lifetime employment. It is estimated that perhaps only one-third of all employees in Japan are guaranteed lifetime employment.[32] Of course, locally hired employees, even if they are Japanese nationals, cannot be protected by the rules of the parent companies in Japan; they are governed by the personnel policies of the subsidiaries.

Even if Japanese expatriates are guaranteed their status in their home companies, some of them are worried about what it will be like when they return. One Japanese manager told me about his concerns for the future and about the worries parents have about their children's education in the United States:

Despite their guarantee, I'm not so sure that I would be treated the same as those who stayed back home. What you say in English? "Out of sight, and out of mind" or something like that? I don't believe I'll lose my job in Japan when I finish my term here. But, I'm not so certain whether I would be rewarded the same as those who stayed in Japan....A company official told me that I would be staying in the Tennessee plant only for three years, but it has been more than that. I'm still here....See, when Japanese overseas ventures were limited, and not many Japanese had opportunities to travel the world, overseas assignments were thought to be a thrill. Because of that, becoming a diplomat upon graduation from a prestigious university with foreign studies was most popular. Not any more. Nowadays, since any Japanese can go to anywhere at anytime, why should one wish to have an overseas assignment? Look, when we came to the United States, the problems were many: Language barrier and separation from family members when you have a child who is in high school and preparing for the college entrance examination. As you know, the competition is so severe that we call the college entrance examination "examination hell." Anyone who finishes high school in Tennessee, even if he or she attends the Japanese Supplementary School in math, Japanese language, and some history, it would be very difficult to pass the entrance examination for the first-rate universities. Even if you learned English better than the average high school student in Japan, such training in English would not help a great deal in making a better score on the Japanese college entrance examination. My kids are very young, so that I was able to bring them with me. But, if they had been in high school, I would not have come. But, see, you cannot simply refuse, when the company asks you to go. In fact, there are many Japanese who did not want to come but who did.

The Japanese Supplementary School (JSS), which is located in Knoxville, Maryville, Memphis, and Murfreesboro in Tennessee, is not a full-time school, as is the Tennessee Meiji Gakuin High School in Sweetwater. As the name indicates, it is "supplementary," providing private education mainly for children of Japanese employees who work for the Japanese firms in Tennessee. To help the students maintain the equivalent level of learning that they would normally achieve in Japan, subjects taught include Japanese language, mathematics, and some history. Teachers are selected by the school board and planning committee of each community from among Japanese professors in the United States, students, and other Japanese people in the community. The schools are partially supported by the Japanese Ministry of Education, monthly tuition fees, and volunteer work from parents and employees of Japanese firms. Classes meet on Saturday; one school uses the facilities of a university near by; one meets in a church building; and another meets in a local secondary school. The school year begins in April and ends in March of the following year.

By and large, the Japanese uneasiness in their assignments in the United States and especially in Tennessee are caused by difficulties with communication in the work setting; lack of social relations with their peers; educational problems of their children, particularly when they are in high school; being unable to keep up with the rapidly changing technological knowledge in Japan; and losing relationships with peers and superiors in the parent company, so that they worry about being "out of sight, out of mind." Merry White's ethnographic account describes the problems that Japanese overseas face and the strategies they pursue to adjust to life in foreign countries and to prepare for what may not be a hospitable welcome when they return to Japan.[33]

When I interviewed a Japanese engineering manager in Westech who had been in Tennessee for three years, he was in a jubilant mood because he was about to go back to Japan. Unusually casual, straightforward, and outspoken, he expressed his opinions without hesitation. He said to me, "Ask me anything you want to ask. I'll tell you what I think about it. I am going to leave for Japan the day after tomorrow anyway." He commented about his years living in Tennessee and working with Tennesseans:

> These Tennessee people are wonderful. They're nice, kind, and friendly. But, because of my language handicap, I just couldn't mingle with them well. Some Americans criticize us for always sticking together, rather than mingling with Americans. Look, believe me I tried very hard to do that. But, when I sit with Americans, we don't have many subjects in common to talk about. Commenting about the recent weather wouldn't take more than a few seconds....When I go to a party—with several bags of potato chips and cans of beer—I have the impression that Americans who come to the party are more uncomfortable than I am. They say, "Hi," and exchange a few words of greeting, and then leave me alone....I'm so glad I'm going back to the place where I belong. I'd like to have a good drinking session with my old friends and talk in the Japanese language as loudly as I can. I missed it very much. Forgive me for my ill manner, but I can't hide my happiness. I regret one thing. I wish I could take the U.S. with me to Japan.

Social gatherings or even social drinking have to be spontaneous and undertaken in a relaxed mood, according to the returning engineering manager. Making a deliberate effort to socialize with Americans is artificial and thus seems superficial. Furthermore, using a foreign language other than his mother tongue makes him tense and tired. "At first, after I attended a few of those parties, I thought I was getting sick," he said.

I can vividly recall my early years of socializing in America right after I was transplanted. Whenever a weekend came, I even prayed not to be invited by American families. Once I was invited, I did not have the courage to say no. I rather liked to be alone, so that I could be relaxed. Once I accepted such a dinner invitation, I would have to smile if not laugh when someone cracked a joke, even though I did not "get it." It is one of the hardest things in the world to pretend to understand when you cannot. I can fully appreciate the engineering manager's candor. His feelings were exactly what mine had been. On one occasion because of mounting tension and nervousness, I told the hostess, "Thank you for your 'hostility,'" rather than "hospitality." Such uncomfortable feelings are not limited to Japanese or other Asians. I have observed many overseas Americans who congregate with fellow Americans to overcome feelings of strangeness. Compatriot groupings are naturally formed in an alien land. It would be a mistake to say that "groupism" is in the Japanese national character, while Americans are individualistic.

For the Japanese expatriate, education is deadly serious and perhaps the single most important factor in an overseas assignment. An assistant vice president and engineering advisor, who is one of the very few Japanese who volunteered to come to Tennessee, told me:

> Although I volunteered to come to Tennessee, as a forty-six-year-old man it is very hard to maintain the life of a bachelor. My wife and a seventeen-year-old son would also like to come to Tennessee, to live with me. But my wife has a small business to run, and my son is preparing for his college entrance examination as a high school student. For a while, I don't believe we will be living together as a family. Even though I volunteered to come, at times I wonder if it is worthwhile to do this, to be away from home and family members. Even Mr. K [refers to president of the company] wouldn't be here if his sons were in high school. He came because his two sons are old enough, one already graduated from college, and the other one in college.

It is understandable why the local school system is such an important factor in site selection for the Japanese firms. Even primary school is important for the education of their children.

As Mikio Sumiya has pointed out, in Japan "the deciding factor in establishing their social status was formal education, but the school education was open to rich and poor....If educated, one was not discriminated against according to one's class origin."[34] An obsession with education has led to severe competition in entrance examinations for each rung on the ladder from kindergarten to college and university. Today, 95 percent of Japanese junior high-school students enter senior high schools.[35] A good many of these high school graduates pursue a higher education. In an ethnography of the Japanese high school system, Thomas P. Rohlen describes the milieu of the Japanese obsession with education that creates such severe competition. In order to be winners, 60 percent of the urban Japanese student population in grades seven, eight, and nine are enrolled in a cram school *(juku)* or are being coached by a private tutor. And one in ten of the country's high school students attends *yobiko,* the advanced analogue of a *juku.*[36] Thus, supplementary school or private tutoring in addition to a regular high school has become a *rite of passage* in order for Japanese high-school students to pass the severely competitive university entrance examination. According to Sumiya, this competitive aspect of Japanese life coexists with the traditional "harmony" of Japanese life.[37]

In order to assist the high-school education of the children of Japanese expatriates, the Meiji Gakuin Foundation established the Tennessee Meiji Gakuin High School. As a private high school, however, tuition is high—$19,000 a year in 1992. Not many Japanese middle managers in the Japanese firms in Tennessee can afford to send their children to such an expensive private academy. In fact, out of 109 students enrolled in spring 1992, only 2 were from Tennessee. Seventy students (64 percent) were from Japan, even though their parents were not working in Japanese firms in the United States. The most students from the United States were from New England (11 students), followed by the Midwest (9 students). The total number of students from the entire eleven southern states was only six. It is ironic to observe that the well-paid, top Japanese executives who can afford such expensive tuition reside outside the South, just as many rich American capitalists live outside the South.

Whether they were forced to come or came by choice, a great majority of the Japanese seem to adjust well and find comfortable living. Instead of socializing with their peers, many Japanese expatriates are learning how to spend more of their time off with family members: husbands and wives have more time together than if they were in Japan. Gradually, they are acculturizing to American life, although the center of their nonwork activities is their families. Surprisingly, the wives of the Japanese working in the Tennessee firms seem to enjoy American life more than do their husbands. The wives adapt quickly to the way of life of the traditional American wife and mother: drive their own automobiles, take their children to school, and attend occasional social gatherings sponsored by lay and church organizations. Many of them take English lessons from a tutorial service; there are plenty of volunteers who are eager to give English instruction to the wives of the Japanese workers in their local communities. A Japanese executive told me at a dinner in my house:

> Actually my wife enjoys living here in Tennessee more than I do. She loves the open space, clean air, and kindly people. Since she is the first daughter of the chairman of the board of the parent company in Japan, if she cannot enjoy living in Tennessee, she can always ask to return to Japan, but there is no indication that is the case. Every once in a while, she visits her parents in Japan. But she rather likes to live here. She actively participates in our children's school events. No matter how wealthy you are, in Japan it would be almost impossible to have a large house such as the one we are living in now. You can't even imagine how inexpensive the housing prices are in Tennessee. I

originally planned to stay three years, since our company has a policy of rotating staff every three years. I have been here more than five years. Now, even our company policy has changed to extend the period of rotation from three years to five years in order to keep some sort of continuity. It seems as if we are going to live in Tennessee for quite a while.

His wife concurred with his remarks. Perhaps the Japanese parent companies' best recruiting tool for overseas workers would be the wives of the expatriate employees.

Nevertheless, after a prolonged period of overseas assignment, repatriating families face a crisis, sometimes traumatic. The personal and social adjustments required by the Japanese, especially the children, when they return home, are well documented by White. White reports a case history of a returnee:

> Mrs. Hayashi...feels there is no joy in Japan for her: She returns to a difficult relationship with her mother-in-law and to jealousy among her former colleagues as well as to a thwarting of her new ambitions. She sees Japan as crowded and polluted and the Japanese as overworked and narrow-minded. She now has few friends she sees regularly, except for a woman whom she met overseas. She says she would like to meet other women outside the circle of mothers at her children's school, but at the moment she has no time. She feels she has had two lives—one a relaxed American-style life and the other a self-conscious Japanese life.[38]

Although repatriating families must cope with their unique circumstances, White reports, "In all the families, we find mothers, fathers, and children who must struggle with threats of spoiled identity, damaged career paths, and, most important of all, [children's] education prospects now greatly at risk."[39]

The most serious concern of the Japanese engineers who remain in the United States for several years is that they will lag behind their colleagues in Japan in acquiring new technological knowledge. An engineer assigned to one of the Tennessee plants told me:

> Before I came to the United States, I worried about everything. At first, I was really "thrown" in a new world, but my wife and I with two little kids are doing much better than we had originally anticipated, thanks to many good Americans [meaning Tennesseans]. In fact, although it is very hard to believe, I am beginning to like it here and am getting used to the American ways of life. But, as an engineer, I worry about keeping up with the new technology that is developing in Japan virtually every minute. Changes in technology, skill, and techniques are so rapid in Japan that, while I am working with the techniques that I acquired when

I was in Japan, they might be already outdated or obsolete. When I return to Japan, I'll be behind my colleagues there. To overcome such a lag, I keep in constant touch with my colleagues in Japan either by telephone or fax. I use fax regularly, at least once a month.

It is ironic to hear from the Japanese that staying in the United States may hinder their keeping up with changing technology when there was a time when they came to the United States to acquire such knowledge. Times have changed.

Considering the strains experienced by the Japanese people living and working in the United States, most Japanese parent companies rotate their personnel every three to five years. Westech, for instance, used to have a three-year term but recently extended it to five years to maintain continuity. Some employees serve beyond the specified five-year term, however, either by choice or because the company needs their skills and talent. One engineer told me, "If you were too good, then you were more likely to stay longer than you wanted to. Then, you come to like it here and you might choose to stay even longer." Yet, I was unable to identify any Japanese who was willing to be intentionally tardy, negligent, or incompetent in order to return to Japan sooner.

Because Japanese personnel resist being relocated to foreign countries, the parent companies of the subsidiaries in Tennessee make every effort to minimize the number of Japanese personnel. When they start up their manufacturing plants, usually a large number of Japanese personnel, mostly engineers and technicians, come to set up and begin the operation. Once the plants are running efficiently and the Japanese personnel have completed the basic training of the American employees, most of the Japanese, except for a few essential personnel, return to their parent companies. In fact, there are fewer than ten Japanese each in both Westech and Midtech. During the construction and start-up stages, Eastech had over fifty Japanese personnel; only twelve engineers remain. The firm anticipates that when the plant reaches its maximum production capacity, very few Japanese nationals will stay on.

COMMUNICATION BARRIER AS AN EVERLASTING IMPEDIMENT

Although a basic principle of international business and industrial operations is effective communication, that principle is not the reality in Japanese firms in Tennessee. Rudimentary communication using the English language takes place, yet lack of understanding of verbal nuances causes confusion at times, and literal translation can misinterpret the real intent of the speaker. Consider the episode arising from President Clinton's comment to Boris Yeltsin at the summit in Vancouver, Canada, in April 1993. Clinton said that when the Japanese say "yes" they often mean "no," which was misinterpreted to mean that he was calling the Japanese liars. Indeed, a Japanese "yes" in its primary context is only an acknowledgement that the other person has heard you. One has to wait for a real reply to the question, and that can be notoriously slow in coming. It has been said facetiously that if Americans had understood the Japanese usage of "yes," we could have avoided World War II. In Japanese industries in Tennessee, when Japanese expatriates follow up their initial "yes" response with comments that sound more like "no," American employees became confused.

Also, the Japanese language does not include gender specification. The Japanese are more accustomed to refer to "a person," regardless of the gender of the person. Unless they are very conscientious when they speak English, a good many Japanese will mix up male and female pronouns, saying "he" while meaning "she" or vice versa. This practice disconcerts American listeners and leads to misunderstandings.

Of course, misinterpretation and misunderstanding are not limited to interactions between Japanese speakers and English speakers. Confusion can reign even among English-speaking people. Ferraro explains: "The U.S. businessperson in London will be in for quite a jolt when his British counterpart, in a genuine attempt to pay a compliment, refers to the American's wife as 'homely,' for in the United States the word means 'plain' or 'ugly' but in the United Kingdom it means 'warm' and 'friendly.'...And just imagine the look on the American businessperson's face when his female British counterpart asks him for a 'rubber' (that is, an eraser) or invites him to 'knock her up' (that is, stop by her house)."[40] Sandra Salmans reports an episode that actually occurred in a business meeting of a British company and an American firm: "[British] executives suggested 'tabling' a key issue. To his amazement, the Americans reacted with outrage. The reason, as he learned shortly, was that while in the UK 'tabling' an item means giving it a prominent place on the agenda, in the US it means deferring it indefinitely."[41] If even English speakers can confound one another, one can imagine how hard it can be to communicate between the Japanese expatriates and American employees in the Japanese plants in Tennessee.

Although almost all Japanese executives, managers, engineers, and technicians have some training in English, almost every Japanese expatriate has difficulties in communicating freely with Tennesseans in English. Almost every Japanese with whom I have talked criticizes the method of English instruction in the Japanese school system. (It seems odd to hear criticism of the Japanese educational system from Japanese, while the American experts on education praise the high quality of the Japanese educational system and criticize the American system of public education.) One Japanese expatriate lamented his English-language education:

The Japanese school teaches English as the primary foreign language beginning in middle school [equivalent to the U.S. junior high school], continuing in high school, and going on even in college as a core curriculum in the freshman year and even sometimes in the sophomore year. Also, I took a course in intensive English offered by the company before I was assigned to America. In school, we spent almost all of our English class learning English grammar, not conversational English. I may be fairly good in English grammar, as good as the average American. But what good is grammar, if you can't speak and you can't understand the language? I may be able to speak some English, but I can't converse well with the natives. I may even be able to say what I really want, even if I say it awkwardly. But my worst problem is listening. I can't understand spoken English. It is very hard to understand what these local people are talking about. The beginning word and also the ending word are unclear.

He was referring to the "Southern drawl," although he was unaware of the term *per se*. In fact, it is difficult for any foreigner who has studied standard English, with clear pronunciations, to understand southern dialects and locutions. Not only do most southerners of limited education speak slowly, but they do not pronounce words clearly. Furthermore, southerners have their own idioms. One Japanese asked me, "Why do they say 'I'm *fixing* to go' when they're going to go somewhere? I thought he was actually fixing something before leaving."

A Japanese manager told me candidly:

Once I called up American workers in my section to chastise them for something. But, let me tell you, it isn't easy to reprimand or chastise Americans using English. I must not hurt their feelings, not be rude, not make sexist remarks, and not be too critical. At the same time, I must point out their mistakes. You know what I did? I ended up complimenting them, saying "You're doing good." Complimenting is easier than chastising. See, American workers often comment that all Japanese are nice, smiling all the time, and not very critical about their work. I was not such a nice guy when I was in Japan. I think many Japanese are doing as I do. But, what can you do? I'm very frustrated about my inability to express my thinking and feelings freely, as I do in the Japanese language....Of course, we have a bilingual interpreter. But, often I can't even tell her about my delicate feelings. Even if I could, it would be very difficult for her to translate my feelings into English. After all, the translated version is not exactly what one intends to say, although the basic meaning or the facts can be translated. Once I translated a Japanese joke literally into English and told some Americans. They tried very hard to laugh about it, but I knew that my joke didn't make any sense to them. It's terrible and frustrating. I often think I'm such a fool.

The manager's comments remind me of a case I observed in a Korean overseas firm. A frustrated Korean manager yelled at an American worker: "You've got to be a stoneheaded man." The manager anticipated that the American worker would be upset and angry about the expression he used. Instead, the American worker hardly reacted at all. The curious manager asked me, "Why didn't he feel bad about what I called him ?" "Stonehead" is a literal translation of a Korean expression meaning "stupid person," meaning one's brain is like stone or inflexible. The American worker was unaware of the Korean usage, and consequently the remark did not make him angry. If the Korean manager had called him "numbskull," the response would have been different.

THE ROLE OF AN INTERPRETER

It is very difficult for any interpreter to translate one language into another without losing the nuances of the original words. Selection of the most appropriate words is a difficult task, especially when dealing with many and changing technical vocabularies.

On one occasion, when I was interviewing a Japanese executive, we ran into some difficulties in communicating with each other. The executive's English was insufficient and, since I had had my last Japanese lesson in 1944, my Japanese was as bad as his English. We decided to bring in the company interpreter. During the process of interpretation, my Japanese was just good enough that I was able to discern whether or not the interpreter was getting close to the original meaning. Although she was skilled, the interpreter at one point translated the word for "fellowship" as "scholarship." My question was whether the company had any fellowship program, meaning fellowship as friendship or companionship, but it was translated as scholarship, referring to a grant-in-aid to a student for schooling, for employees' children.

The Japanese-English interpreters are not always female. While some large Japanese firms such as Eastech employ male interpreters usually with other job titles, small- and medium-sized firms usually hire females who are spouses of Americans—either spouses of former military personnel, as is the case in Westech, or wives of professionals, as is the case of Midtech. By employing spouses of Americans, they usually do not have to pay high wages.

The role of interpreter is indeed important. On one occasion, I asked an American manager to make an arrangement with the company president to ask a certain question. The manager told me, "Since you know the interpreter, why don't you ask her directly about such an arrangement? I mean it. Even if I liked to ask the president about such an arrangement, I'd have to go through the interpreter anyway. Why should you go through another middleperson?" His comment made perfect sense, and also summarizes the importance of an interpreter. Often the interpreter can play the role of a "gatekeeper" in screening who can or cannot see the president and other Japanese executives.

The roles of an interpreter go above and beyond the job description. When wives of Japanese officials go to the hospital to birth their babies, the interpreter has to go with them. When communications between the Japanese managers and American employees break down, the interpreter has to be there. At the executive meetings, she has to translate the important points. No interpreter in the world can be expert on every aspect of business and every technical vocabulary for the complicated components of sophisticated machinery. The hardest part of being an interpreter is that, since the Japanese officials know some English, even though they cannot articulate well, if any interpretations are imprecise, most of the time the interpreter is blamed. One interpreter lamented, "My job would be much easier if they didn't understand English at all."

A newly appointed president of Midtech recently replaced a Japanese American interpreter. It did not take the form of "firing," but a new interpreter was hired as a signal for termination of the other, thus the previous interpreter tendered her resignation. The former interpreter maintained a high ethical standard and did not criticize her former boss and the company she used to work for. I noticed, however, ample allusions to her dissatisfaction with the company's handling of her matter. In fact, her resignation became a major topic of conversation among American employees during the lunch hour and over the coffee break. It appeared that she was well-liked and respected by the American employees. One American woman employee told me her version of the story behind the resignation of the interpreter:

> See, she knows American culture so well that when the Japanese officials asked her to interpret certain statements "literally" to American employees, she modified the statements a bit, because she knew that it would be inappropriate to state it in such a way to Americans. It's rather embarrassing for her as a Japanese American to interpret literally into language that would be unacceptable to Americans, so she would modify into American usage. The Japanese official was angry about it, because he thought she was intentionally altering the original statements. That's a shame....On another occasion, when an executive officer was returning from his business trip, he asked her to clean his house before his return. Perhaps you can do that in Japan. I don't know. But, you can't do it in America, you know. She is an interpreter, not

a cleaning lady. You have to respect a person's profession. She shouldn't do it. She didn't. That is the end of it.

The director of the Japan Center of Tennessee, who hired the terminated interpreter as a consultant, told me:

She was exactly the person the company needs now. She is not a simple interpreter of language, but an interpreter of both cultures and of nonverbal communication. I know her quite well. She is capable of narrowing the gap between the two cultures in the company. It was a great mistake for the new president to let her go. I met the new president. He is different from his predecessor. It appears that he would really like to have an interpreter who has a strong Japanese identity.

The interpreter is a highly educated Japanese American who is married to an American English professor at the nearby university.

Once I had an opportunity to observe a small group meeting on quality at Westech; six American managers and rank-and-file workers, and two Japanese managers along with an interpreter. The meeting was chaired by a Japanese engineering manager and started at 7:00 A.M. As an observer, I was sympathetic toward both groups, the Americans and the Japanese. To a naive anthropologist, the agenda seemed to be rather simple, thus the meeting should last for an hour at the most. But the meeting went on and on. Instead of spending time discussing the substance, the two groups spent most of the time trying to understand each other's statements. At times, the interpreter attempted to clarify or assist the speakers, yet some discussions were too technical and complicated for a person who had no training in the field. The interpreter was a layperson who was hired because she is a native Japanese who is married to an American. She was very good in both languages, but she had difficulties with certain technical terms. Communication was so hard at times that the Japanese manager drew pictures of the components of machines he was explaining. The meeting lasted over two-and-a-half hours, and I was unable to comprehend what it was about.

Eastech is different. During the construction and start-up stages, when the firm had over fifty Japanese engineers and operators, several interpreters were employed. Currently, however, Eastech does not have even one designated interpreter. Because of the firm's long years of experience in English-speaking countries prior to coming to the United States, most of the Japanese personnel were able to speak fluent English. Some have been in the United States more than five years. Furthermore, the firm is reputable enough to attract well-qualified Americans who are bilingual. Some of these Americans have been in Japan; thus, they understand not only the literal Japanese language but also Japanese culture. My informant at

Eastech has spent several years in Japan, having made many trips to Japan, and is married to a Japanese woman. Since the firm employs bilingual American staff, communication between Japanese personnel and American employees is much easier than it is at the other two Japanese subsidiaries.

Even if one is a master of a second language, it takes a good deal of experience and extra effort to read the unspoken body language, or "silent language," as Edward T. Hall has termed it.[42] Faulty communication, resulting from language and cultural differences between Japanese employers and American employees, is indeed a problem to be overcome. So far, however, the priorities of the companies appear to be focusing on production goals, with an obsession about quality rather than about overcoming poor communication. The challenges that Japanese industry faces in working with American employees are like those of a "cross-cultural marriage." In the early stage of the marriage, particularly during the honeymoon, some minor cultural differences can be overcome by love, and the other differences may not be manifest. In later stages of the marriage, however, such minor matters can lead to major problems. Those who are succeeding in their cross-cultural marriages tell us of their everlasting efforts to understand each other's culture.

As I have described, the problems, challenges, and orientation of the three Japanese firms are both the same and different. No general statement about Japanese firms can be made. According to my observations, the ways of managing a Japanese firm and the adaptive strategies required in the American cultural setting depend more on the idiosyncrasies of the top executives of the firm than on the Japanese culture that is shared by all the Japanese expatriates. Nevertheless, it will be interesting to look at the ways that Japanese management adapts the industrial-relations model used at home to the host country, and the major obstacles that the Japanese firms in Tennessee have faced in dealing with the American culture.

_4_

INDUSTRIAL RELATIONS OF JAPANESE INDUSTRY

The industrial-relations practices of the three Japanese companies includ-ed in this study vary. As Malcolm Trevor has indicated, "it is a mistake to interpret the behavior of every single company overseas in the light of broad generalizations or stereotypes. Each company has to decide which strategy will suit its business best."[1]

Since Eastech is well financed, has previous overseas business experi-ence, and has a sister plant located nearby, its operation appears to be smooth. In less than two years since the grand opening, its production level has reached near capacity. On the other hand, Midtech appears to be strug-gling, as evidenced by the replacement of the chief operating officer and the remodeling of the managerial complex of its main building. The new president is younger, energetic, and prone to be more Japanese in his iden-tity and style of managing than his predecessor. Since its establishment in 1987, the firm has been unable to generate a profit. The American eco-nomic recession and concomitant scaled-down auto sales in 1991 and 1992 have stressed this supplier of auto parts. Despite the recession in the auto industry, Westech has been able to sustain itself mainly because of the small scale of its operation. A recent multimillion-dollar contract to manufacture the vibrant absorbers for Nissan trucks has been a booster, and the firm is in the process of hiring additional workers.

Organizational culture, which includes industrial-relations practices, is a separate entity from regional and national cultures.[2] My descriptions in this chapter are based on the particular organizational cultures of the three companies, including managerial practices and attitudes of workers. Nevertheless, the global restructuring of industrial management in the transnational settings is so rapid that the impacts of regional and national cultures on organizational culture are profound and complex, and it is very difficult for me to assess the relationships among the three layers of cul-tures. Perhaps any effort to categorize industrial relations by specific region or country is futile. And yet people continue to perceive that there are unique Japanese industrial-relations practices.

The so-called Japanese "divine treasures" model is one of those mythologized practices, and I use it as my frame of reference. This chapter examines the Japanese industrial-relations model to see to what extent Japanese management adapts the model used in home firms to the host country; and discerns what the major obstacles are that Japanese management in Tennessee faces in dealing with the American South.

THE JAPANESE "DIVINE TREASURES" MODEL

Since the 1970s, the Japanese industrial-relations principles, often called the "divine treasures" model, have received wide publicity, ranging from scholarly work to mass media treatments. The principles deal with guaranteed lifetime employment, length-of-service wages and promotions, and enterprise unionism (union membership that is confined to the permanent employees of each company).[3] Sometimes the principles also include company welfare benefits, recruitment of workers directly upon graduation from school, training and working as team members, task and job rotation, and early retirement with money benefits as additional "treasures."[4] Although the divine treasures may be the most widely known industrial-relations model, it is poorly understood in the minds of ordinary Americans. Some scholars characterize the divine treasures as "myth rather than reality" or as an "idealized model."[5]

Do Japanese industrial firms replicate the treasures model in their plants in Tennessee? Practically speaking, even if Japanese firms in Tennessee wanted to implement the divine treasures model, American laws, norms, and mores would hinder their intentions.[6] As Levine and Ohtsu note:

> Companies that establish subsidiaries or joint ventures abroad often do not have a completely free hand in instituting labor relations practices, especially if the host country is *already well advanced industrially* [italics mine]. The foreign company must contend with long-standing expectations and demands, as well as laws and rules, of the host country's government, workers, unions, and other employers, which are likely to be at variance with home country institutions.[7]

A survey of seventy Japanese-owned firms in Canada in the early 1980s indicates:

> Very few of the companies sampled carried over distinctive labor relations and personnel practices identified with the Japanese divine-treasures model. In eight areas investigated—recruitment, job security, compensation, training, promotion, worker participation in management decision making, group-based teamwork, and employee fringe benefits—the results indicated only a small amount of transplanting

from Japan. The least practiced were group work and employee benefits, while the most frequent, but still relatively little, were employment
security and recruitment. On the whole, the average scores for the firms
revealed that emulation was not emphasized and was perhaps actually
avoided. The Japanese companies pragmatically adapted to Canadian
conditions rather than attempt to install new practices from Japan. Even
among the large units there was no strong resemblance.[8]

Similarly, in my fieldwork I learned that quite a few Japanese small- and
medium-sized firms in the United States copy the industrial-relations
practices of domestic American firms.

My examination of the industrial and labor relations practices of the
three Japanese firms included in this study indicates that, instead of dupli-
cating their Japanese home practices, these firms too have adopted common
American industrial-relations principles. Specifically, the joint venture of
Westech copied exactly the rules of its American parent company. The vice
president of human resources in the American parent company not only
serves as consultant and advisor to Westech, but is also *de facto* vice president for human resources of the joint-venture firm. When the joint venture
was forming, both companies agreed that personnel management would be
exercised by the American partner, while technology and engineering
would be managed by the Japanese partner. The Westech policies, including industrial-relations rules, are spelled out clearly in the company's personnel policy handbook. The handbook begins with an affirmative-action
statement and then discusses policies on sexual harassment, responsibilities
of supervisors and employees, work rules, probationary periods, and transfers. Instead of a lifetime employment guarantee, the handbook deals with
layoffs, recalls, and even terminations. Like that of any other American
firm, the Westech handbook includes the reward system, wages, promotions, retirement, pension programs, and other fringe benefits, including
group insurance.

The policy manual of Midtech is basically the same as that of Westech,
but in certain aspects is more specific, such as in a policy statement on
nepotism. The policy manual states, "In order to avoid potential impropri-
eties and conflict of interest, the company will not employ any applicant if
the company already employs a member of the immediate family.
Immediate family means spouse, brothers, sisters, mother, father, children,
grandparents, and the corresponding 'in-law' and 'step' relationships."

This policy statement on nepotism is quite intriguing to an anthropologist. First of all, nepotism has not traditionally been taboo in Japanese business practices. In the formative period of Japanese capitalization and in corporation, nepotism was common.[9] Its remnants still exist in small- and

medium-sized Japanese corporations. In fact, the parent company of Westech is owned by a single family, and the son-in-law of the Japanese owner is now vice president of Westech. Although Japanese industrial relationships have changed a great deal since World War II, such family-like relationships have not completely disappeared.[10] Thus, a policy against nepotism is a radical departure from traditional Japanese norms.

Also of interest, the policy manual's definition of "immediate family" is much broader than the American definition. To most Americans, the "immediate family" is synonymous with the nuclear family, which consists of a married couple with their unmarried child or children. Not many married Americans include in their concept of the immediate family their siblings, grandparents, and in-laws. So Midtech's policy on nepotism is a hybrid one combining the American taboo against the practice with the Japanese concept of extended family.

Compared with the other two companies, Eastech is a relative newcomer. When I started my fieldwork on this firm, barely one year had passed since its grand opening ceremony in January 1991. Because of its short existence, most policies had not yet been codified, written, and distributed to employees. The earliest publications other than the company brochures that profiled the company and a catalog that displayed the company's products for its employees, were the *Safety Handbook* and the *Benefits Handbook*. The *Benefits Handbook* specifies medical benefits, the dental plan, life insurance, both short and long-term disability insurance plans, and social security disability benefits. The safety and benefits handbooks were printed by the Industrial Training Service of the Tennessee Department of Economic and Community Development, so the rules regarding safety and the benefits are basically the same among the Japanese firms in Tennessee. The policy manual of Eastech, which was finally codified in 1993, is the same as those of Westech and Midtech. My informant in Eastech commented about the similarities of the personnel manual policies between and among the Japanese industries in the United States, "Because, they are all American companies even if the ultimate beneficial owners are foreigners." Nevertheless, Eastech personnel policy favors internal promotion whenever a vacancy occurs and all the applicants have the same qualifications.

LIFETIME EMPLOYMENT

The Japanese executives of all three firms make every effort to provide job security for their employees, even if they do not explicitly commit their companies to guarantee "lifetime employment." Of course, American executives in domestic American firms do not enjoy laying off or terminating their employees, but, according to my observation, the commitment of the Japanese firms to keep their employees on the job is much stronger than that of their American counterparts. As evidence of this, when the U.S. economy was in a deep recession in the early 1990s, the auto industry was also experiencing a severe recession. Sales were down, inventories were high, and unsold automobiles were even filling up the cow patch near the transplanted Japanese auto plant. As an auto-parts supplier, Westech was having extreme difficulties and tried to save money in virtually every corner and by using every angle. Finally, the American president of Westech, upon the recommendation of his managers, decided that he had no choice but to eliminate three positions. Even though the Japanese partner had agreed from the beginning not to interfere with the personnel policies and decisions of the American partner, the Japanese partner expressed reluctance to approve the terminations. When word got around that the American executives wanted to eliminate the positions but that the Japanese executives were opposed, popular opinion gave the Japanese credit for their commitment not to terminate good employees. Finally, a compromise was devised. All eighty-six employees were assembled in one large conference room, where the company president asked who, for whatever personal reasons, was not expecting to be working in the near future. If three employees were planning to quit in the very near future, the company would not have to eliminate three positions. Luckily, three workers announced that they intended to resign soon, one to take another job, another to relocate, and the third to get married and move away. The company was saved from having to terminate its workers against their will, and held onto its reputation for not easily terminating its employees.

During my interview with a Westech worker, a transplanted Yankee from New York, she told me:

> I was really impressed by the Japanese effort to take care of their employees. I worked before in an American carburetor manufacturing plant. The plant closed, because nowadays automobiles don't need carburetors. In that plant, nobody really cared about us [employees]. We were treated almost like part of the equipment. We were treated like nobody. Here, the company is small, and we're treated like somebody. Our associates address each other by first names, including the president, vice president, managers, and whoever. Also, I can talk to everyone if I want to talk. They all know my name. It's a good place to work, knowing that the company cares about you. I wish they paid us more than they're paying now. But if I had a choice, I would rather have a steady job and some security than have an uncertain future. Don't get me wrong. I am not saying that everything's rosy here.

WAGES AND JOB TURNOVER

Since the woman commented on wages, it is worthwhile to add a few words about them. Of course, wages differ from firm to firm, and are based on levels of skill, experience, education, and job performance. Also, wages vary according to the reputation as well as the size of the firm and its geographical location. In Tennessee, the wage scales of East and West Tennessee (other than in Memphis) are lower than that of Middle Tennessee.

At big and better-known firms, such as Nissan in Middle Tennessee, where it is hard to get a job, the starting salary for high-school graduates without any prior work experience was reported in 1991 to be $11.65 per hour, although after the probationary period, a bonus is added to the basic hourly wage. The comparable worker's wage at Eastech was $7.00 (plus $100 annual bonus for perfect attendance or $50 for 99 percent attendance), $7.31 at Midtech, and just over $5.00 of Westech.

Wage scales of Japanese firms run slightly higher than the norm of the wages of the region where they are located. The Japanese are reluctant to pay much more than the established regional norm because they do not want to be blamed for escalating the regional wage scales. In all cases, the wages paid by the three firms in this study in 1991 are lower than the national average of $11.18, and even lower than the state average of $9.91.[11]

Since the Japanese firms offer better job security than do their American counterparts, lateral movement of workers from one company to another is less than the American norm. In the case of Westech, the yearly labor turnover rate in 1990 was 15 percent. Several Westech employees are waiting for any vacancy in an American manufacturing firm located nearby. Since there are quite a few Japanese firms in the vicinity of Midtech, some employees already have moved to better-paying, more reputable companies; in the summer of 1992 alone, 3 out of the 184 Midtech employees joined firms such as Nissan. A quality control manager told me, "I originally came to Tennessee from Illinois to work for Nissan, but I was unable to get a job from Nissan. I ended up working here." He hinted that if any job for which he qualified opened up, he would go to Nissan. Midtech had been his second choice.

Since Eastech has an international reputation and also pays slightly higher wages than any other firm in the region, most Eastech employees are satisfied with their employment. This is reflected in Eastech's labor turnover rate of less than 5 percent annually. However, for the last four years, Eastech's labor turnover raate has increased. In 1994, it reached to 12 percent annually. No one knows for sure why there is an increase. One of my informants in Eastech speculates that it may be in part related to the improvement of job situation in the U.S. domestic firms. It is my observation that the rate of labor turnover and lateral movement are closely asso-ciated with the competitiveness of the job market in a particular firm: the harder it is to get a job, the lower the labor turnover rate. Since Eastech selects one employee out of every twenty applicants, one could anticipate the lower turnover rate. And because the employees are selected from a larger pool of applicants, their qualifications are better than those hired at the small- and medium-sized firms.

The effort made by Japanese industrialists to secure employees' jobs does not preclude their terminating some employees. Midtech, for instance, terminated seven workers in summer 1992 on the basis of incompetency or unfitness. When I interviewed an employee who was terminated that sum-mer, she was very skeptical about the efforts of Japanese executives to secure their employees' jobs. By cross-checking with other employees, how-ever, I learned that she was fired for dishonesty by an American manager, not by any Japanese executives. Despite some terminations, Japanese firms do make deliberate efforts not to terminate their employees against their will. During the recession that pervaded the years of 1991 and 1992, most Japanese firms in Tennessee, in an effort to keep the current work force and obviate terminations later, posted notices informing prospective applicants that "We are not taking any applications at this time." Although Japanese management does try to provide job security, none of the Japanese firms in the United States, including the three firms included in this study, has institutionalized lifetime employment.

The concept of lifetime employment originated in Japan.[12] In his inter-pretation of the institutionalization of permanent employment, James C. Abegglen found that the practice grew out of the loyalty associated with traditional social relationships and master-servant relations.[13] Others, such as Taira, see the system as having developed after World War I,[14] when life-time employment was institutionalized at least partly as a response by man-agement to the high labor turnover rate during the war. The concept con-tinued in the post-World War II period as a union and worker response to job scarcity. Robert E. Cole reports, however, that in the 1960s, "the grow-ing labor shortage, caused by the expanding economy and demographic changes resulting from a declining birth rate, pressures the permanent em-ployment practice and encourages workers to look for alternative job offers. The structure of the labor market increasingly comes to resemble that of other advanced industrial societies."[15] A recent study of Japanese university students indicates that almost half of the sampled students do not want to work in one company for life.[16] Indeed, in 1988, more than 2 million Japa-nese changed their jobs. Almost 26 percent of Japanese business firms believe that the lifetime employment system will fade away, mainly because of rapid technological development and the elimination of the dual economic structure (differentials, in which large firms are better off than small ones). Some Japanese prefer to work in small- and medium-sized firms where they find challenges and opportunities.

The recession in Japan, which began in the early 1990s, threatens the faithful remnant of Japan's lifetime employment practice more than ever before. Not only have Japanese companies in Japan slashed hiring, some are committing the unthinkable and breaking job contracts.[17] "Japan's social contract that promises lifetime employment is unraveling fast."[18] There is ample evidence of the threat to lifetime employment: "Several months ago, a group of labor lawyers set up an advice hot line. The result: Four telephone lines were jammed for two days solid by 584 men and women worried about their jobs. Many of the callers worked at large, well-known Japanese companies that supposedly never lay off employees, and more than half the calls came from people over 45."[19] Despite praise by western scholars of the unique managerial strategies of Japanese auto makers, "Nissan Motor sent shivers through Japan in February when it announced the shutting of its 29-year-old car-assembly plant in Zama, near Tokyo. The factory closure will be one of the biggest ever announced in Japan, leading to the loss of at least 4,000 jobs. With an estimated $248 million in red ink during the last fiscal year, Nissan had little choice but to retrench."[20] Where, then, is the lifetime employment for Nissan workers at the Zama plant? A laid-off Japanese worker lamented, "I wake up by myself in the middle of the night...and I can't control my anger. Sometimes I just cry."[21] For anyone familiar with the rosy description of Japanese industrial management, it is almost impossible to reconcile that description with current reports on the crisis of industry in Japan.

Thus far, the Japanese firms in Tennessee have never experienced a labor shortage, so they do not feel they have to guarantee lifetime employment to attract the work force.[22] Most of all, although lifetime employment is offered in a limited number of Japanese firms in Japan, it is of little consequence when these firms exploit large numbers of temporary workers, part-time workers, women workers, and legal or illegal foreign workers.[23] Since those workers are mostly excluded from the security provided by the divine treasures model, when any company faces financial exigency, it can terminate those workers in order to guarantee the regular work force.

HIRING PRACTICES AND SOCIAL VALUES

To succeed, the concept of lifetime employment has to be supported by careful hiring practices and by social values that stigmatize workers who change their jobs often. In essence, lifetime employment means, according to Cole, that "the worker enters a large firm after school graduation, receives in-company education and training, and remains in the same company until the retirement age of fifty-five."[24] The Japanese method of recruiting workers through senior graduating classes in various high schools, colleges, and universities, has never been used in Tennessee or elsewhere in the United States.[25] A Japanese executive once told me about the possibility of recruiting from the graduating classes of Tennessee's vocational and technical schools, but I do not believe he was serious about it. At no other time in the course of my fieldwork was the recruitment idea brought up, and since applicants outnumber openings in Tennessee, apparently the necessity to recruit has never arisen. Recruiting workers directly from school was tried in New United Motor Manufacturing, Inc. (NUMMI), a fifty-fifty joint venture between General Motors and Toyota, in Faremont, California. Since the majority of the workers in the plant were the workers from the old plant, Toyota management, after initial hesitation, agreed to accept the UAW as the duly certified collective bargaining agent for the employees' wages and abandoned their initial plan to recruit workers directly from school.[26]

In Japan, there is a stigma to workers who change jobs frequently. There is a strong Japanese cultural tradition whereby one's value, status, and dependability tend to be measured by the duration of one's stay in a group. The more one moves around or changes jobs, the less dependable one is thought to be. Employers try to avoid hiring frequent movers. Social values also contribute to lifetime employment even in professional circles. There is, for instance, no tenure system *per se* in Japanese universities, but once a professor is hired, he or she plans—and is expected—to retire from that university.[27]

Since the number of Japanese personnel included in this study is too small to yield any meaningful statistical analysis, I did not survey them, but almost all of the Japanese I interviewed or talked with casually had a negative view of workers who change jobs often. Contrary to this Japanese cultural pattern, in America, able people who stay in one place with the same job are not necessarily viewed as dependable, capable, or even loyal. Following the norms of the Far East—both Japan and Korea—I have taught at the same university for nearly a quarter century. My American colleagues often ask me, only half jokingly, "What's wrong with you?"

LENGTH-OF-SERVICE WAGES AND PROMOTIONS

Length-of-service wages and promotions are another hallmark of the Japanese divine treasures model. The Japanese word *nenkō*, abbreviated from *nenkō joretsu chingin*, has been widely publicized and become a familiar term in western literature. *Nenkō joretsu chingin* means length-of-service wages and promotion.

There are generally two established methods of paying workers. In the *nenkō* system, widely adopted by Japanese firms, employees are paid according to their social status and obligations. Taken into account are age and seniority, gender, marital status, and family obligations. In the system followed by most western industrial firms, payment is based on an employee's job skills, job performance, market demand, and sometimes length of service. In some cases, however, such as in most Korean business firms, various combinations of the two systems are employed.

The reasoning behind the Japanese *nenkō* system is not altogether illogical. As workers age and mature, their knowledge may grow and their skills may improve. This is particularly true among blue-collar workers, whose training is mostly acquired on the job. Thus, pay increases by age and seniority are actually on the basis of the skill and knowledge accumulated as one gets older. Also, the *nenkō* system reflects the Japanese societal value whereby elders are treated with respect. This Japanese attitude is in contrast to the popular western view that getting older does not necessarily mean getting wiser. Instead, in the view of Americans, younger people are energetic and have fresh new ideas, whereas "older" is often viewed as being stagnant and obsolete. When technological innovation is so rapid, young people can keep pace with the changes, while older workers often have difficulties keeping up.

In the fall of 1990, when I was at Hirosaki University in Japan, whenever faculty members in the Division of Humanities got together for informal conversations, the junior members cleaned coffee cups, made coffee, and even served the senior members. I commented that it did not seem fair for the junior members to do such chores all the time. The most senior professor told me, "Oh no, you've been in America too long! This is the fairest system I know of, and the most equitable system in the world. Because every junior faculty member, here and everywhere else in the world, will get older sooner or later. Then, they will be served by the junior members." Hirosaki University does not even have department heads. Most administrative matters are handled by the dean, and each scholarly discipline has been organized around the senior faculty members.

The senior professor's comment serves as the best illustration of the seniority system and its societal equity and justice; not only does it make sense, it explains the reasoning behind the Japanese *nenkō joretsu chingin*.

Related to seniority in the *nenkō* system is a worker's family obligations, which are also an important consideration in determining a worker's wage. The increase in a worker's family obligations results mostly from the increase in a worker's age: the number of children increases as the worker gets older, cost of living expenses increase as the size of the family grows, and additional expenses become unavoidable as the worker's children get older and enroll in schools.

Japanese philosophy and values, then, are behind the seniority concept whereby age and length-of-service play major roles in determining workers' wages.[28] According to an ethnographic report on Japanese factories, in addition to their standard wage, Japanese blue-collar workers are paid a family allowance (2 percent of their total monthly income) and a housing allowance (3 percent of their total wage). Adding in the various allowances, the average Japanese worker's wage is 56 percent of his or her total monthly paycheck. In Japan, a yearly raise is not determined by performance but by the yearly "base up" [an across-the-board raise].[29] Such a yearly "base up" and seniority rating succeeds best when the firms hire the workers directly upon graduation from schools each year, as most Japanese firms do. Then, seniority of each individual worker can be marked and tracked clearly.

None of the three firms included in this study replicate their home practices of *nenkō* system in pure form in their transplanted firms in Tennessee. This does not mean to say, however, that Japanese management in Tennessee completely abandons the *nenkō* system or ignores its spirit altogether. The personnel policies of these firms specify a partial consideration of seniority in determining wage increases as well as promotions. Since the personnel policies of all of them are almost identical, I will cite the case of Westech:

The Merit Review System provides for periodic wage increases based upon individual performance, attitude, initiative, frequency of accidents, and attendance. Each new employee shall be rated three separate times during the first year.... Wage increases will be granted for employees reaching the maximum rate based on *length of service* as follows:

Length of Service Based on Hire Date	Percentage of Wage Increase over Maximum Rate
5 -9 Years	25%
10–20 Years	50%
21–30 Years	75%
30 Years and Over	100%

Length of service increases will not apply to merit increase. Should an employee not be at the maximum rate but the annual review will take the employee over the maximum, they will receive 100% of the increase necessary to reach maximum and then the length of service percentage on the remainder of the review will apply.

The formula for merit review differs from most domestic business and industrial firms.

There are specific rules for promotion and transfer (or lateral move) from one position to another: "In the advancement of employees to higher paid jobs where ability, merit, and capacity are equal, *cumulative employment service* [italics mine] shall be given preference....Cumulative employment service will also be considered in filling job openings as set forth in the Job Bidding Procedure." Midtech is quite specific about the role of seniority and length-of-service: "in matters of promotion, transfers and training opportunities, merit and qualifications will be the *deciding factor* [italics mine]. Seniority or length of continuous service will be used as a 'tie breaker' between two more equally qualified employees. In cases where the hire date is the same, the 'tie breaker' will be alphabetical using A–Z in odd numbered years and Z–A in even numbered years." While seniority is used as a "tie breaker," as Midtech expresses it, seniority is the determining factor in the scheduling of vacations: "In the scheduling of vacations within a department, seniority will be 'the' deciding factor and senior employees will be given the first opportunity to request vacation dates."

The descriptions above indicate that even if the transplanted Japanese firms do not replicate the traditional *nenkō* system as it is practiced in Japan, the basic spirit of seniority has not been abandoned altogether, though its role is limited to "tie breaker" cases where other factors are equal, or it is given preference only in deciding mundane matters or making trivial decisions.

ENTERPRISE UNION

The Japanese "enterprise union" (company union) is one component of the three divine treasures. Before discussing labor unionism in the Japanese firms in Tennessee and in the three firms included in this study in particular, a few comments on the basic nature of the Japanese labor union and its genesis are necessary in order to dispel some myths surrounding the topic.[30]

First of all, a good many Americans believe that in Japan either there are no labor unions or, even if there are, that their relationships with management are cordial, docile, meek, and therefore virtually ineffective. Anyone who remembers the tense, hostile, and often violent confrontations of labor with management in Japan in the 1950s and the early 1960s, however, cannot easily generalize that labor and management relationships in Japan have been always peaceful and harmonious.[31] It took a long time of fierce struggles to overcome the friction between Japanese employers and employees and to finally change a confrontational relationship to a cooperative one. A word has to be said here that, even though relations between Japanese employers and employees are cooperative, demands from Japanese industrial workers are not nonexistent.

Although the Japanese had labor unions prior to World War II, during the war the Japanese militarists who were in power disbanded all labor unions. After the war, the General Headquarters of the Occupational Forces encouraged the formation of Japanese labor unions, trusting that unions would be useful for the Japanese industrial workers. Instead of organizing workers in national unions, with chapters in individual plants, however, the Japanese organized separate unions in each plant or enterprise—hence, the term "enterprise union." Mikio Sumiya, a native Japanese scholar and a member of the research team that studied Japanese labor unions extensively in 1947-48, relates, "The enterprise union in Japan was not established because it was thought that the enterprise type was appropriate; rather labor unions were first established and then, after investigation, were found to be enterprise unions."[32]

Sumiya traces the genesis of this peculiar or even unique form of Japanese enterprise or company union to the particular culture of Japanese business:

> There is a strong social background causing unions to become enterprise unions, namely *lifetime employment* [italics mine]. It is difficult for Japanese workers to find comradeship in striking together for a labor movement outside of their own enterprises. When the enterprise is doing well, there is no fear of being fired and the possibility for improvement of working conditions is great. When the enterprise is not doing well, there is the danger of bankruptcy and unemployment and, of course, no hope for improving working conditions. Further, there is no opportunity for discussion with workers of other enterprises because of the rather closed nature of lifetime employment, and there is nothing to gain by organizing with workers from enterprises that are not doing well. When workers under lifetime employment organize a union, they find it natural to do so separately within each enterprise.[33]

It would be difficult, if not impossible, for the Japanese to duplicate the Japanese enterprise union in the American sociocultural setting, especially with established American labor unions such as the UAW and the Teamsters in place. The Japanese enterprise labor union is incompatible with the existing organizational structure of the American labor unions. Consequently, even some Japanese firms in the United States that have labor unions duplicate the American type, as in the case of NUMMI, cited above.

Another unfounded American belief is that Japanese firms are so worried about American labor unions that they confine themselves to establishing their U.S. subsidiaries in states that have right-to-work laws. As discussed previously, Japanese manufacturing firms are not as fearful of labor unions as one might expect. In fact, surprisingly, many Japanese manufacturing firms have established their plants in states where there are no right-to-work laws. Honda in Ohio and Toyota in Kentucky (the only southern state that does not have a right-to-work law) are two examples. It appears that, as far as labor unions are concerned, Japanese manufacturers are as flexible as American workers. Most Japanese industrial firms, having had experience dealing with a labor union at home, have learned to live with unionism:

> It should be noted, however, that resistance to unionism by large-scale Japanese companies at home is not characteristic. Most big enterprises,especially in manufacturing, have long been organized, albeit with the enterprise union structure, for several decades. Few have experienced organizing drives, as in the United States, and when they do occur, they do not entail the complex American election procedures for establishing representation rights for a union under the law. While at times it is asserted that Japanese managements accept unionism only because the union membership is confined to the permanent employees of each company, it is more likely that their resistance in the United States follows the advice of American labor relations consultants whom they call upon for guidance.[34]

The Japanese firms seem to prefer establishing their manufacturing facilities in states with right-to-work laws, if everything else is equal, and Tennessee, like most other southern states, has a right-to-work law. Some Japanese firms here have American-style labor unions, such as Bridgestone with United Rubber Workers Local 1055, but others, even big firms like Nissan, do not.

In the case of Bridgestone Tire Company in La Vergne, Tennessee, which took over the ailing Firestone in 1983, the Japanese management has cultivated an unusual rapport with the rank-and-file members of the union inherited from Firestone. The unusual affinity and comradeship has been widely publicized:

> In July 1985 [two years after the acquisition from Firestone], Bridgestone president Ishikure announced that Lex McCarthy, who was selling shrubs in Lakeland, Florida, six hundred miles away and five years from his last job at Firestone, would be coming back to work, the last of the laid-off Firestone workers put back on the payroll under Bridgestone management. Mr. Ishikure praised United Rubber Workers Local 1055 for helping to locate the last few workers. And he praised the workers themselves, for improving quality and tripling production of the plant's radial truck tires in the two and a half years since Bridgestone had taken over.[35]

One does not have to be a genius to figure the outcome of such a congenial effort by the management to search for the workers who were laid off under different management. The recovered workers would naturally be loyal to the new management; quality of work would be improved; and the union, which consists of those rank-and-file workers, would be cooperative instead of confrontational. As a unionized Japanese firm in America, producing quality products and winning the support of its labor union, Bridgestone is an example of success, as is NUMMI in California.[36] These cases suggest that Japanese management does not have to have the enterprise as a structural model and that Japanese management can work with the existing American labor unions using adaptive strategies of its own.

It would be a mistake, however, for anyone to believe that all Japanese management in the United States has been as successful as Bridgestone, NUMMI, and others. Levine and Ohtsu report a different case:

> Worker hostility, for example, emerged at the Kawasaki motorcycle factory soon after it started up in Lincoln, Nebraska, in 1975. The apparent issue there involved health insurance coverage for the em-ployees. For the following few years there was a running battle over attempts by the United Automobile Workers (UAW) to organize the 700 employees, with two union representation elections held in 1978 and 1979 declared invalid by the National Labor Relations Board be-cause of charges of unfair labor practice against management. While the management apparently staved off unionization, it also seemed to refrain from instituting employment practices that departed widely from familiar American approaches, notably in recruitment, job security, communication, pay criteria, and the like.[37]

The Kawasaki case is an indication that the skills of Japanese management are neither by-products of a unique Japanese industrial culture nor inherent Japanese managerial art. Rather, successful management depends on the skills and the strategies of the managers in each firm and on the adaptability of each firm to a new sociocultural milieu.

Most Japanese firms in Tennessee appear to keep their options open regarding labor unions. Some firms, such as Nissan, announced themselves antiunion from the start and wanted, like Nissan, to be located "in a part of the country where the chances of...ever becoming unionized would be minimal."[38] In light of its antiunion stance, Nissan's choice of Tennessee for its plant site is logical, although Nissan's experience with American labor unions started even before the plant began to operate. In response to Nissan's employment as general contractor of a nonunion construction company from Greenville, South Carolina, a rowdy building-trades union demonstration marred the ground-breaking ceremonies at the Nissan plant in Smyrna:

On February 3, 1981, when the ceremony took place, several hundred union construction workers showed up to protest. An airplane flew overhead trailing a banner reading: "Boycott Datsun [Nissan]. Put America back to work." Big, burly men carried signs saying: "Quality projects with skilled UNION workers. Boycott Datsun," and cries of "Go home, Japs," drowned out the words of the speakers. When the driver of the snowplow truck that was supposed to break ground tried to move forward, he discovered that his tires had been slashed.[39]

Embarrassed Tennesseans, Lamar Alexander remembers, "poured letters of support into the Nissan offices in Smyrna and Tokyo. Even members of the state AFL-CIO helped to repair the damage, and participated in our Japan Forum in 1982, designed to teach us all more about Japan."[40] "The demonstration so shocked the community, and the national TV people, that they came down heavy on the union. The next day the legislature passed a resolution condemning the building trades union....The union spent a lot of money saying how sorry they were. They ran full-page ads saying, 'Hey, we apologize. We didn't really mean it. Things got out of hand.'"[41]

An extreme form of demonstration, including racial slurs, did not receive any support from the public, even from the union sympathizers. The Smyrna protesters garnered bad publicity and tarnished the public image of the union, all of which had a profound impact on the UAW's efforts to organize a union in Nissan. Despite the persistent and zealous effort of the UAW and the personal dedication of Jim Turner, the UAW organizer, at a union representation election in August 1989, workers voted against the union, two to one. The UAW's defeat in Smyrna had a long-lasting negative impact on any labor movement in Japanese industries in Tennessee.

None of the three firms included in this study has a labor union. Eastech does not have a labor union, although it is the largest one. There has been no movement to organize a union. Aside from Westech being too small to organize a union, the parent company of the American partner has not had a union in the quarter-century history of its company. "Midtech as a major part supplier to Nissan," as one manager said, "will not have a labor union as long as Nissan does not have one." The recession in 1991–92 in the state and the nation as a whole, which hit the manufacturing sector and auto-related industries in particular, did not create favorable socioeconomic conditions for a strong labor union movement.

Because most southern states have passed right-to-work laws, and because southern states stand at the bottom of the list in terms of the percentage of workers belonging to unions, the South is known to be anti-union.[42] Recently, however, a growing number of historians have started questioning the image of southern workers as distinctly nonunion or anti-union in character. Robert H. Zieger points out specifically, "In recent years, teachers and other public employees have made substantial gains in the South and it appears that in the past two decades of organized labor's protracted decline, Southern unions have held their own better than their counterparts elsewhere. Today Southern workers constitute the highest percentage of labor movement's ranks in history."[43] Gilbert J. Gall illustrates the fallacy of an antiunion sentiment among southerners by employing elaborate statistical analyses on two southern states, Arkansas and Florida, and concludes:

> The aggregate response of the southern industrial working class to a pro-union electoral measure indicates that simple generalizations about the existence of an indigenous "antiunion" culture in the South's working class are overdrawn....[A]s the measures in Arkansas imply, they could at times be even more sympathetic toward trade-union goals such as preventing the prohibition of union security restrictions. By inference, this suggests that the primary reason and/or reasons for organized labor's failure to breach the South in organizing might be more strongly associated with factors extraneous to the supposed anti-union bias of southern industrial workers.[44]

Gall may be correct, but if there had been no antiunion sentiment, would Tennessee's state legislature have passed a resolution condemning the building-trades union's demonstration against Nissan's opening ceremony? Gelsanliter reports that Fred Harris, Governor Alexander's assistant during that commotion, was very surprised about the prompt action of the state legislature and commented, "Can you imagine any general assembly in these United States doing that? I couldn't. But they did."[45]

I asked several workers who seemed to be satisfied with their work in the Japanese firms about antiunion sentiment. Their answers in essence were almost identical: "I don't have any antiunion feeling, but I am skeptical about the union's role in these recession-ridden years." One worker asked me, "Tell me what a union can do for me, now? I'm glad I've got a job." When I asked the same question of several midwesterners who work for a Korean manufacturing firm, their answers were basically no different from those of the Tennessee workers. One commented, "I used to work for a union plant. I was laid off, and I'm here. I ended up working for a foreign firm. I'm not going to pay the dues for nothing. I'm not going to put up with it any more. Don't you know what the union did for Caterpillar workers? Nothing." He preferred to maintain good rapport with the company and thus secure his job. Perhaps I carried out my fieldwork at the wrong time to ask about the union. If the economy had been going well and if the unemployment rate had not been as bad as it was in 1991–92, workers' responses to my questions about labor unions might have been different.

When I questioned Japanese executives about antiunion sentiments, one executive replied promptly and straightforwardly, "I hope we will not have a union in this company. If there is going to be one, then so be it. We will have to learn to live with it. But, let me tell you, honestly: If there were a union and collective bargaining and so on, to a certain extent my job would be easier than what I'm doing now. We would go by the collective bargaining contract, no more and no less. Wouldn't it be easy?" What the Japanese executive was suggesting was that the management cares more about the welfare of its employees than the union can. Such an answer differs from several reported cases whereby rather well-known Japanese-owned companies, such as Nissan, have resisted or avoided unionization. When some Nissan workers, for instance, organized an antiunion committee to campaign against union organizers, the company made effective use of its in-house video system to combat the union's assertions. Gelsanliter reports: "Gail Newman, Nissan's general counsel and vice-president for human resources, had once made a speech in which she said, 'We have an in-house video system that reaches over a hundres locations by means of monitores we've put in every work area and in key locations in administration and the cafeterias. When it was installed, we knew it would help us communicate quickly and accurately with our employees. But none of us forewaw how valuable a communications tool it would become....Turner's comment: 'They're using the in-house video to combat our organizing drive. They have professional actors and negative news—about GM closing a plant or laying off people. They never show anything positive'."[46] This action is similar to action undertaken by American managements.[47] Although the three firms included in this study have not made any deliberate efforts to stop unionization in their firms, it is fair to say that the need for unionization in those firms has not yet arisen.

Employees who were terminated from Japanese firms, however, have definite opinions about the need for a union. A woman worker terminated by Midtech for insubordination expressed her frustration and anger over her termination: "You know, a union is the only answer to this [her termination]. My lawyer told me that I can't even sue the company over my termination, because Tennessee has a law prohibiting any litigation about terminations.[48] But, if they keep on doing that, the union will come to the company. As far as I know, some union representatives came to the company several times, and met several workers." According to her, the union is going to be organized in the plant imminently. In my judgment, however, as long as Midtech remains a parts supplier delivering most of their products to nonunionized Nissan, any possibility of having a labor union there is remote. The grievances of a few workers are likely to remain as isolated personal complaints. As long as the Tennessee law on termination of workers remains on the books, dismissed workers will have little chance to win against their employers in a Tennessee court unless the case deals with a violation of Civil Rights, with sexual harassment, or is part of a class action suit.

EMPLOYMENT OF WOMEN

Since I have touched on litigation, this may be an appropriate place to comment on Japanese labor practices concerning women. Beginning in the mid–1980s, the Japanese were accused of, and in a few cases actually cited for, unfair labor practices, especially the under-employment of women and minority workers in the United States. The Sumitomo sex-discrimination suit was a landmark case. It was settled in 1987 for $2.7 million plus guaranteed raises averaging 16 percent for Sumitomo's thirteen women workers.[49]

The three firms included in this study could not be accused of practicing sex discrimination. Depending on the nature of the work involved, the Japanese firms in Tennessee employ a variety of ethnic and racial minorities and as many women as men. Furthermore, there are several women in managerial positions in all three firms. The work force at Midtech, which produces air filters and other plastic parts for automobiles and other vehicles, is dominated by women: over 60 percent of its work force is female, and there are women managers, too. The proportion of women workers in Eastech is over 35 percent and, in Westech, 49 percent. Among manufacturing industries other than the garment industry, the proportion of women in the work forces of Japanese-owned firms in the United States is impressive. I am in agreement with the observations of others that some Japanese-owned companies employ more women workers than do their American counterparts. In the Toyota plant in Georgetown, Kentucky, Gelsanliter reports "more women work on the assembly line than at most Big Three plants."[50] Also "Recognizing that in the United States two thirds of new car purchases are made or influenced by women, Toyota saw women as deserving of particular attention."[51] One informant told me, "The Japanese executives are impressed by women workers, because they usually make higher scores on the dexterity test that we require in hiring new employees. You know, the Japanese demand a great deal of dexterity on the job. There's no reason why they would avoid hiring anyone who has better skills and potential to acquire better skills."

REPRESENTATION OF MINORITIES

Under-employment of minority workers, especially blacks, is a touchy issue. A Japanese executive questioned whether any mainstream American firm should criticize the employment practices of the Japanese. He teased me by saying, "If Americans are doing so well, why do they bother to have 'affirmative action,' and so forth?" Indeed, I was not prepared to respond to his comment. Despite the general criticism of Japanese hiring practices, the firms in this study employ more than their share of minority members in the region.

Minorities at Eastech make up 10 percent of the work force, while the minority population in the county where the firm is located is 2.7 percent: 21 percent of the work force at Westech is minority, while its county minority population is 10.1 percent; Midtech's minority population is 12 percent of its total work force, even though the county's minority population is 9 percent. Even at Nissan, blacks comprise over 17 percent of the total work force, although the black population of the surrounding three counties, where most workers come from, is less than 10 percent.

A young black manager in the oil filter line in Midtech defended Japanese management's treatment of American minority workers and expressed his satisfaction in working for them:

> I really can't speak for anyone else, but Japanese companies in Tennessee did a lot of good for me and my family. My brother works for Nissan. I wanted to work for Nissan, too, but I didn't make it....Before this job, after high school, I worked for two different American companies, but I was always temporary. For the last one, I worked for seven years, but I was still temporary....In this company, I was one of very few who started to work from the beginning. You know Jim, right? He hired me. I worked really hard to show them that I can do my job as well as the others. In May 1990, the company sent me to Japan for training. I guess the Japanese management thought I was manager ma-terial. I was very impressed by the hardwork and discipline of Japanese workers.... This company has been particularly good for me, giving me a steady job so that I can plan my life. I'm not a temporary worker anymore. I'm doing the best I can for the company. You know? I've never missed a single working day ever since I started to work for this company. I think the Japanese know that it is wrong to generalize all black people into one category, either good or bad.

In fact, everyone in Midtech confirms that the black manager has been an excellent worker and a good manager.

In summary, it seems to me that the Japanese have made an art of managing employees. No Japanese firms in Tennessee have institutionalized a system of lifetime employment, but their employees tend to believe that their jobs are safe and to trust that they will be treated fairly with or without the presence of a labor union. One worker answered me when I inquired about job security by saying, "Almost everyone has a sort of trust that the Japanese will do everything they can to secure our jobs." Instead of offering words, they have demonstrated their guarantee of job security, so long as workers are productive and reliable. In fact, at Nissan, despite the commotion over an organized drive for a union; "Nissan didn't lay off, not any technicians, not even any of its 'temporary' contract employees. Instead, the company slowed line speed from 64 to 57 vehicles an hour and over the next several months gave fifteen hundred employees a week's extra training in safety, shop floor management, or communications."[52] Indeed, Japanese managers go to extraordinary lengths to avoid laying off any regular employees by having a layer of temporary workers—security and maintenance contract workers—as a buffer or cushion, as they were accustomed to in Japan.

OTHER JAPANESE INDUSTRIAL-RELATIONS PRACTICES

Not only do the transplanted Japanese firms not replicate the "three divine treasures," but they also do not follow other well-publicized Japanese labor-relations practices, such as generous company welfare benefits, early paid retirement, task or job rotation, and training and work as team members. As far as company welfare benefits and retirement are concerned, the Japanese expatriates follow the existing American practices and laws, and they grant no additional fringe benefits, which are common in Japan, such as scholarships for employees' children, housing and family allowances, and free meals during the working hours. The retirement age is uniformly sixty-five, and pensions for retirees are almost identical with those of the domestic U.S. firms.

Job rotation, as practiced in Japan, is the reallocation of workers from one specialty to another as needed, to insure a lean operation. For instance, a plumber, whose service is not critically demanded, can switch to work as an electrician, depending on which service is needed. To the employee's benefit, while the position of plumber may have to be eliminated, the worker's job is saved. Even in white-collar jobs, Japanese training requires new employees to have experience in almost every department or division by periodic rotation. Even when one becomes a manager or top executive, one (almost always a male) will have a keen knowledge of how each division or department functions as an integrated part of the whole. Rotation is in stark contrast to the western practice whereby workers pursue specialized career paths within a firm or by moving from one firm to another.[53]

Japanese managers in the United States appear to be reluctant to alter the existing American preference for employee specialization. They are aware of American workers' pride in their own specialties, territories, or turfs. For most Americans, keeping their own specialized fields seems to be as important as owning their own properties. "Comes with the territory" is a common American phrase. Regarding turf, an illustrative episode took place in the building where my department is housed. A cat was trapped in the basement of the building. When the department secretary asked the maintenance office to free the "poor cat," she was told that, if the cat were dead, the maintenance department would take the dead cat out, but, since the cat was alive, then the job belonged to the department of safety and security! One can understand why not many Japanese managers would dare try to impose a job rotation system on American workers.

Significantly, most manufacturing jobs assigned to American workers in the three firms in Tennessee demand very little skill. They appear to be repetitive and machine controlled; thus, if necessary, jobs can be rotated without institutionalizing a rotation system. Yet the three firms neither institutionalize nor practice rotation. Instead of institutionalizing a rotating system, Japanese management reduces the number of job classifications to a minimum. For example, since Toyota's joint venture with GM started, NUMMI reduced job classifications from eighty to a mere four. All three firms included in this study have fewer than eight job classifications.

Although a lot of publicity has centered on how the Japanese train and work as a team, these Japanese labor practices are almost invisible in Japanese plants in the United States. In posters, manuals, and elsewhere, the spirit of teamwork is manifest, yet I did not observe any tangible efforts toward training for teamwork. My attendance at management meetings also leads me to believe that teamwork is publicized more than it is practiced. My informant in Midtech told me:

> When one of our customers returned some of our products because of poor quality and defects, one Japanese executive wanted to display them in the cafeteria where everyone could see them, so that everyone could see the defects and who authorized the shipment. By doing that, the executive said, "We'll reduce, if not eliminate, such mistakes." I advised him not to do that, because I don't believe that is the spirit of teamwork. That's an attempt to humiliate a particular worker. You can't promote teamwork by doing that. I can understand now how the Japanese managers can yell at their workers in front of others, even in front of foreign visitors like us.

In another case, I was told of an episode that occurred at Eastech, when a zealous American worker was insulted by the teamwork spirit. The worker, exercising his ingenuity and independence, was fixing his malfunctioning machine when a red light began flashing. A team of Japanese engineers dashed to the scene and tried to help the worker fix the machine. The American worker was not only embarrassed but also frustrated and even angered, because he knew that he could fix the machine, even if it would take him a little longer than it would take the Japanese experts. To the Japanese engineers, it seemed natural to assist a struggling fellow worker, and it was very difficult for them to understand why the American worker was upset. Why was he not gratified by the prompt assistance from a team of Japanese engineers? The American ethos of self-reliance could hardly be understood by many Japanese, whose cultural orientation is centered on group achievement and collective goals.

Some cutting-edge American firms, such as GM's Saturn plant, maximize teamwork in their operations more than their Japanese counterparts do. As widely reported, the "Japanese-inspired team concept" is applied much more at the U.S. Saturn plant than it is in the plant's counterpart in Japan:

> Beyond sharing power at top levels, the labor agreement established some 165 [about 3,000 team members] work teams, which have been given more power than assembly-line workers anywhere else in GM or at any Japanese plant. They are allowed to interview and approve new hires for their teams (average size: 10 workers). They are given wide responsibility to decide how to run their own areas; when workers see a problem on the assembly line, they can pull on a blue handle and shut down the entire line. They are even given budget responsibility. One team in Saturn's final-assembly area voted to reject some proposed pneumatic car assembly equipment and went to another supplier to buy electronic gear that its members believed to be safer. Says Hoalcraft: "I don't know of another U.A.W. person who has ever decided on the purchase and installation of equipment."...Saturn philosophy is that all teams must be committed to decisions affecting them before those changes are put into place, from choosing an ad agency to selecting an outside supplier. "That means a lot of yelling sometimes, and everything takes a lot longer," says U.A.W. official Jack O'Toole, who oversees Spring Hill personnel, "but once they come out of that meeting room, they're 100% committed.[55]

Saturn's teamwork concept revolutionizes the relationship between labor and management, changing it from confrontation to cooperation, not unlike the relationship achieved by the Japanese enterprise union. *TIME* describes this companionship between labor and management:

> The company president walks around in a polo shirt with a pocket logo right out of *Star Trek*, allows workers to call him "Skip" and describes his position as "team member." He and the union boss (who goes by "Dick") have a strange, collegial relationship. As for the rank and file, they don't punch a time clock and they get to handpick the people they work alongside.... The core of Saturn's system is one of the most radical labor-management agreements ever developed in this country, one that involves the

United Auto Workers in every aspect of the business. The executive suite in Spring Hill is shared by president LeFauve and U.A.W. co–ordinator Richard Hoalcraft, who often travel together and conduct much of the company's business in each other's presence.[56]

It is interesting to note that Japanese firms in the South, particularly in Tennessee, have initiated very little change in existing American labor relations–practices. Consequently, the well-publicized Japanese industrial relations–principles, especially the divine treasures, have not been replicated and, to a certain extent, have even been avoided. Ironically, domestic American firms, as evidenced by GM's Saturn plant in the very state of Tennessee, emulate the Japanese practices that the Japanese firms in the United States eschew. In small towns in Tennessee and other parts of Dixieland, it seems as if these two distinct industrial giants, Japan and the United States, rather than employing their own indigenous practices, are learning and adopting from each other.

JAPANESE INDUSTRIAL STRATEGIES

Any attempt to generalize about Japanese strategies for succeeding in their manufacturing operations in the South is difficult and can be misleading. Even among the three firms included in this study, strategies vary. Each firm, as evidenced by Midtech, changes its strategy over time in order to cope with external changes.

There are, however, some major strategies uniformly adopted by Japanese firms in Tennessee: flexibility, adaptability, and the ability to borrow from another culture. All of these strategies can be attributed to the cultural pattern of Japanese "inclusiveness." As they learn to produce industrial goods, the Japanese make every effort to find the strengths and weaknesses in their procedures and to change quickly to build on the former and eliminate the latter. Although it is widely documented that the Japanese are notoriously slow in reaching decisions, it is not as well known that, once they make a decision, they execute it very briskly.

Japanese strategists rapidly figured out that their home-grown industrial–relations practices, the divine treasures in particular, would be difficult to duplicate on alien turf, so they quickly adopted American industrial-relations practices. By doing so, they promoted American strengths. Indeed, when moving into a foreign culture, Japanese industrialists, as a matter of principle, make every effort to show their eagerness to conform to the regional norms rather than to impose Japanese culture on them. Because of this strategy, the Japanese as a group in Tennessee and elsewhere in the South make every attempt not to appear snobbish or arrogant, or to have a "colonial attitude."[57] Consequently, even when Japan-bashing was at its height, no violent incidents ever took place in Tennessee or in the South.

Instead of trying to replicate their home practices in their entirety, the Japanese expatriates apply certain industrial-relations principles selectively and partially, and they modify some of them to complement and/or promote American strengths. For example, the Japanese expatriates try to promote American workers' egalitarianism by addressing them and each other by first names and encouraging the workers to do the same. They also encourage and welcome workers' suggestions and ideas, and American blue-collar workers are receptive to the Japanese efforts. One young black worker in Westech told me with pleasure:

> I was tickled to death when my suggestion was adopted as a company policy. See [he showed me some boxes used to ship their final products to their customers], we used to use stamps for marking all these boxes before shipment. No one could read the stamped marks. I suggested the company use magic pens to write rather than use the stamps. It takes about the same time, but we can read it clearly. The company accepted my suggestion, and it's in use. It's great to see such a thing. This is the first time such a thing has happened to me. I'm proud of it.

He appeared to be highly motivated.

An observation made by Yoshihara is virtually identical to that of mine, and true to the firms I have studied:

> In American and European factories, as a general trend, workers are treated as though they were machines. Workers are supposed to be mere robot-like executors of the instructions given by their superiors and by specialists. Under the Japanese production system, workers are not machine-like individuals doing their jobs, but are expected to use their minds while working. One of the features of the Japanese production system is the so-called bottom-up approach. Workers on the job site are encouraged to express their ideas and to make proposals to their superiors and the company's specialists, who in turn, receive them constructively. Then, improvements in the work routine developed jointly by the workers, their supervisors, and the experts are put into use....Based on egalitarianism, efforts are made to reduce the differences between workers and superiors or specialists as much as possible. They all use the same cafeteria, choose food from the same menu, use a common toilet, etc. Every effort is made to give the worker the same treatment received by the specialist or supervisor. Moreover, once or twice a year, and in some places a month, company presidents hold regular meetings. During these meetings, over-all business results as well as information on the environmental conditions surrounding the firm are also presented to all the employees, including factory workers. The information is also inspired by egalitarianism.[58]

When I attended a quality control meeting at Westech, the Japanese engineers, despite the difficulties in communication, seemed very receptive to the workers' difficulties, problems, and criticism. Some suggestions made by a rank-and-file American worker at the meeting did not have enough merit to warrant any attention at all, yet the Japanese engineers wrote the suggestions down in their notes as if they were important ideas. The American worker seemed happy about the Japanese engineers' serious attention to his suggestions. The Japanese are accomplished at winning American workers' support and confidence.

The Japanese expatriates do not of course modify all of their industrial-relations practices to please American employees. Two of the Japanese home practices that have not been compromised or abandoned are *kaizen* and the so-called 5s movement. One Japanese executive commented about *kaizen*:

> I do not believe the term *kaizen* is correctly understood by many Americans, even those who preach it. As far as improving is concerned, every industrialist has been doing that. Look at American vehicles for instance. Each year, American auto makers have introduced new models, and improved some models each year, but their improvements have had almost nothing to do with the wishes and expectations of customers. They tend to be arrogant, to think that they are the only ones who know everything, including the tastes of customers. They think the customers will buy whatever products they turn out, because the products are good and improved. The essence of *kaizen* is, of course, continuous improvement, yet its goal has to be toward the wishes and expectations of customers.

Indeed, Masaaki Imai defines *kaizen* as "a customer-driven strategy for improvement."[59] To the Japanese, customers are the "kings," as one Japanese executive calls them. According to my observation, *kaizen* begins with very small things and is a continuous process. When I attended a *kaizen* meeting—virtually every meeting is for *kaizen*—both Japanese American engineers, American foremen, and some American rank-and-file workers spent over two hours discussing how neatly they could cut tiny rubber hoses, and what type of blade could improve the neatness. In a sense, their discussions went beyond quality and extended to appearance and beauty. The same subject was the agenda of the next three meetings. This is a tiny example of Japanese *kaizen*.

Japanese management aims for small improvements day by day in their equipment, measuring instruments, and tools, which are improved and replaced frequently. The Japanese trust that plant workers, on the basis of their daily job experiences, can make the improvements. The parent company of Eastech, for instance, gathered more than six million suggestions from its employees in 1985. Eastech initiated its suggestion program officially in 1994. During the year of 1994, 150 suggestions were made by its (Eastech's) employees. Because of its short history, any meaningful comparison cannot be made. However, my informant told me, "*As an Americn company* [emphasis mine], it isn't bad at all."

Suggestions made by rank-and-file workers of a company can improve not only the quality of products and working conditions but also save a company from bankruptcy. U.S. Steel's Gary Works in Gary, Indiana, is a most remarkable example of this feat. Five union and rank-and-file workers at the Gary Works' mill saved contracts and the plant by suggesting ideas gleaned from their fact-finding mission to their dissatisfied customers. They relayed their findings to the plant manager, who implemented the change. The story goes:

> U.S. Steel's Gary Works was all but banished from General Motors' supplier rolls. Ford Motor was threatening the same....It also was losing more than $100 million a year. The heart of Big Steel [the biggest mill in the biggest steel company] was about to stop beating....Five steel workers were freed from mill jobs to visit automotive customers' plants and see problems for themselves....They [after the visits] demanded rubber pads on flatbed trucks to cushion the steel. [Workers at the plant] created plastic rings to protect the rolls from crane damage. They persuaded workers who package and load each roll or stack to take responsibility for its condition.... Automotive customers, who buy almost half of Gary Works' steel, now reject just 0.6%, down from an industry-worst 2.6% in 1987....Word spread, and other auto plants demanded Gary Works' liaisons. Even GM came around and has increased Gary Works purchases fivefold since 1987.[60]

Gary Works was the winner of the 1992 Quality Cup in manufacturing.[61] The most significant aspect of a worker-led suggestion program is identified best by the workers themselves. One of the five-member team of Gary Works said, "We have to give power to the people, and then we can beat the Japanese. We're more innovative than they are, and we don't need all the committees and meetings they do....But if we don't give power to the people, we'll keep on that downhill slide the Japanese have us on."[62]

After *kaizen*, the practice that Japanese managers stubbornly insist on retaining is a clean work place, known as the "5s" movement. The 5s are the initial letters of the Japanese words: *seiri* (arrangement, adjustment, regulation), *seiton* (good order, proper arrangement), *seisō* (cleaning), *seiketsu* (cleanliness), and *shitsuke* (training, discipline). Anyone who has ever been inside Japanese manufacturing plants can understand what they mean by the 5s movement and its dutiful practice.

I have spent a good deal of time in industrial plants in Korea and in the United States, but I have never seen anything like the Japanese manufac-

4.1 • A Clean and Orderly Scene inside the Eastech Plant

turing plants in terms of cleanliness and orderliness. Whether the firm is small, large, or even a joint venture makes no difference. My immediate reaction as I enter Japanese plants and shops is, "My God, even if I dropped food on the floor, I could pick it up and eat it without feeling the need to clean or wash it." During my stay in Japan, I observed that things everywhere were clean and orderly, but I did not anticipate that manufacturing plants would also be kept so clean and neat.

In the Tennessee plants, with or without any notice or poster about the 5s policy, all the Japanese workers seem to be well trained in the 5s and to have persuaded American workers and managers to keep their factory floors clean and to arrange their tools and parts in their proper places. Smoking inside the shops is strictly prohibited except for designated areas, as is drinking coffee or other beverages. In Westech, there is a poster of the 5s in English along with the Japanese version in the cafeteria, where everyone goes at least once a day during working hours. In addition to the 5s poster, there is a poster with plain English words that reads: "Your mom does not work here!" One Japanese commented, "Perhaps that sign carries a clearer message to the average American than 5s in the Japanese words."

Observing the Japanese industrial operations and their strategies, it is very difficult, if not confusing, to categorize the inherent Japanese traits and the hybrid ones. If "globalization of industrial management" is going to be a future trend, categorization of industrial-relations principles by specific countries may be rendered futile and meaningless.

The Japanese facility of blending other cultures into their own is nothing new. Sumiya eloquently summarized flexible Japanese wisdom:

> Japan, under the influence of Confucian rationalism in the middle of the nineteenth century, when faced with Western advanced technology, accepted it within the context of "Eastern morality and Western technology." While retaining its traditional worldview as its value system, Japan accepted Western culture aggressively in the field of production technology. Every nation has these two facets, but with different nuances. We are two kinds of societies; one accepts rationalism with production technology, and the other almost totally rejects it. Japan, while recognizing the confrontation between the two, retained both aspects. If one carefully examines Japanese society, it is easy to see both. For example, even when modern, high-rise office buildings are constructed, built on top of them are small shrines where prayer is offered for company security and prosperity....In the case of Japan, while there have been some problems, one can say that this coexistence has worked out rather well.[63]

Such Japanese adaptability can be seen by foreign observers as dualism or contradiction—cruel warriors driven by a spartan code of ethics called *bushido* on the one hand, and harmony-loving worker bees on the other; an artistic, somewhat feminized chrysanthemum in one hand, and in the other a masculine, assertive sword, in the *samurai* tradition, as delineated in Ruth Benedict's celebrated book, *The Chrysanthemum and the Sword*.[64]

Combining the best of both industrial cultures certainly would be desirable, but even if it is not achieved, the impact of Japanese industrial-relations principles and managerial strategies is beginning to be felt. As Ralph Linton recognized, cultural changes and exchanges took place long before we even acknowledged such changes:

> There can be no question about the average American's Americanism or his desire to preserve this precious heritage at all costs. Nevertheless, some insidious foreign ideas have already wormed their way into his civilization without his realizing what was going on. Thus dawn finds the unsuspecting patriot garbed in pajamas, a garment of East Indian origin;...Breakfast over, he places upon his head a molded piece of felt, invented by the nomads of Eastern Asia, and, if it looks like rain, puts on outer shoes of rubber, discovered by the ancient Mexicans....At the station he pauses for a moment to buy a newspaper, paying for it with coins invented in an-cient Lydia....Meanwhile, he reads the news of the day, imprinted in characters invented by the ancient Semites by a process invented in Ger-many upon a material invented in China. As he scans the latest editorial pointing out the dire results to our institutions of accepting foreign ideas, he will not fail to thank a Hebrew God in an Indo-European language that he is a one-

hundred per cent (decimal system invented by the Greeks) American (from Americus Vespucci, Italian geographer).[65]

Civilization is indeed an outcome of those changes, exchanges, and constant interactions between and among various cultures, and the industrial domain cannot be excluded. Many managerial practices employed in Japan, including the famous quality control, have their origins in America.

Levine and Ohtsu astutely delineate the most recent exchanges between the industrial cultures of the United States and Japan:

> It is now possible that Japanese-owned companies in the United States are emulating what they believe to be the best American practice of employee involvement. Labor-management cooperation is not new to American industrial relations—prominent cases can be traced back to the early part of this century....It is well known that in the 1920s major Japanese corporations looked to the example of the Americans in pursuing their own paternalistic labor policies at that time....American assistance for Japan's postwar recovery also helped Japanese management to learn much from the Americans, the leading example being the influence of W. E. Deming and other industrial engineers and statisticians in introducing quality controls in production. Thus, one way to interpret the approach of the large Japanese companies toward accepting worker participation, egalitarianism, employment security, and even unionism in America is that these are the very features that U.S. labor relations themselves have been attempting to achieve.[66]

Similarly, it now appears that many American executives in manufacturing sectors are seriously examining the ways of their Japanese counterparts, and some are adapting the traits claimed to be inherent Japanese practices, thereby becoming competitive and successful. American competitive strength in the semiconductor arena is a good example. Up until the early 1990s, Japan's chip makers maintained global leadership and beat back American competition, but the times are changing:

> In 1988, for example, Japan controlled half the world semiconductor market, while the United States saw its share, which had reached nearly 60 percent in 1980, sink to below 40 percent. Now, U.S. manufacturers are racking up record sales and profits, while Mitsubishi and other Japanese chip producers slash capital spending as profits plummet. Last year [1991], according to VLSI Research, a technology-information firm, America regained the top spot in the $65.6 billion global semiconductor business, claiming a 43.8 percent share of market, compared with Japan's 43.1 percent. At the same time, California-based Intel shot ahead of Japanese rivals NEC and Toshiba to become the world's largest semiconductor supplier, with over 5 billion in sales.[67]

_5_

RESPONSE OF SOUTHERNERS TO THE JAPANESE CHALLENGES

The response of southerners to the Japanese manufacturing presence in the South varies, ranging from extremely negative to neutral to very hospitable. Focusing on Henry Companies, I will examine the various responses of southerners toward Japanese investment in their native turf, the impact of the Japanese on southern life, and the influence of the Japanese-owned industries on southern manufacturing industry.

THE JAPANESE VIEW OF AMERICAN MANUFACTURING WORKERS

Despite the Japanese's pervasive criticism of American workers in Japan,[1] the Japanese expatriates in the American South view American workers quite positively. Since the three firms in this study are manufacturing plants, the observations made by the Japanese interviewed are largely about American blue-collar workers.

Their remarks add up to: American workers are as good as Japanese workers. In fact, one executive told me that: "American workers are even better than their Japanese counterparts. Their work ethic is the same as that of the Japanese. Simply, American workers have not been highly motivated to work hard." Another executive elaborated:

> When I first looked at an American worker, I thought he couldn't do the job, because he didn't show any enthusiasm. But, in the end, he finished his assignment in the given hour. It's like the way Americans work on their highway constructions. From the way they work, it would seem almost impossible that they would complete the highway. But, somehow and someway, they complete the job. They don't show off or brag about the work they do. But, when we give them a job, they do it. Maybe we Japanese are too crabby about the way Americans work.

Another commented:

> Some Japanese people complain about American workers' lack of skill and knowledge, but they're more machine-oriented than the average Japanese. I guess it has a lot to do with their acquaintance with machinery from an early age, growing up on farms with tractors. How many Japanese living in Tokyo can fix their own cars? Here, they work on them, and fix them themselves. They're not like people living in Third World countries, where mechanical knowledge is still alien. When you give them clear directions, American workers can do better than any other people. I'm so impressed by their willingness to help when someone needs help. If I tell them that I need their help to accomplish so and so, and if they see that it's a necessity, they don't mind helping me in order to meet the goal. Some Japanese complain a lot that American workers avoid overtime work, while Japanese workers would not dare to. That is not true. Even in Japan nowadays many young people avoid overtime work, especially when it is unexpected. But, in Amer-ica, you have to approach the workers right. If I can explain and appeal to them for their help, and if they see it's urgent, then they will help. They're very straightforward and frank, and they even seem naive and trusting. I'm sometimes afraid to say things, because they become too serious about what I say.

Notwithstanding their favorable comments, most Japanese expatriates cautiously point out the shortcomings of some American workers. They find that, unlike their Japanese counterparts, American workers are not committed and loyal to their companies. According to the Japanese, American workers see the company as a place to work and earn wages. They do not view the plant as they do their home, and fellow workers as family members. A Japanese manager commented, "It seems to me that most Americans have their friends elsewhere rather than among their workmates. Their homeward rush is so swift that it looks as if they would run over somebody in the parking lot." An executive commented, "Don't get me wrong. They do their jobs while they're working for us but whenever they find other jobs that pay better, they don't mind leaving us, just like that! Sometimes, I really hate to see someone leaves us, but there's nothing I can do about it."

Another Japanese manager wondered about American workers' initiative: "Perhaps it may be unfair to say this about high-school graduates and blue-collar workers, but I haven't witnessed much initiative among blue-collar workers. They do okay when we instruct them to do certain jobs, but they don't go beyond the instructions. They don't want to think or to figure out their jobs. I've heard this is the 'volunteer state,' they don't seem to go above or beyond the given job." Perhaps in the better-known Japanese firms, such as Nissan, where employment is more competitive, the motivation and initiative of the workers is different. Nissan is an exceptional case, however. Since the three firms included in this study, other than Eastech, are typical small- and medium-sized Japanese firms, perhaps the manager's assessment of American workers may be true of most American workers.

Various Japanese expatriates may assess American workers somewhat differently; nevertheless, almost all of the Japanese expatriates expressed a common complaint about American workers: the lack of basic knowledge and skills.

LACK OF BASIC KNOWLEDGE AND SKILLS

The Japanese expatriates are surprised to find a wide gap between the level of educational attainment of American workers and their basic knowledge and skills. One commented; "Some American workers claim that they have high-school diplomas, but they cannot function as high-school graduates should." A Japanese manager who has been in Tennessee for three years told me how startled he was to learn about the American public high-school system: "Someone told me that in America quite a few can graduate from high school without knowing how to read and write. I couldn't believe that! Now I know why some American workers who are high-school graduates cannot meet our expectations." In fact, an educational program director for a southern industry points out that having a high-school diploma does not necessarily mean the holder can read.[2]

According to the 1990 Census, in the state of Tennessee, 67.1 percent of the people twenty-five years old and over graduated from high school or better. That Japanese manager might not be surprised that nobody knows how many of those high-school graduates can read and write; he might be surprised, however, to know that there are different kinds of high-school diplomas in the United States: a high honor diploma; a standard diploma; a special education diploma; and a diploma for attendance, just putting the time in without making the grades. "A diploma's significance varies from state to state and from locality to locality, and many people don't know that."[3]

Certainly, I was unaware of the various standards for American high-school graduation until I started this study. Except for a few big Japanese firms, where employment is highly competitive, a good many small- and medium-sized Japanese firms have had to hire some of those marginally educated high-school graduates, and their criticism of the functional illiteracy of these workers is legitimate and valid. Halberstam substantiates that the weakness of the American industrial worker is the public-school system and the low level of literacy.[4] Some Japanese are tempted to explain this paradox as part of American culture. But an illiterate high-school graduate, however common today, is a relatively new phenomenon in the United States, hardly part of American traditional heritage.

NATIVE RESPONSES

Japanese direct investment in the United States was not met with open arms and an open-hearted welcome. Some Americans viewed Japanese direct investment in the United States as a "threat": "Given the size of the trade imbalances, Japan's competitiveness in high technology fields, and anxiety that the ANIEs [Asian Newly Industrializing Economies] are catching up technologically, it is understandable that the United States might view Asian economic strength as a threat."[5] According to a U.S. public opinion survey in October 1989, 33 percent of the people who were asked, "Which do you think is a greater threat to the United States?" opted for Soviet Union military strength (before the union was divided into several republics), while 52 percent cited Japanese economic strength.[6] Others worry that the intent of heavy Japanese investment is "buying into America" or "Japanization" of the host country's economy.[7] In reporting Sony's acquisition of Columbia Pictures Entertainment for $3.4 billion, *TIME* wrote, "Some entertainment-industry observers suggested that Congress should challenge the Sony deal as well. For one thing, entertainment is the second largest U.S. export industry (aerospace is first)."[8] Still others see Japanese direct investment as a "Japanese challenge," just as operations of the American-based firms in Europe have been viewed as an American challenge.[9]

From my view, the so-called silent majority of southerners, including Tennesseans, welcome Japan's money and the jobs provided by Japanese manufacturing firms, but little else. "More than 75% of U.S. adults surveyed in a poll conducted last spring [1988] for a group of Japanese firms agreed that foreign acquisitions have boosted U.S. economic growth, employment and competitiveness. Nevertheless, nearly 75% viewed the increased foreign presence as undesirable."[10]

Southerners are wondering: What has happened to America and Americans? All of sudden, the very Japanese who surrendered "unconditionally" to Americans during the war and who were starving afterward are bringing money to the heartland of America and offering jobs to Americans! Many southerners cannot accept the reality of Japanese ascendancy in certain manufacturing industries. It is a matter of pride. For many uneducated Southerners, America is the center of the world for everything.

Some southerners' responses to the Japanese challenge have been explicit and direct. There was a cross-burning incident in the schoolyard of the Tennessee Meiji Gakuin school. When Nissan announced its decision to locate in Smyrna, Tennessee, Carl Montgomery, a patriotic southerner and retired Air Force colonel from World War II, demanded that the County Commission rename the access road to the plant "Pearl Harbor Boulevard."[11] While most southern industrial promoters, politicians, and governors have been stouthearted advocates, recruiters, and promoters, some southern governors were against incentive packages to recruit the Japanese plants. Wallace Wilkinson campaigned against the Toyota incentive package,[12] and his victory in the gubernatorial election in 1987 was a manifestation of public sentiment against the over-generous incentive package to recruit Toyota that has been prepared by his predecessor, Martha Layne Collins.

Whenever I visited the Tennessee towns where the Japanese plants are located, I was almost always misidentified in local shops and restaurants as a Japanese executive. This mistake allowed me to empathize with the Japanese and to experience firsthand the local attitudes toward the Japanese. This fieldwork was quite different from the experiences I had in southern towns before Japanese investment in the South began. During my previous fieldwork in the 1960s, I received more help than I needed: When I asked for directions, they took me to my destination. Assuming that "an Asian guest" needs help, they displayed southern hospitality to me as a foreigner.[13] In contrast, consider a rainy day in late February 1992, when I needed to check the air pressure of the tires on my car during a field trip to a Japanese firm in Tennessee. I pulled my car into a full-service section of a gas station, but instead of checking my tires for me, an attendant handed me the air-pressure gauge. I happen to drive a Japanese-made car. Without any doubt, the attendant thought I was Japanese, and he could not stand to serve a Japanese. It would have been worse if I was in Detroit.[14]

Despite the hysterical commotions and the tragedies that occurred in the Midwest, however, in general, most southerners remained calm, although sullen, with the Japanese. I noticed this churlishness more in towns where there are Japanese plants. This sullenness comes not only from the sentiment that the American manufacturing industry is losing its competitive edge to the Japanese but also from the belief that the Japanese demand too much hard work from southern workers. A University of Kentucky survey reveals that the residents of a Kentucky county are disenchanted with the Japanese work demand: "Few found fault with the Japanese as individuals—they were seen as hardworking, family-oriented, and religious—but nearly 40 percent thought Toyota might work its employees too hard, up from just 12 percent the year before."[15]

In contrast to such negative views, many Southerners, as well as other Americans—especially some perceptive politicians, progressive intellectuals, and renowned political economists—view Japanese direct investment in the United States, including the South, as positive and functional to the region and to the nation. Alexander, who was instrumental in recruiting many

Japanese firms to Tennessee, believes that a certain ambivalence toward Japanese direct investment on the part of Tennesseans and other Americans results from a "sad lack" of American understanding of Japan and its importance to Americans: "This is the most ridiculous charge of all [that the Japanese are buying up America]. Despite the large amount of Japanese investment in Tennessee, the English, the Germans, and the Dutch each own about as much of us as the Japanese do. Altogether, foreign investment in Tennessee is about the same as GM's investment in the new Saturn Plant, $5 billion, only about five percent of our manufacturing base."[16]

Robert B. Reich advocates that "we should encourage, not discourage foreign direct investment."[17] His advice is pragmatic, because foreign manufacturers, particularly the Japanese in Tennessee, have recently created more jobs in the United States than have American-owned manufacturing companies. On the one hand, "America's 500 largest industrial companies failed to create a single net new job between 1975 and 1990, their share of the civilian labor force dropping from 17 percent to less than 10 percent."[18] On the other hand, American-owned multinationals employed large numbers of foreigners:

> Forty percent of IBM's world employees are foreign....IBM Japan boasts 18,000 Japanese employees....Whirlpool now employs 43,500 people around the world in 45 countries—most of them non-Americans. TI employs over 5,000 people in Japan alone....American corporations now employ 11% of the industrial work force of North-ern Ireland....More than 100,000 Singaporians work for more than 200 U.S. corporations....[M]ore than one-third of Taiwan's notorious trade surplus with the United States comes from U.S. corporations making or buying things there, then selling or using them back in the United States.[19]

Reich's list goes on. He concludes that "Overall, the evidence suggests that U.S. companies have not lost their competitive edge over the last 20 years—they've just moved their base of operations."[20]

In response to the recession and corporate losses, in the early 1990s scores of major American industrial giants announced their intentions to reduce their work forces and terminated numbers of their employees.[21] At the same time, the Japanese firms in Tennessee, for instance, expanded and increased their employment. In January 1992, the Japanese-owned Sharp Manufacturing Company of America, founded in 1979 and located in Memphis, Tennessee, held a groundbreaking ceremony to add its third plant in Memphis. By the end of 1994, its 200 new workers will join Sharp's existing local work force of 830.[22] Also in January 1992, Nissan in Smyrna announced a $490 million expansion (to make the total investment of $1.2 billion) that prompted the hiring of 1,500 more workers, and the plant's work force grew to 6,000 by summer 1992. Nissan also purchased 958 acres in Decherd, Tennessee, 60 miles southeast of Smyrna, for an engine plant that is projected to employ up to 1,000 people by the late 1990s.[23]

Reich sees other benefits of foreign direct investment in the United States:

> ...[I]n the process of supplanting the American company, the foreign-owned operation can transfer the superior know-how to its American work force—giving American workers the tools they need to be more productive, more skilled, and more competitive. Thus foreign companies create good jobs in the United States. In 1986 (the last date for which such data are available), the average American employee of a foreign-owned manufacturing company earned $32,887, while the average American employee of an American-owned manufacturer earned $28,954. This process is precisely what happened in Europe in the 1950s and 1960s. Europeans publicly fretted about the invasion of American-owned multinationals and the onset of "the American challenge." But the net result of these operations in Europe has been to make Europeans more productive, upgrade European skills, and thus enhance the standard of living of Europeans.[24]

Reich holds strongly that foreign direct investment in the United States is not a threat, because the United States can control foreign assets in the United States much more than it can control American assets abroad.[25]

ECONOMIC IMPACT

That the Japanese investment in the South and in Tennessee in particular has helped the economic health of the region is well known. Alexander concludes:

> Between 1980 and 1985, the number of Japanese companies in Tennessee more than doubled, from fourteen to thirty-two. The amount of Japanese investment in Tennessee jumped ten times, to about $1.2 billion. The number of Tennesseans directly employed at those Japanese enterprises grew one thousand to nearly eight thousand; construction, purchases of parts and supplies, and the turnover of an annual $154 million in Japanese payrolls creates three to four times more jobs than that.[26]

U.S. News & World Report assessed: "Now, it's the Japanese yen that's keeping Tennesseans home and luring new blood from places as close as Kentucky and Alabama and as far away as New York and California. Outside investments have helped push Tennessee several rungs up the economic ladder, from the 45th state in per capita income as recently as 1979 to 38th now [1988]."[27] As late as November 1994, 113 Japanese firms, including sales and distribution firms, employed over 26,840 Tennesseans, investing $4.8 billion in the state.

Perhaps greater than the direct impact of Japanese investment is the indirect impact, as Alexander asserts:

> These [Japanese firms] operations produce other benefits for Tennessee.... That helped to sell American plants on Tennessee, too. *Many people think that General Motors put its Saturn plant in Spring Hill in 1985 because Nissan had done so well in the Tennessee environment* [italics mine]. We were the envy of every other state because the $5 billion Saturn plant is the largest single business investment in U.S. history.... Now *The Washington Post* describes Tennessee as the "new industrial wonderland of American industry." Would this have happened if the Japanese had not found us first?[28]

Alexander may be correct. Not only have the Japanese investments induced American companies to come to Tennessee, but they have generated an "imitation effect," as Yoshihara has termed it: "Local manufacturers attempt to introduce some good features of the Japanese system, and as a result, production systems in the local industry improve."[29]

During the general election of 1992, *U.S. News & World Report* rated the "economic health" of the fifty U.S. states and the District of Columbia on the basis of five economic variables: the rates of income growth, employment growth, unemployment decline, home price increases, and business

Table 5.1 • Rankings of States by Economic Health

Ranking of State	Income Growth Rate	Employment Growth Rate	Unemployment Decline Rate	Home-Price Growth Rank	Business Bankruptcy Rate
Oklahoma	14	14	6	9	9
Kentucky	2	13	9	7	31
Arkansas	8	1	11	1	41
Kansas	7	8	3	30	20
South Dakota	4	37	5	16	8
Montana	3	3	2	29	35
Mississippi	5	35	16	14	5
Indiana	18	4	41	12	4
Texas	11	12	29	24	10
Tennessee	19	27	8	26	6
Idaho	13	10	20	22	22
Alabama	20	7	38	13	11
Michigan	10	2	21	28	29

(Table 5.1 cont.)

Ranking of State	Income Growth Rate	Employment Growth Rate	Unemployment Decline Rate	Home-Price Growth Rank	Business Bankruptcy Rate
Ohio	33	6	39	3	14
Illinois	31	26	4	11	25
Iowa	12	20	15	6	50
Wisconsin	16	19	23	4	48
Maine	37	5	1	48	19
North Carolina	17	31	26	17	23
Utah	24	17	10	27	36
West Virginia	23	46	22	8	16
South Carolina	49	23	28	15	2
Virginia	45	16	27	10	21
Massachusetts	29	9	7	36	40
Nebraska	15	21	32	21	34
Alaska	43	22	33	25	1
North Dakota	1	47	42	2	33
Minnesota	22	39	12	20	32
Louisiana	9	48	30	31	7
Maryland	47	15	40	5	28
New Hampshire	28	49	13	46	3
Missouri	21	18	14	47	44
Oregon	30	40	45	19	13
New Mexico	32	36	25	34	26
Pennsylvania	34	25	36	18	43
Rhode Island	46	24	24	45	18
Washington, DC	6	50	35	33	39
Wyoming	25	42	43	37	17
Colorado	26	44	44	23	30
Florida	48	28	37	32	24
Arizona	42	33	47	35	12
Connecticut	40	43	11	43	38
Vermont	35	29	18	50	46
Washington	39	34	34	38	37
Georgia	38	38	50	42	15
Nevada	51	11	46	39	45
Delaware	50	32	9	44	47
New York	27	45	31	49	49
California	44	30	48	40	42
New Jersey	36	51	49	51	27
Hawaii	41	41	51	41	51

Source: *U.S. News & World Report,* 14 September 1992: 62–66.
Note: Southern states' names highlighted in italics

bankruptcy. Oklahoma was rated first, and Hawaii last.[30] As shown in Table 5.1, among the top ten states, four are southern: Kentucky, Arkansas, Mississippi, and Tennessee. If one defines the South broadly to include Oklahoma and Texas, six out of the ten top performing states are southern. The report specifically points out that the performance of Tennessee is directly related to foreign direct investment, especially Japanese investment. The analysis indicates, "International businesses are responsible for investing $9.1 billion and creating more than 60,000 jobs in Tennessee."[31]

Table 5.1 should be interpreted cautiously, however. The ranking of a state's economic health does not necessarily depend on Japanese or other foreign investment. According to Table 5.2, for instance, Georgia rates fourth in hosting the most Japanese firms, yet (on Table 5.1) it is seventh from the bottom in the ranking of economic health. States such as California, New York, and Pennsylvania host large numbers of foreign manufacturers, including the Japanese, yet they trail a number of other states in the economic health rankings. Perhaps the benefits of foreign direct investments, including those of the Japanese, have been overrated. Certainly, foreign direct investments do not account for the entire economic health of the states.

Japanese direct investment, however, helped Tennessee's economic condition, and Japanese investments indirectly contributed to attracting a giant American corporation, GM's Saturn. It should be added that the economic health of Tennessee was also the result of the state's tight fiscal policy and frugality. In fact, Tennessee's Constitution requires a balanced state budget.

CULTURAL IMPACT

In addition to their economic impact on Tennessee, some consider that Japanese industrial firms and their personnel have made the regional culture richer than ever before.[32] To a certain extent, Japanese culture has affected even the eating habits of Southerners. Looking back, when I first came to the American South in 1965, I was unable to find any food store that carried Japanese food. In order to buy a small bottle of *shoyu* (Japanese soybean sauce) and some *soba* (Japanese noodles), I had to drive all over the city of Atlanta. Nowadays, almost every southern grocery story carries *shoyu* and *ramen* (dried soup with noodles). *Tofu* (beancurd) is also a common sight in the typical American grocery store. Even squid balls and garlic pills can be found in some southern grocery stores.

Tennesseans still prefer barbecue and whiskey to *sushi* and *sake* (Japanese rice wine or rum), and many Southerners are still fond of fried chicken, fried catfish, or country ham with hush-puppies or corn bread instead of *soba*, *ramen*, and *sashimi*. Nevertheless, rice used to be found in

Table 5.2 • Top Ten States in Economic Health, Number of Foreign
Manufacturers, and Number of Japanese Manufacturers

	Ranking of States by	
Economic Health[a]	Number of Foreign Manufacturers[b]	Number of Japanese Manufacturers[b]
Oklahoma	California	California
Kentucky	Illinois	Illinois
Arkansas	Texas	Ohio
Kansas	New York	Georgia
South Dakota	New Jersey	Michigan
Montana	Pensylvania	Texas
Mississippi	Georgia	New York
Indiana	Ohio	Indiana
Texas	Florida	New Jersey
Tennessee	Michigan	North Carolina/Pennsylvania

Source: [a] "How the States Stack up," U.S. News & World Report, 14 September 1992: 62–66.
[b] U.S. Department of Commerce, Foreign Direct Investment in the United States (1994), table F-22.

the supermarket only in a small bag, but now bags weighing up to 100 pounds are available as the numbers of rice-loving Japanese expatriates and American converts increase in the American South.

If I had told American friends thirty years ago, "I want to eat raw fish [*sashimi* in Japanese] and fish eyes," they wouldn't want to discuss the subject. No southerners would dare to try raw fish for lunch. Now, *shoyu, ramen, sashimi, sukiyaki*, and *sushi* are oft-spoken words in the conversation of southerners; many have tried them, and some are fond of them. A Japanese grocery in Murfreesboro, Tennessee, receives fresh fish via Atlanta and rents Japanese-language videos. Nashville and Murfreesboro together have ten Japanese restaurants. Knoxville has one Japanese restaurant, and recently a Japanese restaurant opened in Smyrna. The food in these restaurants is typically Japanese rather than a hybrid version of Japanese food to please the American taste. There are plenty of native Japanese who wish to have their familiar cuisine without any modification.

With the exception of Japanese foodways, however, as yet no other aspect of Japanese culture, including Japanese popular culture, has made major inroads into ordinary consumer marketing. Not many southerners enjoy listening to Japanese music, although many have heard about *karaoke*, the Japanese pastime of singing along to instrumental sound tracks of popular songs. The Hibari restaurant in Lexington, Kentucky, near the Hitachi auto parts factory, features *karaoke*, and Japanese expatriates occasionally

5.1 • A Japanese Restaurant in Memphis, Tennessee

5.2 • A Class on Japanese Culture at the Cumberland Museum and Science Center
(Courtesy of the Japan Center of Tennessee)

go on Saturday night to loosen up with fellow employees. A Japanese executive in Westech told me that he has a *karaoke* set at home.

Fortune magazine reports the marketing of Japanese popular culture as a commercial venture: "Smith & Hawken, a specialized mail-order house, does well with Japanese garden tools....Kellogg has introduced what it calls an 'Oriental cereal' named 'Kenmei' with a bold ideogram on the box meaning grain plant. The stuff is like Rice Krispies minus the snap-crackle-pop....Perhaps wisely, ads for Anheuser-Busch's successful Bud Dry beer don't mention that the lengthy dry brewing process, which causes extra fermentation, comes from Japan."[33] None of those products have made much noise in the American consumer marketplace. It is less likely that Japanese influence will have a major impact on consumer goods in any foreseeable future.

As time passes, southerners view the Japanese as odd-looking aliens less and less. Before many southerners were aware of what was occurring, Japanese became their nextdoor neighbors, classmates, students, and bosses. When I asked directions to a Japanese executive's home, one southerner who lives miles away from him knew about his house and pronounced his name more accurately than I could have. I do not believe many southerners are going to start wearing *kimonos*, but it is true that they have become more cosmopolitan than before. Many southerners are beginning to learn and practice "cultural relativism"—instead of viewing one culture as superior to another, they see the other culture in terms of its own value.

American workers and managers who are associated with Japanese firms prefer to use the Japanese word *kaizen* rather than the English translation "continuous improvement." "*San*" (a Japanese honorific for a senior) instead of "Mr." is commonly used by American employees in the Japanese-owned firms. It is difficult to calculate an exact figure, but it is reported that throughout the United States over 35,000 Americans are taking college-level courses in Japanese, and enrollments continue to rise.[34] Indeed, Japanese language courses are no longer offered just by the "elite" colleges and universities. Traditionally, in most American colleges and universities, the East Asian languages, including Japanese, were thought to be "exotic" languages as compared with the Western European languages; thus the departments of modern foreign languages seldom taught Japanese. But examining the bulletin of job announcements of the Association for Asian Studies, one sees that teaching positions in Japanese language/culture outnumber those in any other field. And some states offer Japanese language courses at the precollege level.

A potential source for cultural influence is the Japan Center, located in Middle Tennessee State Univeristy, Murfreesboro, Tennessee. Supported by the state as well as Japanese and American corporations, it could have launched major Japanese cultural programs, such as sponsoring course offerings, including Japanese language courses, in various colleges and universities throughout the state. The center might have found additional financial support from the big Japanese corporations, but it is my impression that the Japanese corporations are very cautious and sensitive about launching an aggressive campaign to transplant Japanese culture to the South and wish to keep a low profile. They make every effort and seem eager to fit into the host culture rather than to impose Japanese culture on American southerners. Besides the center's efforts, Smyrna's First Baptist Church offers Japanese wives English classes, Bible studies, and an occasional fashion show. The Tennessee Meiji Gakuin High School has a Japanese art center to exhibit Japanese culture, yet it limits its role and keeps a low profile, although presumably its purpose is similar to that of the Japan Center.

RESPONSES OF AMERICAN WORKERS TO THEIR JAPANESE BOSSES

Despite a wide variation in the ways American workers view the Japanese, there are several common characteristics. Although Japanese management goes to great effort to give the impression that the transplanted firms are American, not many American workers perceive that as true. Almost all American employees in Japanese firms refer to the Japanese in the third person plural—they, them, their—and to themselves in the first persons plural—we, us, our. By and large, Americans are ambivalent about working in a foreign-owned firm and about telling the foreign-born researcher that they are happy to work for foreign firms. Some southern workers seem to think that working for foreign firms is unpatriotic. One worker told me, "What can you do? No American plants are hiring me." The president of Westech answered me almost apologetically when I asked about the machines the company uses: "Right now we're using machines that are made in Japan exclusively, but we're planning to use some American-made machines, also." In fact, the plant manager of Westech, who is an American, told me, "Even though we use machines that are made in Japan, we have to make many adjustments to meet the high safety standards set by the Occupational Safety and Health Administration [OSHA]. We can use machines made in the U.S. without making adjustments."

Notwithstanding such ambivalent feelings, a surprisingly large number of American workers who work for Japanese firms seem to be satisfied. This is true particularly among those who worked previously for American manufacturing firms and were terminated or laid off. My observation concurs with a 1989 survey: "More than 75% of U.S. adults surveyed in a poll conducted last spring for a group of Japanese firms agreed that foreign

acquisitions have boosted U.S. economic growth, employment and competitiveness. Nonetheless, nearly 75% viewed the increased foreign presence as
undesirable."[35]

White-collar managers and blue-collar workers differ in their views of
Japanese management. White-collar workers in Japanese manufacturing
firms fall largely into two groups: managers or semi-executives; and support staff, including office clerks, secretaries, and receptionists. Since white-
collar workers have ample opportunity to observe decision making and discussions at the executive level, they are frustrated by slow decision making
and poor communication, resulting from the language barrier. One manager put it: "It takes a lot of guts to talk to your executive directly, but when
you have to go through a third party—an interpreter—in order to communicate, it's hell." Even in informal social circles, American managers are
confused. One manager told me, "Whenever we have gatherings, official or
unofficial, I'm not so sure whether I should be there or not."

A purchasing manager of Midtech complimented her company but also
revealed her frustrations with the Japanese way of doing business. She said:

> I'm tired of their indecisiveness and slow decision making. I'm not talk-
> ing about any big decision over a major matter. I'm talking about a
> minor...matter...I had twenty days training in Japan about my area.
> Since it was a short training, it was observational in nature. But the final
> week I spent in their purchasing department. They explained to me
> their practices. I thought, "My God, it wouldn't work in the U.S. large-
> ly because our laws wouldn't allow us to duplicate their practices." I told
> the president upon my return. He seems to understand that.Since this
> is a small company, relatively new, executives of the company seem to be
> receptive to my suggestions. Opinions and voices are well accepted.
> Even if they did not accept my suggestions, at least they are serious
> about my suggestions....I've heard about the Japanese style of decision
> making by consensus, I'm not sure whether or not that is the case of
> every Japanese firm.

She gave me the impression that American middle managers find themselves in the uncomfortable position of having to explain to their Japanese
bosses why "You can't do that here in America!" The Japanese are then
frustrated by not being able to implement their ideas. The situation leaves
both parties with unpleasant feelings.

An American middle manager in Westech summarized his view of
working for a Japanese company:

> We can complain that the important decisions are made by the Japa-
> nese. But think of it. Suppose you had invested such a large amount
> of money, and were operating the same kind of business in Japan,

wouldn't you want to make the decisions? Talking about promotion, how many American middle managers think of becoming a president or vice president in a Japanese-owned firm? If you do, then you're wrong. Particularly in a company of this size, I don't think many would think about getting a promotion to the top executive. About the clarity of objectives, logic, and so on, these problems are mainly because of the language barrier. I've often felt sorry for those guys having to speak a foreign language. I admire them. Why don't they complain about us not learning Japanese? A guy told me once, "They [Japanese] talk about us, don't they?" I told him, "They may talk about the weather, who knows?" About the meetings, the Japanese are blamed for having many time-consuming meetings. I agree that they do. But doesn't any American company have many meetings? I've been in an American company. Let me tell you. We probably had more meetings than I have had in this company. The only problem I see is that because of the language barrier, our meetings usually last longer.

The Westech manager's comments are comparable to Yoshihara's list of the criticisms made by American managers in Japanese firms.[36] The president of Westech commented about his frustration, "I wish the Japanese parent company could transfer their know-how quickly, so that we could produce the goods. They take all the time in the world. They are notoriously slow and extremely cautious and sensitive about transferring the know-how to us."

Is the Japanese practice of not transferring their know-how to the American plants a strategy? Reich and Mankin believe it is: "The Japanese investment in U.S. factories gives the American experience in component *assembly* [italics mine] but not component design and production. Time after time, the Japanese reserve for themselves the part of the value-added chain that pays the highest wages and offers the greatest opportunity for controlling the next generation of production and product technology...The U.S. strategy appears dangerously shortsighted. In exchange for a few lower skilled, lower paying jobs and easy access to our competitors' high-quality, low-cost products, we are apparently prepared to sacrifice our competitiveness in a host of industries—autos, machine tools, consumer electronics, and semiconductors today, and others in the future."[37]

Blue-collar workers' views of Japanese management are more positive than those of white-collar employees, but not totally free of negative criticism. *Ms. Magazine* reports, "As a rule, blue-collar women working the fast-moving assembly lines see very few Japanese. At the Toshiba plant in Lebanon, Tennessee, there are only 14 Japanese in a work force of 650. And just 13 among 3,172 at Nissan's Smyrna, Tennessee, plant (where recently a spate of sexual harrassment grievances were filed, caused, the women thought by, insufficient supervision by the far-off Japanese owners over Detroit-trained male managers and women on the line)."[38] During the UAW's campaign to organize a union at Nissan, union organizers cited worker injuries and production lines that moved too fast to be safe, despite Nissan's insistence that its safety record is better than others and that the line speed of sixty-four units an hour is average for the industry.[39] An official of the Mental Health Center of Maryville, Ohio, where a Honda plant is located, has witnessed an increasing number of referrals of Honda associates [enployees] who complain of headaches, of chronic backpain, and of stomach aches, presumably resulting fron work-related stress.[40] In a recent survey of Scott County residents in Kentucky conducted by the University of Kentucky, "nearly 40 percent thought Toyota might work its employees too hard."[41]

During my study of the three Tennessee firms, I did not encounter anyone who complained about the hard work. Nor did I even hear about any American employees suffering from stress resulting from hard work imposed on them by the Japanese. One woman worker at Westech who came from the Northeast was very candid in relating her feelings about the Japanese expatriates: "They're very nice, kind, and every good word you can think of. But I just can't stand it when a Japanese engineer acts as if he were smarter than we are. It's related to my pride." When I asked the woman's male coworker, a southerner, about her reaction, he commented, "Didn't you know she is a Yankee? Pride might be very important to the Yankees, but we've been accustomed not to care much about pride. If we could get used to the Yankees, we can put up with the Japanese. Life down here goes on."

Workers whom I interviewed did not complain about their jobs being difficult. One compared work in industry to farm work: "We talk about hard work here in the plant. But think about what if you were working in the field out there now, under the blazing sun. Also, we don't make any money from farming. You know, farming is not work or a job. For a lot of folks down here, farming has been a way of life. My preparation for hard work was on the farm, I guess." Most employees of the three Japanese plants, except a few managers, are natives of the towns or of nearby towns where the plants are located. They are fully aware of and used to hard work.

Surprisingly, a large number of American blue-collar workers are satisfied with working in the Japanese-owned plants, although employees of Japanese-owned plants are not any better off than employees of comparable American plants in terms of their wages.[42] Their satisfaction in working with the Japanese firms does not stem from wages and fringe benefits, which are the same as those of domestic American firms, but largely from two sources: job security and being treated equally and with respect, which appeals to the American core value of equality.

As stated previously, no Japanese firm in Tennessee or in the United State has institutionalized guaranteed lifetime employment, yet the Japanese have managed to assure American workers that, as long as their work is good and they are reliable, their jobs are well secured. By action and deed rather than by words, the Japanese have been able to convince their workers and their potential workers of their efforts to retain their work force. In fact, no matter how severe the recession might have been in the early 1990s, most Japanese firms in Tennessee terminated only a few workers against their will, and most of these workers were at fault. Some Japanese companies even expanded their facilities in those hard times, and thereby increased the work force. It is understandable why applicants flock in whenever a large Japanese firm announces its opening. The Japanese companies' records of providing job security have resulted in their successful recruitment of the most qualified and productive workers. Not many American plants would fail if they could acquire such high-quality work forces.

Employees of almost all Japanese-owned firms wear uniforms, and all employees, from president to rank-and-file workers, are identified by first names on their uniforms. Everyone is asked to use first names, regardless of titles or rankings. In a society where individual identity is becoming meaningless and where impersonalized numbers are becoming important, people welcome the personal touch of using first names. We are living in a world where "John's son" is no longer a useful identification, without adding UAW Local 111, for instance, or a nine-digit social security number. If a term of address serves a functional purpose, then why not let it be the individual worker's personal name? The practice is symbolic of the company's recognition of the worker as a person, as an individual. And when a gray-haired Japanese president and an eighteen-year-old American worker address each other by their first names, the concept of equality is in play. This spirit of egalitarianism carries over into the Japanese practice of paying equal pay for equal work in the American plants.

So quite a number of blue-collar workers like to work in the Japanese firms and have publicized their satisfaction, even in news media. Expressions vary from person to person, but generally they can be summarized as: I've worked other jobs, and this is the best thing that ever happened to me; this company has been good to me, and I'm going to be good to the company. Perhaps the Japanese have made an art of making friends. When Nissan announced its intention to establish a plant in Smyrna, an ex-Air Force colonel demanded that the county commission rename the access road to the plant "Pearl Harbor Boulevard." Four years later, the same colonel was pictured on the front page of the local *Rutherford Courier* nominating a Nissan executive from Japan for membership in the Rotary Club.[43]

FROM FARMING TOWNS TO MANUFACTURING CENTERS

The Japanese impact on the southern way of life in Tennessee can be described as profound, notwithstanding a conscious effort on the part of the Japanese expatriates to keep a low profile and to uphold the existing norms of the South. With the addition of another ethnic group to the traditional pattern of blacks and whites, southerners are becoming somewhat cosmopolitan. Despite the wishes of small-town Southerners to retain small-town identity and values, no longer can Smyrna, La Vergne, and Spring Hill be identified as little farming towns in Tennessee. Rather they are identified now as huge manufacturing towns and auto and electronic capitals of America and the world. The small southern town of the past has become a mecca for job seekers across the southern region.

Some small-town southerners have naively believed that they can receive the benefits from the Japanese firms and still maintain their traditional way of life. Ann E. Kingsolver reported the impact of Toyota on the lives of rural Kentuckians and the way the people resisted having to choose among farming, industry, or a combination of both.[44] Small-town farmers are beginning to see that their political powers have been overshadowed by new players—the management of new American and Japanese industries working in global factories.

Journalists file report after report about the inevitable changes that result from the establishment of Japanese plants in rural areas. The most tangible evidence of change is in the annual budgets of these towns. The *Asian Wall Street Journal* reports about Georgetown, Kentucky, which hosts Toyota:

> The town's annual budget has tripled in six years, to $6.7 million. The previous mayor was a part-timer who was paid $7,200 a year and drove a school bus on the side; Mayor Prather earns $40,400. The police department has swelled to 29 people from 16, despite almost no increase in crime. All officers have their own police vehicles now, and their firepower has been upgraded to 14-shot semiautomatics. "We seem to be searching for ways to spend money," complains Clay McKnight, a county attorney. There have also been trips to Japan for the mayor and other city officials, with Toyota paying for accommodations. School Superintendent John Herlihy Jr. has gone twice, and says Toyota also includes him in its major functions....At the Scott County High School north of town, students study Japanese.[45]

The same phenomenon is taking place in Smyrna, in Rutherford County, Tennessee, where Nissan has its plant:

> "When you have a major company make an investment in a community, it's a tremendous advertisement," said Ralph Vaughn, president of the

Rutherford County Chamber of Commerce. "It says to the corporate world, 'This is a good place to do business.'" Nissan has attracted other companies to Rutherford County. At least seven of the 40 manufacturing newcomers or expansions since 1980 are direct suppliers to the auto plant. The county's population grew 46 percent, to 123,000 people, between 1980 and 1990. And, while nearly 10 percent of the county's residents were unemployed in 1983 when the Nissan plant opened, the unemployment rate has remained a steady 5 percent since.[46]

One native Tennessean who returned home upon retiring from his job in Chicago gave me his views on the recent southern prosperity:

We used to go to Chicago and other northern or midwestern industrial cities to get any kind of jobs in those hard years, particularly during the Depression. Look now what's happening. A whole bunch of north-ern-ers and midwesterners are coming to the South. They used to come down to the South to see the South and put us down. But now, they're coming down to work and live in the South. If you go to Spring Hill, you find a bunch of Yankees. Those folks used to live outside the South [GM's Saturn workers were recruited from UAW locals in 38 states]. They do the same thing that we southern folks did before.

In fact, I had been wondering why a weekly newspaper in a tiny town in Tennessee always carried a column of "Chicago News." I learned that during the Depression so many towners went to Chicago to find work that the town newspaper had to report on them, and the column had become a tradition. Who knows? In the future midwestern and northeastern town papers may report about their townspeople who went South for work.

MEETING THE JAPANESE CHALLENGE

The most important impact that Japanese direct investment is having on the South is to stimulate, stir up, and provide an example to American industry. "Stimulus diffusion"—borrowing ideas or cultural traits of others—between the Japanese industrial culture and American industry has begun quite vigorously in Dixie.

Let me begin with my own story. As a graduate student, I purchased a secondhand 1966 Chrysler automobile in 1969, which had a chronic starter problem. Worse than the nonstarting was that whenever I needed to stop the engine went dead as I hit the brake; I had to wait until the engine cooled to restart it. To pay for repairs, I mortgaged one-third of my assistantship, yet the problem persisted. I had to learn to live with the problem by using both brake and accelerator at the same time to keep the engine running. In spite of the car's faults, I stayed with a Chrysler product when I bought a new car in 1971. With the excitement of owning a new car for the first time in my life, I was driving around that afternoon to get a feel for it. As I was driving on a gravel road in the vicinity of our town, all of a sudden all the gauges stopped functioning; I was unable to tell whether I was speeding or not and whether I had enough gas. In 1982, frustrated with Chrysler, I purchased a GM product. That car did not serve me well either. I had to add water to the radiator as often as I filled up the gas tank. The dealer replaced the gasket twice, yet the symptom was never cured. In 1989, I switched to a Ford product, whose fuel efficiency was a great improvement but whose tires wore unevenly. When I took the car to an auto repair shop, the mechanic told me that the wheel-balancing of the car had not been checked when it was assembled.

With a few exceptions, car stories like mine are now ancient history. The excellence of Japanese automobiles has had a salutary effect on the American automobile industry. No longer can American auto makers dwell on complacency. In fact, American automobile manufacturers are winning back market share from the Japanese. *TIME* reports that, by July 1993,

American manufacturers have sharply narrowed—and in some cases eliminated—the gap between their own and Japanese cars. Seven of the 10 most improved autos in the latest J.D. Power survey carried U.S. name plates. (Three U.S. brands made the Power list of the 10 highest-rated cars in terms of owner satisfaction, up from one model when the survey began in 1986.)...Americans bought cars and trucks at an annual rate of 14 million units in the first half of 1993, the briskest pace in four years. The recovery continued in the first 10 days of July, car companies reported last week, as sales of North American–made vehicles rose 14.6% over the same period a year ago. Virtually all the first-half gains were by U.S. manufacturers, who have raised their domestic market share from 72.5% last January to 75% today, while the Japanese have slipped from 24.6% to 22.7%.[47]

By forcing American industry and the U.S. government to face their competitive challenges, the Japanese are having an enormous impact on the American manufacturing industry. The brightest result of the challenge is seen in the changes in the rank-and-file workers. As I cited earlier in the text, the once-silent voices of American industrial workers are now heard, speaking out rather loudly in response to the Japanese success. The voices say: It's our own damn fault. It's the end of an illusion we've had since the battle of Midway, that if America does it, it's the best. We have to give power to the people, and then we can beat the Japanese. We're more innovative than they are, and we don't need all the committees and meetings they do. We can get things done. But if we don't give power to the people, we'll keep on that downhill slide the Japanese have us on. And so on. The Japanese challenges are stimulating a movement at the grassroots level by American workers themselves, a movement led by neither executives nor the government.

This movement is not limited to the rank-and-file workers, however; it has spread to management. A classic example is the bold, near-revolutionary GM Saturn project in Spring Hill, Tennessee, where the Japanese-inspired attempt to manage the plant on the concept of teamwork goes beyond even the practices of the Japanese themselves. The collaboration and exceptional rapport between Saturn's management and the UAW workers have changed the fundamental attitudes of both workers and management toward labor unions, from the traditional view of confrontation and conflict to one of cooperation and reciprocity. Although it may be too early to evaluate the Saturn plant as a complete success, both workers and management are striving to get their own houses in order to meet the Japanese challenge on a level playing field in Tennessee.

HENRY COMPANIES RESPONDS TO THE JAPANESE CHALLENGE

Instead of selecting a huge company like Saturn, which has a financial edge and can recruit a better-than-average work force, I have chosen to relate the success story of a medium-sized firm, pseudonymously called Henry Companies. Henry Companies is typical of American manufacturing firms that hire many American workers, and the story of its survival in the midst of the well-financed Japanese competition is meaningful.

The many interesting features of the industrial culture of Henry Companies warrants a book-length ethnography at a later date. In this book, I have to be ruthlessly selective and parsimoniously brief in delineating the ways Henry Companies does business. My intention is to document an American response to the Japanese challenge in Tennessee, where manufacuring industries are becoming increasingly global.

BACKGROUND OF HENRY COMPANIES

Henry Companies manufactures and sells predominantly extruded products, including fuel hoses, emission hoses, heater hoses, and coolant hoses, and injection-molded products, including solid rubber air ducts as well as silicone oil pans and rocker cover gaskets. Eighty percent of the company's products are sold to the automotive industries and aftermarket, and the other 20 percent goes into the marine, appliance, industrial, and highway construction markets. A family-owned firm, Henry Companies draws its work force from a limited regional labor pool. The firm's survival and eventual success are based on the unconventional managerial strategy of the executives, who understood the tactics of a Judo match and thereby achieved a competitive advantage.

Michael E. Porter points out that companies achieve competitive advantage through acts of innovation. But "much innovation is *mundane* and *incremental* [italics mine], depending more on a cumulation of small insights and advances than on a single, major technological breakthrough. It often involves ideas that are not even 'new'—ideas that have been around, but never vigorously pursued....Some innovations create competitive advantage by perceiving an entirely new market opportunity or by serving a market segment that others have ignored."[48]

Henry Companies did what Porter advocates. In order to attain competitive advantage, Henry Companies adopted a global strategy, which Porter lists as a prerequisite.[49] Also, the strategy of Henry Companies is a combination of folk wisdom, common sense, and scientific management. Most of all, the firm has taken on the challenge of Japanese competition and turned it into an opportunity.

It is not an easy task for a company located in a little-developed, remote town of Northwest Tennessee to adopt a global strategy. The firm is nowhere near a major highway, and the unemployment rate of the county where the company is located is 8.3 percent, which is higher than the state average of 6.4 percent. The county's per capita GNP is $10,423, which is lower than the state average of $12,255 in 1990, and barely 60 percent of population aged 25 years or older has finished high school.

Despite all the company's handicaps in terms of its location, the oldest son of the founder of the company, who was appointed chairman in 1988, started a global campaign in 1983, when he was 33–years old. He had begun his career in the company in 1972 as a lab technician earning $2.00 an hour. He told me: "We—executives, managers, and workers—think globally, talk globally, and act globally." The chairman has made the statement to his managers: "We are not trying to be Japanese—our mission is to become an International Company and serve an International Market." The company logo, shown under a globe of the world, changed in 1992 from "Spanning the Globe" to "Our Place of Business."

FOLK WISDOM AND COMMON SENSE

My interview with the founder of Henry Companies, who is retired, took place in his farm office. He is calm, gracious, and gentle, and has all the qualities of a traditional "southern gentleman," although he is a transplanted midwesterner from Ohio by way of Indiana. I was unable to discern any characteristics that would identify him as a shrewd businessperson or a dynamic entrepreneur. Preferring to hear from me rather than to talk about his own business strategies and success stories, he said, "Now you've had a chance to look around our operations. Tell me what you think." Instead of responding, I asked him, "Was there any negative response from the residents when you started your business in a small southern community?" "None whatsoever," said he, without any hesitation. He began to explain his background:

> My education was in accounting. I am a CPA. I have been engaged in the management of business for the past twenty-five years [twenty-one years CEO and four years board member]. I'm a beneficiary of the GI Bill. I served in the army during the war against the Japanese. I even published in our newsletter, "Anyone who drives a Japanese-made car shouldn't park in our company parking lot. He or she should park across the street," or something like that. It sounds awful, but you have to keep in mind that my generation of Americans were taught to hate the Japanese, you know. One day, the oldest of my four sons [the current chairman] told me, "Dad you can't do that. Not only your parking policy, but we must have business with the Japanese. We can't ignore them in this global era." At that moment, I went further than what my son told me. "Son, if they [referring to the Nissan management] buy our products, not only will I allow those who drive the Japanese cars to park in our company parking lot, I will buy the first car rolling out of their [the Nissan] production line." My son can tell you how hard it is to sell our products to the Japanese. But, at any event, they bought our products. At that point, I realized that it was the right time for me to retire and let the next generation of Americans [baby boomers], who have not been taught to hate the Japanese, take over the company. I enjoy my life here at the farm, looking at how the company is running every now and then, and watching my grandchildren grow. I'm worrying about my grandchildren's generation, which sees nothing but plenty. Will they be frugal?

From our conversation, I learned that his training in accounting taught him to be fiscally conservative. His modest office, dress, and manner, as well as his remarks about his grandchildren, indicated this. Most of all, he displayed a keen awareness that succeeding in business in the global era requires new leadership. Although he may be a businessperson of the older generation, many of the programs that fostered the growth and prosperity of Henry Companies were initiated and improved during his tenure as chair and CEO. In commenting on his programs, he was humble: "I was not an expert on running a manufacturing industry. If any program worked, then it was based on folk wisdom and a lot of common sense." He added, "If I had any principle in my business, it was a belief that 'Our customers are the kings,' and 'They're right.' Our troubles in our manufacturing industries in this country stem from ignoring our customers. Manufacturers design, test, and then manufacture industrial goods in accordance with their own imagination, without knowing what customers really want."

He gave me a brief history of the company, as it was printed in his company's newsletter, a "Special 20th Anniversary Issue." He started his company in November 1967, with a co-owner, to manufacture rubber products. It was a small, family-owned operation, and his wife served as secretary. "The transition period was 'touch and go.' The company needed orders and working capital was very tight. Equipment was old, requiring constant maintenance. Some employees wanted to organize, but, in a very close election, the employees voted to stay nonunion." Despite the hardship of his early years, Henry Companies made remarkable progress.

Instead of delineating each stage, let me display some key statistics that show the growth and development of the company over the past quarter of a century (see Table 5.3) then describe several key programs. Indeed, the growth is remarkable: the number of employees increased from 35 in 1967 to 1,223 in 1992. Over a 25-year period, sales grew from $600,000 to almost $68 million. The firm is now the ninth largest privately owned rubber company in the United States and sells its products to eight countries: the United States, England, Germany, Australia, Sweden, Scotland, France, and Japan (plus Japanese firms in the United States). The company is indeed global in its operation.

The founder of the firm explained in simple words his success: "We had a unique way of combining equipment, materials, labor, and money to produce rubber parts." What he means above by folk wisdom and common sense is continuous improvement: *kaizen*. He commented:

> We did not use that term [*kaizen*] then, but here is how it worked in actual practice. It is one of our characteristics to never be satisfied. It didn't take long for us to embrace the concept of working to improve existing standards and goals. For example: When an extruder crew was able to produce 3,000 feet an hour of a certain product, we'd talk about and ultimately get 4,000 feet an hour, or 6,000 feet an hour. When a press operator was able to produce 10 heats of a certain product per hour, we'd talk about getting 12 or 15 heats and would ultimately get it. There are hundreds of examples of setting goals and then trying to do better than the goal. So, continuous improvement has always been a part of our culture. Since the highest motivator has been continuous improvement, there has always been a feeling of confidence that we can do better tomorrow, next week, and next year.

So *kaizen* is nothing new, according to the founder of the company. He has been practicing it ever since he started the company.

Table 5.3 • Growth and Development of Henry Companies

Year	No. of Employees	Total Sales	Property, Plant, & Equipment Per Year ($ million)	Total Assets Net Change by Year ($ million)
1967	35	—	—	—
1968	35	0.6	305	408
1969	68	0.9	54	64
1970	69	0.8	8	86
1971	70	1.1	13	82
1972	105	2.1	68	225
1973	197	3.6	216	466
1974	301	5.2	361	1,228
1975	371	7.2	588	1,320
1976	454	11.5	(54)	460
1977	604	7.7	1,169	2,552
1978	675	22.1	1,454	2,360
1979	684	25.9	(100)	718
1980	600	26.4	606	2,586
1981	715	33.8	1,396	3,503
1982	558	30.9	(479)	(959)
1983	776	34.8	449	2,778
1984	768	44.2	756	(804)
1985	770	42.6	4,310	4,621
1986	822	48.1	1,622	2,608
1987	930	56.4	1,680	4,689
1988	999	67.2	2,169	4,599
1989	1,020	72.8	262	480
1990	965	67.5	(1,776)	(925)
1991	966	67.8	2,210	6,075
1992	1,223	81.6	(676)	(412)
Fiscal Year End Total			$16,611	$38,808

Source: Henry Companies.

He talked about the role of education:

Any comprehensive reflection on the past twenty-five years would include something about education. It is my opinion that twenty-five years ago only a handful of people recognized that education would become such an important issue. Certainly we didn't recognize that. The way we worked, in the beginning, was relatively primitive. It was like a farmer using a team of horses and a singlebottom plow to plow. Little or no education was required to produce the parts we made. Most of the thinking was done by a manager and the workers carried out the in-structions. When we began to buy sophisticated injection-molding presses, laser-controlled measuring devices, and modern lab equipment, it became readily apparent that a higher level of education was required to operate the equipment and produce better parts.

The founder of Henry Companies commented modestly and rather casually on various innovative practices the company adopted, as if they had all come about effortlessly. The company developed a concrete mission statement and a ten-point management plan to carry out the company's mission. These ten points and the mission statement all deal with "quality" and a tireless commitment to continuous improvement. To succeed in its mission, the company recognized the importance of involving the workers, mainly by providing educational and training programs and a workers' suggestion plan. The company published a comprehensive statement on quality improvement entitled *The Quest for Perfection.*

In dealing with his managers about continuous improvement, the current chairman and eldest son of the founder of the firm uses a sports analogy:

Carl Lewis set the world record in the 100 meter race. The difference between number one and number two was 0.02 seconds. The difference between Carl Lewis and who finished sixth was 0.1 second. That 0.02 to 0.1 will probably mean the difference between who survives as an auto supplier and who doesn't in the twenty-first century....We've got to remember, just as in this example, people only remember number one, regardless of how close a race may be...whether it is the 100-meter dash or the race to supply auto companies with parts.

Henry Companies' record speaks for its quality control, which has been recognized by a General Motors "Mark of Excellence Award," which fewer than 1 percent of GM's 7,000 worldwide suppliers have been able to earn. Henry Companies is one of only thirteen firms in the world to receive the Ford Motor Company's conferment for "Total Quality Excellence." The company has achieved Nissan's "Quality Master" rating four years in a row and has been awarded the "Pentastar," Chrysler's highest quality award. In

Table 5.4 • Research and Development Costs of Henry Companies

Fiscal Year	Amount ($)	Percent of Gross Sales
1985–86	1,759,556	3.66
1986–87	2,625,993	4.65
1987–88	2,854,097	4.25
1988–89	2,570,581	3.53
1989–90	2,189,459	3.25
1990–91	2,241,833	3.31

SOURCE: Henry Companies.

1990, Henry Companies won the "LIFT" [Labor Investing for Tomorrow] award for training and education in the workplace.

It is difficult for any foreign company to meet Japanese quality standards, yet Henry Companies has successfully done business with several Japanese firms, including Mitsubishi, Hitachi Cable, and Nissan. (The company's current market includes Diamond Star and Kawasaki.) Impressed by the quality of Henry Companies' products, two Japanese firms asked the company to join them to create a joint-venture firm, which was established in 1987, with production starting in 1988. It is ironic that Henry Companies, whose former chair would not even allow a Japanese-made car in the parking lot, has a joint venture business with the Japanese.

To maintain quality and to continuously improve, the company consistently allocates over 3 percent of its gross sales revenues to research and development, as shown in Table 5.4. (In 1992, the percentage increased to four.) One manager told me, "It's amazing to invest such an amount of money for research and development in a year like this [referring to the recession, especially in the auto industry, in 1991–92]." Another manager, referring to the company's being family owned, commented: "I guess Henry's boys do not have to spend their share of the company's profit, so they have it to invest. That's good."

Another successful and popular program for continuous improvement is Savings and Sharing, which started with a campaign against waste called War on Waste (WOW), initiated in 1985. In an attempt to improve various processes and eliminate scrap, WOW evolved into the Savings and Sharing program, in which any saving resulting from the reduction of waste was divided equally between the company and the employees. This program not only reduces the waste of raw materials, often called scrap, but it also offers workers incentives to reduce the cost of operations. In a typical year, the average share for each worker is $832, which the workers call "Wal-Mart Money"—extra income available to buy something at Wal-Mart.

Although Savings and Sharing involves employees directly, worker participation is more systematically and efficiently fostered by a "Sugges-tion Program, which is a way of harnessing one of America's strengths, ingenuity. The Suggestion Program has a full-time director, who is in charge of promoting the program, evaluating suggestions, and rewarding those suggestions that are worthy of an award and of company-wide adoption. The Henry Companies' Suggestion Program, initiated in 1973, evolved into the Suggestion and Award Program in 1984. The rules, criteria, and award structure of the program are revised annually, and workers participate in the program with enthusiasm. The number of suggestions made by employees during fiscal year 1991 reached 1,098. According to the National Association of Suggestion Systems' statistical report, in 1990, the number of employees submitting suggestions per 100 eligible employees was 9, and the adoption rate of the suggestions was 32 percent.[50] If these are the national averages, then the Henry Companies' Suggestion Program is a remarkable success story (see *Table* 5.5). Note the "supervisor incentive" category in the table: to avoid any jealousy on the part of supervisors of employees who make good suggestions, the Suggestion Program rewards the supervisors as well as the employees.

Although the average award per suggestion appears to be small, it is much higher than that of many Japanese companies, according to the director of the program. Indeed, according to 1990 statistics complied by the National Association of Suggestion Systems, the average award payment of Honda of America MFG is $22.46; Mazda, $22.43; Nippondenso MFG., $13.01; and Calsonic MFG Corporation, $0. Only Nissan SA (PTY) Ltd, with $263.38, and Toyota Motor MFG UAS, with $45, are higher than that of Henry Companies with $37.93.[51] The director emphasizes: "The philosophy of the Suggestion Program is not to buy ideas or suggestions from employees. The program is designed to inspire workers to participate and to think while working."

In fiscal year 1991, a forty-year-old quality engineer and laboratory supervisor made twenty-three suggestions that saved an estimated total amount of $23,000. He told me:

> Even if my award for the particular suggestion might not be impressive, others benefit, including my immediate supervisor and my fellow employees, because the money saved from my suggestion will go into the pot of the savings and sharing fund. Think about it. My suggestions can be beneficial to all employees. More than anything else, when my suggestions are adopted, it is a wonderful feeling. Even if I end up working extra hours to implement the suggestions, I like being involved in the process.

Table 5.5 • Data on Henry Companies' Suggestion Program

	FY 1989	FY 1990	FY 1991
Suggestion Data			
Number of Employees Eligible	1,010	891	927
Suggestions Reviewed	782	825	1,098
Suggestions Adopted	434	415	598
Adoption Rate (%)	55	50	54
Participation Rate (%)	44	36	59
Award Payment			
Primary Award	$4,885	$5,628	$5,480
FOY*	$1,660	0	0
Gift Incentive	$9,104	$4,084	$3,264
Supervisor Incentive	$2,360	$5,628	$1,420
Quarterly/Annual Award	$400	$400	$400
Total	$18,409	$15,740	$10,564
Average Cost Per Adoption	$42.41	$37.92	$17.66
Estimated Savings			
Gross Savings	$259,747	$306,191	$266,379
Implementation Cost	($42,099)	($25,477)	($49,147)
Award Cost	($16,049)	($10,112)	($9,144)
Supervisor Incentive	($2,360)	($5,628)	($1,420)
Estimated Net Savings	$199,239	$264,979	$206,668
Average Savings Per Adoption	$459	$639	$346

SOURCE: Henry Companies.
* Administrative expenses for the first of the year for the program development.

The supervisor showed me a machine in the mixing shop in his lab, which is a by-product of his suggestion:

> This machine is made in America by Americans. It costs almost half of the fancy-looking one over there, which was made in Japan. Why should we have to use the Japanese machine? Folks working over there [pointing at a joint-venture firm] have to use the Japanese machines....I can't understand how the Japanese can say we're lazy. Boy, I've never seen any people who are so slow to make decisions. I don't know how they can make money. Do they? or Don't they?...Let's talk about quality. Ask the Japanese whether the quality of our products is bad.

His two assistants working in his lab were nodding, and one seemed almost ready to say "Amen!" because he was heartily agreeing with his supervisor.

The background and college training of this laboratory supervisor and star of the Suggestion Program are intriguing. He did not major in engineering or technology; his degree was a B.S. in nursing. After working two years in an insurance company, he joined Henry Companies three years ago. Anyone doubting American ingenuity has to meet this "nurse-turned-engineer." Since he graduated from the university where I teach and where he still has many friends, we felt comfortable with each other and talked endlessly. His conclusion about quality was, "Thus far, many American industrial workers don't have many opportunities to demonstrate their maximum potential, what they can do. I'm happy to see some American executives and managers, like the ones in Henry Companies, provide such opportunities to their employees. It shouldn't take too long to catch up with the Japanese."

To catch up with the Japanese takes educated and trained workers, and the management of Henry Companies saw education as an American weakness. Most workers in the company are by-products of the public schools: some hold high-school diplomas yet are functionally half illiterate; others are high-school dropouts. In 1982, the company started offering a GED program, and eventually benefited from its success. By 1988, forty employees of Henry Companies had voluntarily attended GED classes, and in 1989 thirty employees were honored at a county-wide GED graduation ceremony. The founder of the company has been moved by some of the results of his company's GED degree program:

> Some of my most delightful experiences were attending luncheons where GED graduates were recognized for the attainment of their degree. I remember a grandmother telling about receiving a letter in the mail, which she knew contained the grades for her examination. She was so terrified of perhaps having failed, she couldn't open the letter. So a granddaughter opened the letter and read it and said, "Grandma, you passed!" and the grandmother cried with happiness. It's difficult to capture all of the emotion of such a story, because many of us have taken a high-school diploma and graduation for granted. How valuable is a high-school diploma? Certainly valuable if you don't have it!

Other educational programs, combined with training, have been a company priority, as indicated in their ten-point management plan.

The 1990 projection for education at Henry Companies states:

> Our goal for continuing education is that we will add 900 hours of training each month for employees. The training will include subjects ranging from basic mathematics to design of experiments. We are committed and dedicated to customer satisfaction through continuous improvement in quality and productivity. Our program of education includes all

employees. We plan that each one will receive training that will enhance our ability to consistently produce a product of superior quality.

In addition to job training, the company offers Japanese-language classes. One year (fiscal year 1991–92), Henry Companies spent $440,996 for education and training, which is not a small amount considering the size of the company.

An important feature of the educational program is that it is handled by professional people. Again, not many manufacturing companies the size of Henry Companies would hire a former university professor with an Ed.D. degree, a specialist in adult education. This professional educator, who has even published a technical book on improving work-force basic skills, plans and executes the company's educational programs. Consequently, the company earned several prestigious awards for its educational efforts: the previously mentioned LIFT award from the United States Department of Labor in 1990, Tennessee's Sequoyah Literacy Award for Education in 1991, and honorable mention for the George S. Dively Award for "Excellence in Education" from Harvard University.

The young, globally aware chairman hired as company president an MBA graduate from a first-class university. Besides running the day-to-day operations of the firm, the president is involved in promoting teamwork and developing team training. It is as uncommon to see a rurally based auto-parts supplier hire an elite business school graduate to run the company professionally as it is to see such a company hire a former professor and adult education specialist to run the company's educational programs. The chairman's keen view of the global market and his winning strategies are impressive.

The company harnesses American strengths and makes efforts to overcome American weaknesses—principal ploys of Judo and Sumo in order to meet the foreign competition. Many Americans, both workers and managers, are learning the Japanese Judo tactics of using the power and strength of the opponent against the opponent and then going beyond the Japanese strategies. At the same time, one should give credit to the Japanese, who inspired Americans to move from complacency to competitiveness and combativeness in the global business market. Increasing awareness on the part of government, on both federal and state levels (as evidenced by Tennessee's Industrial Infrastructure Program), and stepping up efforts to improve America's infrastructure, physical as well as mental, are right steps and positive ones.

— 6 —

THE ETHNOGRAPHER'S VIEW OF JAPANESE
INDUSTRY IN THE SOUTH

By casting this study as an actor-oriented ethnography, I have made an effort to report the perspectives of the respondents, informants, and the existing literature. In so doing, I have minimized my personal views. In concluding this book, I would like to add my personal perceptions and interpretations to the questions I have raised during the course of this study: Why have Japanese industries come to the American South? Do they replicate the industrial-relations model used in Japan? What are the Southerners' reactions?

Most of the existing literature has focused on highly aggregated and abstracted analysis on the basis of an idealized industrial-relations model that may be applicable to a few exceptional Japanese transplants, predominantly those in the auto industry. Despite the fact that small- and medium-sized Japanese industries are vital to foreign direct investment and also in overall economic activities in Japan, the story of a concrete nexus of social relations in a particular industrial setting that the small- and medium-sized Japanese industry to function is yet untold. In fact, very limited information deals with the voices of people—both Japanese and American—who manage and work in those transplants, even the exceptional auto giants. This book may help fill the gap in our knowledge.

My unique identity of being an insider who has lived in the region for years and is at the same time an outsider who has not yet been fully integrated into the regional culture as a marginal person serves this study well. Thus far, western scholars have tended to emphasize the positive aspects of traditional values and practices for Japanese industry and have often idealized them, even romanticized them, at times. Hence, those works have a value comparable to the sound, as Zen philosophers say, of one hand clapping. By using my bicultural experiences, being equipped with an anthropological approach and relating the voices of the people, I hope to provide the "other hand" so vital to produce a distinct sound.

DID THE JAPANESE "REDISCOVER" THE SOUTH?

There is a general belief that Japanese industrialists are coming to the South because they have done their homework so well that they have been keenly aware of and able to exploit the characteristics of the South and southerners. Such a public perception has been formed largely on the basis of Americans' tendency to overestimate Japanese abilities, including their abilities to understand regional cultural variations in the United States. This belief has been further reinforced by the inherent stereotype of the South in the minds of many Americans, coupled with a long history of industrial hunting records of the South's political economy in "selling" the South to the other regions.

This perception is incorrect. The Japanese knowledge of the South is very limited, much less than the American public may suspect. For instance, Japanese businessmen, who are fond of drinking Jack Daniels (which is very popular in East Asia) may know that it is distilled in the Tennessee town of Lynchburg, but hardly anyone knows that Moore County, which hosts the distillery, is a "dry county."[1] (Most Japanese do not know the meaning of that phrase.) And, if the Japanese are so knowledgeable about the South and southern characteristics that they can take advantage of them, then why have they built their plants outside the South, including in the so-called "Rust Belt" of the Northeast and Midwest?

In contrast to common belief, the Japanese are not the ones who discovered the South and southerners. Instead, the southern political apparatuses—aggressive governors, supportive state legislatures, and business circles equipped with attractive incentive packages—discovered the Japanese industrialists in Tokyo. Most ordinary southerners, even the job seekers, learned about the coming of Japanese industries to their states and communities through the news media. If anyone believes that southerners, who as citizens and taxpayers eventually pay for the incentive packages, have been fully informed and participated in recruiting Japanese industries, they are wrong. It is equally fallacious to believe in a highly developed Japanese knowledge of southern regional cultural variations.

For Japanese industrialists considering overseas locations, political assurance from the hosting government—be it state, municipal, or local—is more important than any other factors in site selection. That is the main reason why the industrial selection factors for Japanese industries differ from those of domestic ones. In fact, for the Japanese, the close ties between the government and private industries have a long history and have formed a tradition. As Edward S. Mason and his associates note, "Students of the Japanese growth 'miracle' have frequently attributed importance to the close cooperation of government and business in that country, and, to emphasize the closeness, have referred to 'Japan, Incorporated.'"[2] If there were any choice between the government support and other site selection factors, Japanese industrialists would not hesitate to choose the governmental assurance and support. Consequently, some southern states have been very successful in convincing the Japanese industrialists of their political support and commitment. Then, the remaining factors that are unique to the South become bonuses. In stressing the vital role of the state, a state official who had participated in an industrial recruiting trip to Japan offered me an interesting analogy: "No matter how famous you have been, the final count of the attendants at your funeral depends on the weather of the day." All other factors are secondary to the assertive recruiting effort made by the state government.

Nevertheless, in assessing the success of some southern states in recruiting Japanese industries, one should not be ahistorical. Southern strategies for industrial recruitment have been developing throughout the history of the region. The strategies have been developed, refined, and elaborated by combining old and new methods in accordance with the shift of the global economy. Ironically, however, other states' political leaders, especially those of the Rust Belt, have learned and are learning and even competing with the southern states in the recruiting endeavor. Certainly, the former Ohio governor during his industrial hunting trips to Tokyo could feel for the many southern governors who had made such trips to his state in the past. The shifting global economy has made things turn around.

Although southern political and business elite discovered the Japanese industrialists in Tokyo first, the Japanese expatriates are the ones who "rediscovered" the South and southerners after they were transplanted there. The Japanese have begun to realize that the commitments made to the state recruiters have been well served and that the South offers more than they had bargained for. Because of this, the site-selection factors given by the Japanese industrialists are similar, if not identical, to the list used by the state officials for their recruitment. The most surprising Japanese rediscovery is not so much of economic and related factors, but of a peculiar form of southern hospitality that has made the Japanese expatriates feel comfortable in the South.

Southern hospitality has not raised any confusion or question about the status of the Japanese in a multiracial society. Traditionally, the Japanese have been treated the same as whites in the South. Even when racial segregation was an institutionalized pattern in most of the South, for instance in Memphis, Tennessee, Japanese Americans used the same section as the whites, although Chinese Americans were buried in the black section of the cemetery.[3] Because they are still rare enough in the South to be considered exotic, the Japanese find themselves treated somewhat like celebrities. Unlike the other newly emigrated Asians, the Japanese are not competing with southerners for jobs but rather are creators of new jobs. Southerners even grant Japanese a "scarcity value." as well as some privileges as celebrities. One Japanese executive told me, "I've a bad habit of overspeeding. But, whenever I was caught by the local police officers for my overspeeding, they seldom issue tickets. I have been in a way spoiled."

It did not take long for the Japanese to learn that they would be welcome as long as they remain "outsiders" and "foreign guests"—not challenging the existing southern ways of life, not launching a crusade in racial equality, not getting deeply involved in community affairs. Robert Perrucci reports, "Nissan made an effort to get involved in domestic politics that went awry. It sponsored a five-hundred-dollar-per-couple fund-raiser for a Tennessee congressman who fought against 'domestic content' legislation that would negatively affect transplants. Two senators from Tennessee and one congressman announced they would not attend the fund-raiser because of concern about a foreign firm getting involved in domestic politics."[4] In addition, because of their uneasiness in socializing with southerners resulting from cultural differences largely stemming from the language barrier, the Japanese expatriates and their families tend to keep a distance from the rest of people in their hosting communities. They even established their own high school in a remote town in the foothills of the Smoky Mountains. They have made a deliberate effort to keep a low profile. Other than some limited contacts in local schools for their children and the occasional *origami* demonstration in local schools, their spheres of interaction are confined to their business circles. Some Japanese expatriates want to be less Japanese and more American, yet the sociocultural milieu of the American South expects them to remain "Japanese" and to conform to the norms of Japan, even if the "Japan-ness" is difficult to characterize. They may be a new "aristocracy" in the New South.

ARE THE JAPANESE OVERPUBLICIZED?

Japanese industrial operations in America, especially in some southern states, have taken advantage of American taxpayers' money. The Japanese have also taken full benefit of American media coverage at the American's expense even before starting up their industrial operations. The recent trend of reverse ethnocentrism further contributed to this end, as if Japanese could cure the backward state of American manufacturing industries by transplanting their miraculous management skills with their home-grown structure of industrial organization. The enthusiasm displayed by the American media, especially regional, state, and local, in hailing the arrival of Japanese transplants has been no less apparent than that demonstrated by the political and economic elite of the states. The coverage has been extensive and positive, mapping each step in the journey: X Japanese company is considering coming to the United States; the company's site selection teams are coming; the company has narrowed its choices down to three states for a possible site; it has chosen to the site; it is there; new era has begun for the county and the state; more jobs for states expected.[5]

The positive aspects of Japanese industrial organization have been understood in terms of their greater commitment to job security, their egalitarian appearance, their attention to work at the shop-floor level, their emphasis on quality and pride in work, and their careful selection of workers.[6] These may be the characteristics of a few large Japanese industrial organizations, but they are not uniquely Japanese any more: some domestic competitors are doing more. The focus on uniforms, exercise sessions, parking, addressing all employees on a first-name basis, an egalitarian appearance, and other slogans are thought to be mundane and superficial by most American workers.

If the Japanese transplants are doing well and if there is a deciding factor, then it is their careful selection of workers out of an unusually large applicant pool—one generated by the American media. Perrucci reports: "The *Louisville Courier-Journal* (September 10, 1986) reported that the state expected 200,000 people to apply for 3,000 jobs at Toyota. The *Lafayette Journal and Courier* (June 14, 1987) estimated that 50,000 are expected to apply for 1,700 jobs at SIA [Subaru-Isuzu auto]. Mazda reported having a pool of 96,500 job applicants for 3,500 jobs."[7] Without a doubt, the Japanese can select the best workers out of such a huge applicant pool. After hiring, the applicants at Nissan were required to take 40 to 200 hours of unpaid preemployment training, which they could do at night or on weekends, so as not to interfere with other jobs.[8] If an industrial firm can draw workers with the best intellectual, physical, and attitudinal qualities and commitment, it does not take much managerial skill and organizational structure to be successful. Any domestic American industrial worker can be as productive as a Japanese, maybe more so.

In addition, the states' service extends even to the recruitment. Perrucci reports:

> In cases of Toyota, Nissan, and SIA, the earliest stages of recruitment were handled by the states' Department of Employment. Moreover, some aspect of the selection process (or training process after selection) was paid for with state funds, whether it be the $5 per hour that Kentucky paid for time spent in assessment, the $10.20 an hour paid by Kentucky for up to six months of in-plant training, or Indiana's

payment of transportation, lodging, and meals for the hundreds of team leaders who are trained in Japan."[9]

Nevertheless, except for a few well-known and well-publicized Japanese industries, most small- and medium-sized Japanese firms take less qualified workers. Consequently, the well-publicized Japanese managerial skills or even the modified version do not seem to be an explanatin for productivity. The small- and medium-sized Japanese plants are struggling and face an American challenge, as evidenced in the case of the Henry Companies.

Even in the case of highly publicized companies, the genuine feelings of the workers who have passed such elaborate selection requirements are rarely heard. The big transplants seldom allow social scientists to study their employees. A rare description of an auto worker was reported in the *Lexington Herald-Leader* on April 23, 1986: "You're not going to get an accurate picture of this because everybody will lie because they're scared of losing their jobs. They just do as they please in there. The Union is in the pocket of management. You don't want this in Kentucky. This sucks."[10] The public assumes that workers are very happy in the Japanese transplants. In small- and medium-sized firms, however, American workers are not as happy as others presume them to be.

One very positive aspect is that most American workers trust the Japanese industries for their greater commitment to job security, although it is implicit. Thus far, the Japanese have been able to keep their commitment. Others report, "There is some evidence that workers at transplants believe that they have job security, often because of the employment of several hundred temporary workers who can be laid off if there is a slowdown."[11] It is, of course, too early to tell if the Japanese will be able to keep their commitment to job security, as one hears of layoffs in home plants in Japan. If the commitment were to be broken for reasons even beyond their control, then the American public might hear the voices of the silent people clearly and loudly.

APATHETIC SOUTHERNERS?

Despite the enthusiasm displayed by state officials, news media, and businesspersons whose businesses are directly or indirectly related to the Japanese transplants, most southerners seem to be unusually apathetic toward the Japanese transplants. Since they confine themselves to their spheres of business and industry, the presence of Japanese in southern communities is considered to be harmless.

Most southerners also do not comprehend the complex configuration of incentives and what they are worth to their economy. When people's jobs are at stake, not many have the heart to question the use of public funds to attract Japanese industries, and general attitudes seem to reflect the bent of "how much is too much when jobs are at stake?" Perceptions of the scholarly and intellectual communities across the South are not any different, although there is some skepticism about all the publicity over the economic impact of Japanese industries in the South, a skepticism that can be heard in former president Ronald Reagan's, "Here we go again," this time referring to the South's effort in the past to lure industries from the Northeast and Midwest. Above all, most southern intellectuals are so preoccupied by the guilt of the past's racial segregation and discrimination that they are too cautious to say anything about Japanese industries. They are reluctant to be accused as "Japan-bashers"—a code word for the racists.

This is not to say that there has been no resentment against excessively favorable incentive packages for Japanese investment. For instance, three weeks after Nissan announced it was coming to Smyrna, the County Farm Bureau expressed its opposition against the Nissan project, saying it would so increase land values that farming would become unprofitable; there was also a public protest by labor unions at the Nissan groundbreaking ceremony. In Kentucky opposition has been stronger than in Tennessee, especially from labor representatives. Nevertheless, reactions and voices of labor representatives and environmental groups have been overwhelmed by the persuasion of special-interest groups aided by a powerful media campaign. There is, however, growing demand to take a close look at the full impact of Japanese direct investment. Recently, one county commissioner of West Tennessee echoed such a sentiment by saying, "We've gone about as far as we should, and maybe we went a bit too far." [12]

> Annual surveys of Scott County, Kentucky, residents between 1986 and 1990 indicate that between 51 and 56 percent of those surveyed believe that the "Toyota plant will benefit the people of Kentucky enough to justify the expense." At the same time, they also express less agreement with the statement "I support the idea of state funding for the Toyota plant in Scott County." In 1986 there was 45 percent agreement with the statement, and it declined to 37 percent in 1990. [13]

Is the honeymoon over?

As the U.S. economy recovers from the recession, the job situation improves, and American manufacturers—by improving the quality of products—recover their competitive edge while the Japanese recession persists, we may hear some local voices not only from labor representatives and environmental groups but also from ordinary southerners. Time will dictate the bottom line in the economic balance sheet that weighs Japanese investment that contributed to the states' economies against the public funds used to facilitate Japanese industries to come. At present, the matter is uncertain. Everyone hopes that it is not just another case of corporate welfare, with public money being provided to Japanese industries that pursue business opportunities without obligations and long-term commitments to the states and communities in which they are located.

The presence of the Japanese in southern communities may contrib-ute to a certain extent to reduce the southern bias toward Japanese: certain Japanese words have been adopted by the southern industrialists, and Japanese cuisine may alter some southerners' taste. But it is presumptuous to assume that the Japanese cultural impact on southern culture will be profound. According to my observations, its impact is superficial at the most.

There is, however, a known outcome of the Japanese impact. The Japanese have caused Americans to awaken from their complacency. Many Americans consider that facing up to the challenge of the Japanese "might be the best thing that had ever happened to the American economy."[14] The American competitive spirit is rising, especially among the rank-and-file manufacturing workers. *Fortune* reported the lament of a frustrated worker, a union pipefitter who worked sixty-hour weeks at a Dow Corning plant before being laid off, saying "I don't like the Japs....It's our own damn fault."[15]

Small- and medium-sized American manufacturers—the backbone of the national industrial growth and development—are becoming competitive with those of the Japanese, as illustrated in the case of the Henry Companies. Many American companies make a conscious effort to adopt more Japanese-inspired industrial-relations practices than their Japanese counterparts do. Perhaps it is too early to draw conclusions about the success of GM's Saturn automobile, yet the Saturn plant practices the teamwork concept more conscientiously than do any Japanese firms in the United States and apparently without engendering hostility in its individualistic American workers. The morale of union members at GM's Saturn plant is reportedly high, which hints that maintaining a cooperative rather than a confrontational atmosphere between labor and management may not be incompatible with American culture. Recent studies find that Japanese success results largely from innovative managerial strategies rather than from any inherent cultural advantage.[16] During the course of this study, in fact, no Japanese personnel told me that American cultural factors hinder their industrial operations.

The conventional western view perceived quality control as arriving naturally to the Japanese because of their cultural orientation toward group activities. Nowadays, however, almost all American manufacturing industries practice quality control no less zealously than do their Japanese counterparts without any resentment from American workers, whose cultural orientation is believed to be "individualistic." In fact, J.D. Power's auto survey in 1992 found "71 problems per 100 cars built at GM's top-rated plant, one fewer than at Toyota's Corolla plant in Cambridge, Ontario, which took top honors last year....GM's Saturn plant, which opened in 1990, shows up in 10th place, with 109 problems per 100 cars."[17]

The improvement in quality of American industrial products creates a Japanese dilemma. Thus far, the Japanese have been successful in selling their industrial products in the American market by presenting their superior quality without investing much effort in marketing. Now, American industrial products offer improved quality at either the same level as or superior to those of the Japanese and at lower prices. The Japanese have to invest money and effort to develop new marketing strategies equal to those of Americans or superior if they want to be competitive. They have to invent the "new wheels," so to speak, for marketing.

ANTHROPOLOGISTS AS THE MYTHMAKERS?

Conventional western scholarship once romanticized Japanese success by crediting unique features of Japanese society and culture. William G. Ouchi points out, as have others, "Characteristically, our social scientists suspect any theory claiming that phenomena differ as a consequence of culture. This is a reaction to an earlier period when some scholars claimed simply that the differences were cultural and therefore not susceptible to scientific analysis, as though cultures were unique in a way that foreclosed scientific analysis genetically transmitted."[18]

It is most intriguing for the anthropologist to recognize the uses, misuses, and abuses of the concept of culture in industrial settings. While the concept of culture seems so obvious to some anthropologists, it is confusing to many others. Because increasing numbers of anthropologists are engaging in organizational studies, discussions on the concept of culture used in various formal organizations have been reexamined in recent anthropological literature.[19] Susan Wright summarizes the culture concept used in organizational studies in four ways:

> First, it refers to problems of managing companies with production processes or service outlets distributed across the globe, each located in a different "national culture". Second, it is used when management is trying to integrate people with different ethnicities into a workforce in one plant. Third, it can mean the informal "concepts, attitudes and values" of a workforce; or, fourth, "company culture" can refer to the formal organizational values and practices imposed by management as a "glue" to hold the workforce together and to make it capable of responding as a body to fast changing and global competition.[20]

Nevertheless, industrialists and workers, both American and Japanese, who are included in this study use the concept of culture quite differently than do anthropologists. The workers seem to be conversant with the concept of culture. Sometimes they use it in an insightful manner, but frequently they use it to explain away or justify their behavior and the behavior of others. Consequently, the concept of culture becomes a convenient tool to explain an unexplainable encounter with others. Often what is called culture has nothing to do with the traditional heritage of either people. Japanese tend to explain the fact of an illiterate high-school graduate, however common, as part of American culture. It is, however, hardly part of America's traditional heritage.

The movement toward globalizing industry and the cross-cultural blending of industrial management practices may require scholars to reexamine the role of culture in explaining Japan's success in economic and industrial development.[21] The field of anthropology should be assigned a vital mission to enhance our awareness of the utility, power, and reality of culture in the areas of business and industry.

From my personal remarks, one may argue that my perceptions and interpretations stem from too few sites with too little data to reach such a broad conclusion. Nevertheless, Geertz's observation on the anthropological orientation gives me support: "The anthropologist characteristically approaches such broader interpretations and more abstract analyses from the direction of exceedingly extended acquaintances with extremely small matters."[22] This is the "very" strength of ethnography—and also its weakness. Notwithstanding, as Miles Richardson has asked, "If the anthropologist does not tell the human myth, then who will?"[23]

NOTES

ACKNOWLEDGMENTS

1. Choong Soon Kim, *The Culture of Korean Industry: An Ethnography of Poongsan Corporation* (Tucson: Univ. of Arizona Press, 1992).

2. For a description of the Japanese spring offensive of the enterprise union and its members, see Robert E. Cole, *Japanese Blue Collar: The Changing Tradition* (Berkeley: Univ. of California Press, 1971), 226.

3. Robert Jackall, *Moral Mazes: The World of Corporate Managers* (New York: Oxford Univ. Press, 1988), 13.

4. Choong Soon Kim, *An Asian Anthropologist in the South: Field Experiences with Blacks, Indians, and Whites* (Knoxville: Univ. of Tennessee Press, 1977).

INTRODUCTION

1. Rafael Aguayo, *Dr. Deming: The American Who Taught the Japanese about Quality* (Secaucus, NJ: Carol Publishing, 1990); Andrea Gabor, *The Man Who Discovered Quality: How W. Edwards Deming Brought the Quality Revolution to America: The Stories of Ford, Xerox, and GM* (New York: Times Books, 1990); D.A. Garvin, *Managing Quality: The Strategic and Competitive Edge* (New York: Free Press, 1988), 179–99, See also Malcolm Trevor, "The Overseas Strategies of Japanese Corporations," *The Annals of the American Academy of Political and Social Science* 513 (January 1991): 90–101.

2. David Halberstam, *The Reckoning* (New York: William Morrow, 1986), 43–44.

3. Clifford Geertz defines ethnography as "thick description" (Clifford Geertz, *The Interpretation of Culture: Selected Essays* [New York: Basic Books, 1973], 5), and E.E. Evans-Pritchard terms it "translation" (E.E. Evans-Pritchard, *Social Anthropology and Other Essays* [New York: Free Press, 1962], 61).

4. Gary P. Ferraro, *The Cultural Dimension of International Business*, 2nd. ed. (Englewood Cliffs, NJ: Prentice-Hall, 1994), 7.

5. R.D. Hays, "Expatriate Selection: Insuring Success and Avoiding Failure," *Journal of International Business Studies* 5 (1974): 25–37; Rosalie L. Tung, "Selection and Training of Personnel for Overseas Assignments," *Columbia Journal of World Business*, Spring 1981: 68–78.

6. World Almanac, *The World Almanac and Book of Facts* (New York: World Almanac, 1992), 153.

7. U.S. Department of Commerce, *Foreign Direct Investment in the United States: Operations of U.S. Affiliates of Foreign Companies*. Revised 1991 Estimates (Washington, DC: U.S. Department of Commerce, 1994), tables F-3, F-14, and F-17.

8. Marietta Baba, *Business and Industrial Anthropology: An Overview*. NAPA Bulletin, no. 2 (Washington, D.C.: American Anthropological Association, 1986), 6. See also Carol S. Holzberg and Maureen J. Giovannini, "Anthropology and Industry: Reappraisal and New Directions," *Annual Review of Anthropology* 10 (1981): 317–60.

9. James L. Peacock, *The Anthropological Lens: Harsh Light, Soft Focus* (New York: Cambridge Univ. Press, 1986), 83.

10. Ryutaro Komiya and Ryuhei Wakasugi, "Japan's Foreign Direct Investment," *The Annals of the American Academy of Political and Social Science* 513 (1991): 57n.

11. David Friedman, *The Misunderstood Miracle: Industrial Development and Political Change in Japan* (Ithaca: Cornell Univ. Press, 1988), 43; Komiya and Wakasugi, "Japan's Foreign Direct Investment," 48–61.

12. Roger L. Janelli had the same experience as I had in his study of a Korean conglomerate. See Roger L. Janelli and Dawnhee Yim, *Making Capitalism: The Social and Cultural Construction of a South Korean Conglomerate* (Stanford: Stanford Univ. Press, 1993), 10.

13. Some social scientists have begun to questions the merit of constructing theories designed to have universal applicability. See Christopher Baker, "Economic Reorganization and the Slump in South and South-East Asia," *Comparative Studies in Society and History*, 23 (1981): 325–49; David Booth, "Marxism and Development Sociology: Interpreting the Impass," *World Development* 13 (1984): 761–87; Charles F. Keyes, "Peasant Strategies in Asian Societies: Moral and Rational Economic Approaches—A Symposium" *Journal of Asian Studies* 42 (1983): 753–68). Still others have indicated that highly aggregated statistics and abstract economic analyses can be misleading and uninterpretable. See Gary G. Hamilton and Narco Orru, "Organizational Structure of East Asian Companies," in *Korean Managerial Dynamics*, eds. Kae H. Chung and Hak Chong Lee, 39–47 (New York: Praeger, 1989).

14. Francis L.K. Hsu, "Intercultural Understanding: Genuine and Spurious," *Anthropology & Education Quarterly* 8 (1977): 206.

15. Geertz, *The Interpretation of Cultures*, 5.

16. James W. Fernandez, *Bwiti: An Ethnography of the Religious Imagination in Africa* (Princeton: Princeton Univ. Press, 1982), xx.

17. *Ibid*.

18. The term ethnology has been defined in several different ways by different anthropologists. "It is sometimes used broadly as a synonym for cultural anthropology, and in the past it has also been employed to refer to the historical approach to the study of cultures. In recent years, however, a more systematic meaning has emerged which identifies ethnology with a general strategy in the search for knowledge about cultures. In this now widely accepted sense of ethnology is the comparative study of cultures" (David E. Hunter and Phillip Whitten, eds., *Encyclopedia of Anthropology* [New York: Harper & Row, 1976], 149).

19. Sheila K. Johnson, *The Japanese Through American Eyes* (Stanford: Stanford Univ. Press, 1988), 3–4.

20. Paul Thomas Welty, *The Asians: Their Evolving Heritage* (New York: Harper & Row, 1984), 10.

21. Francis L.K. Hsu, *Americans and Chinese: Purpose and Fulfillment in Great Civilizations* (Garden City, NY: Natural History Press, 1970), 341; Eugene Franklin Wong, *On Visual Media Racism: Asians in the American Motion Pictures* (New York: Arno, 1978).

22. Ezra F. Vogel, *Japanese as Number One: Lessons for America* (New York: Harper Colophon Books, 1979).

23. Ronald Dore, *Taking Japan Seriously: A Confucian Perspective on Leading Economic Issues* (Stanford: Stanford Univ. Press, 1987).

24. Robert E. Cole, *Strategies for Learning: Small-Group Activities in American, Japanese, and Swedish Industry* (Berkeley: Univ. of California Press, 1989), 8.

25. Friedman, *The Misunderstood Miracle*, 15.

26. James P. Womack, Daniel T. Jones, and Daniel Roos, *The Machine That Changed the World* (New York: Rawson Assoc., 1990), 13.

27. Hsu, *Americans and Chinese*, 280.

28. Lamar Alexander, *Friends: Japanese and Tennesseans* (New York: Kodansha International, 1986), 150.

29. Masaaki Imai, *Kaizen (Ky'zen): The Key to Japan's Competitive Success* (New York: McGraw Hill, 1986).

30. Before Nissan built its American manufacturing plant in Smyrna, Tennessee, in 1980, Nissans were sold under the name of Datsun, meaning "son of fast rabbit." Nissan represents the first letters of Nihin Sangyo, the holding company of which Nissan is a part. See Halberstam, *The Reckoning*, 263–68; Michael A. Cusumano, *The Japanese Automobile Industry: Technology and Management at Nissan and Toyota* (Cambridge, MA: The Council on East Asian Studies, Harvard Univ., 1985), 34–35.

31. Halberstam, *The Reckoning*, 268–70.

32. *Ibid.*, 88. Toyoda for surname spells differently from Toyota for the name of automobile.

33. Miyohei Schinohara, "Japan as a World Economic Power," *The Annals of the American Academy of Political and Social Science* 513 (1991): 13.

34. John E. Woodruff reports about the Japanese overwork that:

Overwork has grown worse as Japan has built itself into the world's second-biggest economic power. More and more commentators speak of it as one of the little-discussed keys to Japan's postwar "economic miracle." No one claims to have reliable statistics, but all hands agree at least tens of thousands of Japanese become seriously ill from overwork every year. Possibly thousands, according to lawyers and some doctors who deal with the consequences, die of overwork every year. In recent years, that kind of death has come to have a name, "karoshi" (John E. Woodruff, "Workers' Stress Is Price Japan Pays for Progress," The *Commercial Appeal*, 6 January 1991: A12).

35. "Claiming the Waters: Morita to Japan," *TIME*, 3 February 1992: 39.

36. Shogo Imoto, "Not All Japanese, or Ants, Really Work So Hard," The *Ceder Rapids Gazette*, 17 May 1992: 7A

37. Thorstein Veblen, *Imperial Germany and the Industrial Revolution* (New York: Macmillan, 1915), ch. 2–4.

38. "Fixing,"*Business Week*, 29 March 1993: 68–69.

39. *Ibid.*, 69.

40. James Fallows, *More Like Us: Making America Great Again* (Boston: Houghton Mifflin, 1989), 6.

41. The Japanese polled cited as problems for the United States: drugs and alcohol addiction (93 percent); lazy workers (66 percent); too many racial and ethnic groups (57 percent); not enough long-term investment (55 percent); workers and bosses too greedy (53 percent). See "What Japan Thinks of Us,"*Newsweek*, 2 April 1990: 18–24.

42. Lance Morrow, "Japan in the Mind of America," *TIME*, 10 February 1992: 16–21.

43. Barry Hillenbrand, "America in the Mind of Japan," *TIME*, 10 February 1992: 22.

44. Janice Castro, "Work Ethic—In Spades," *TIME*, 17 February 1992: 57.

45. Janice Lawlor, "Facts Don't Support Charge that U.S. Works Lazy," *USA Today*, 27 January 1992: 1B.

46. Juliet B. Schor, *The Overworked American: The Unexpected Decline of Leisure* (New York: Basic Books, 1991).

47. Even one year before the manifest outburst of Japan-bashing in January 1992, Friedman and LeBard warned that an actual war between the United States and Japan within twenty years is inevitable (George Friedman and Meredith LeBard, *The Coming War with Japan* [New York: St. Martin's, 1991], 13–14).

48. The *Korea Times Chicago Edition*, 27 February 1992: 1.

49. Sam Allis, et al., "Japan Bashing on the Campaign Trail," *TIME*, February, 10 1992: 23–24

50. U.S. Commission on Civil Rights, *Civil Rights Issues Facing Asian Americans in the 1990s* (Washington, DC U.S. Commission on Civil Rights, 1992).

51. Jim Berry, "'Buy American' Guilt Trip," The *Commercial Appeal*, 15 March, 1992: b5.

52. Kevin Anderson, "'Made in USA' Isn't Anymore," *USA Today*, 27 January, 1992: 2B

53. Cole has warned us that cultural determinism (culture the sole or dominant factor that explains the phenomenon) can lead to "a gross distortion of what actually happened and the amount of 'sweat' involved in making it happen" (Cole, *Strategies for Learning*, 12). At the same time, Okimoto and Rohlen have cautioned us that there is little to be gained by either asserting cultural determinism or ignoring the influence of culture altogether (Daniel I. Okimoto and Thomas P. Rohlen, eds., *Inside the Japanese System: Readings on Contemporary Society and Political Economy* [Stanford: Stanford Univ. Press, 1988], 1).

54. Edward Tylor, *Primitive Culture,* vol. 1 (New York: Harper & Row, 1958 [orig. 1871], 1.

55. Peacock, *The Anthropological Lens*, 7.

56. *Ibid.*, 3.

57. Geertz, *The Interpretation of Cultures*, 89.

58. *Ibid.*, 10.

59. *Ibid.*, 14.

60. *Ibid.*, 15.

61. Magoroh Maruyama, "Epistemology of Social Science Research: Explorations Inculture Researchers," *Dialectica* 23 (1969): 229–80.

62. Yi Ŏ-yŏng, *Ch'ukso Chihyang-ŭi Ilbon-in* [Japanese ethos toward miniaturization] (Seoul: Kirin-wŏn, 1986), 293.

63. Geertz, *The Interpretation of Cultures*, 412–53.

64. Fallows, *More Like Us.*

65. Mitsukuni Yoshida, Ikko Tanaka, and Tsune Sesoko, *The Compact Culture: The Ethos of Japanese Life* (Hiroshima, Japan: Toyo Kogyo, 1982), 26.

66. Yi, *Ch'ukso Chihyang-ŭi Ilbon-in*, 292.

67. Hsu traces the attribute of inclusiveness from the father-son dominant kinship dyad. See Francis L.K. Hsu, *Rugged Individualism Reconsidered: Essays in Psychological Anthropology* (Knoxville: Univ. of Tennessee Press, 1983), 217–47.

68. Harumi Befu, *Japan: An Anthrpological Introduction* (New York: Thomas Y. Crowell, 1971), 96.

69. *Ibid.*, 183–84.

70. Choong Soon Kim and Wilfrid C. Bailey, *Community Factors in Productivity of Pulpwood Harvesting Operations* (Atlanta: American

Pulpwood Association Harvesting Research Project, 1971); Choong Soon Kim, "Life Patterns of Pulpwood Workers in a South Georgia Community" (Ph.D. diss., Univ. of Georgia, 1972); *idem, An Asian Anthropologist in the South.*

71. Choong Soon Kim, "Can an Anthropologist Go Home Again?" *American Anthropologist* 89 (1987): 943–45; *idem, Faithful Endurance: An Ethnography of Korean Family Dispersal* (Tucson: Univ. of Arizona Press, 1988), 10–14; *idem*, "The Role of the Non-Western Anthropologist Reconsidered: Illusion versus Reality," *Current Anthropology* 31 (1990): 196–201.

72. Alexander, *Friends*, 150–51.

73. John Shelton Reed, *The Enduring South: Subcultural Persistence in Mass Society* (Chapel Hill: Univ. of North Carolina Press, 1972), 85.

74. William McWhirter and Barry Hillenbrand, "The Bruising Battle Abroad," *TIME*, 27 May 1991: 42.

75. Gabriel A. Almond, *The American People and Foreign Policy* (New York: Praeger, 1967).

76. Hsu, "Intercultural Understanding," 204.

77. Ronald E. Dolan and Robert L. Worden, eds., *Japan: A Country Study.* Area Handbook Series (Washington, DC: Federal Research Division, Library of Congress, 1992), 90.

78. Of interest, about 6 percent of Koreans and people of Korean ancestry are living overseas, the highest percentage among the three Far Eastern nations, for the special historical reason that the Japanese colonized Korea (1910–45). During the colonial rule many Koreans fled to China to escape Japanese rule, and many others were taken to Japan involuntarily to fill the manpower shortage created by World War II (Kim, *Faithful Endurance*).

79. Geertz, *The Interpretation of Cultures*, 22.

80. Institutionalized patterns of Japanese racial discrimination against Koreans in Japan are well documented in Changsoo Lee and George DeVos, *Koreans in Japan: Ethnic Conflict and Accommodation* (Berkeley: Univ. of California Press, 1981).

81. Kim, *An Asian Anthropologist in the South*, 123.

CHAPTER 1
THE SOUTH AND SELLING OF THE SOUTH

1. Larry T. McGehee, "Anthropologists Can Weep," *Fulton Daily Leader*, 20 February 1989: 2.

2. William H. Nicholls, *Southern Tradition and Regional Progress* (Chapel Hill: Univ. of North Carolina Press, 1960), 34.

3. James C. Cobb, *The Selling of the South: The Southern Crusade for Industrial Development, 1936–1980* (Baton Rouge: Louisiana State Univ. Press, 1982), 130.

4. Glenn E. McLaughlin and Stefan Robock, *Why Industry Moves South: A Study of Factors Influencing the Recent Location of Manufacturing Plants in the South*. NPA Committee of the South Report III (Kingsport, TN: Kingsport Press, 1949), 3.

5. Gavin Wright, *Old South, New South: Revolutions in the Southern Economy Since the Civil War* (New York: Basic Books, 1986), 272.

6. Edward Wellin, "Review" of: *An Asian Anthropologist in the South* by Choong Soon Kim, *Rural Sociology* 43 (1978): 312–14; cf. Kim, *An Asian Anthropologist in the South.*

7. Harold Franklin McGee, Jr., "Comments" on: "Anthropological Studies in the American South" by Carole E. Hill *Current Anthropology* 18 (1977): 319.

8. *Webster's New World Dictionary of American English* (3d ed., 1988), 401.

9. The *World Book Encyclopedia* (Chicago: Field Enterprises, 1975), vol. 5, 211.

10. Lewis M. Killian, *White Southerners* (New York: Random House, 1970), 10.

11. George B. Tindall, *The Emergence of the New South, 1913–1945* (Baton Rouge: Louisiana State Univ. Press, 1967), x.

12. Howard W. Odum, *Southern Regions of the United States* (Chapel Hill: Univ. of North Carolina Press, 1936), 6–9, 219; Rudolf Heberle, "Regionalism: Some Critical Observations," *Social Forces* 21 (1943): 283.

13. The American Institute of Public Opinion includes in the South the states of North Carolina, South Carolina, Virginia, Georgia, Alabama, Arkansas, Florida, Kentucky, Louisiana, Mississippi, Oklahoma, Tennessee, and Texas. Cobb defines the South as the Confederate South plus Kentucky and Oklahoma. See James C. Cobb, *Industrialization and Southern Society, 1877–1984* (Lexington, KY: The Univ. Press of Kentucky, 1984), 7.

14. It should be noted that the U.S. Department of Commerce includes the South under the Southeast as a regional subdivision of the United States that includes West Virginia in addition to Odum's list of the Old South.

15. John Shelton Reed, *One South: An Ethnic Approach to Regional Culture* (Baton Rouge: Louisiana State Univ. Press, 1982), 71.

16. *Ibid.*, 72.

17. Rosalie H. Wax, *Doing Fieldwork: Warnings and Advice* (Chicago: Univ. of Chicago Press, 1971), 43.

18. McGehee, "Anthropologists Can Weep," 1.

19. H.L. Mencken, *A Mencken Chrestomathy* (New York: Knopf, 1949), 184.

20. Killian, *White Southerners*, xi.

21. See Monroe L. Billington, ed., *The South: A Central Theme?* (New York: Holt, Rinehart and Winston, 1969); Hodding Carter, *Southern Legacy* (Baton Rouge: Louisiana State Univ. Press, 1950); W.T. Couch, ed., *Culture in the South* (Chapel Hill: Univ. of North Carolina Press, 1935); John Egerton, *Americanization of Dixie: The Southernization of America* (New York: Harper, 1974); Alfred O. Hess, *The Southerner and World Affairs* (Baton Rouge: Louisiana State Univ. Press, 1965); Valdimer O. Key, *Southern Politics in State and Nation* (New York: Knopf, 1949); Ralph McGill, *The South and the Southerner* (Boston: Little Brown, 1964); Nicholls, *Southern Tradition and Regional Progress*; John Shelton Reed, *Southern Folk, Plain & Fancy* (Athens: Univ. of Georgia Press, 1986); Allen Tate, ed., *A Southern Vanguard* (New York: Prentice-Hall, 1947); C. Vann Woodward, *Origins of the New South, 1877–1913* (Baton Rouge: Louisiana State Univ. Press, 1951); *idem*, *The Strange Career of Jim Crow* (New York: Oxford Univ. Press, 1957); *idem, The Burden of Southern History* (Baton Rouge: Louisiana State Univ. Press, 1960).

22. Carole E. Hill, "Anthropological Studies in the American South: Review and Directions," *Current Anthropology* 18 (1977): 309–26.

23. David Bertelson, *The Lazy South* (New York: Oxford Univ. Press, 1967); W. J. Cash, *The Mind of the South* (New York: Knopf, 1941); Shelton Hackney, "Southern Violence," *American Historical Review* 74 (1969): 906–25; Killian, *White Southerners*; Ulrich B. Phillips, "The Central Theme of Southern History," *American Historical Review* 34 (1928): 30–43; *idem, Life and Labor in the Old South* (Boston: Little, Brown, 1929); Charles Ramsdell, "The Southern Heritage," in *Culture in the South*. ed. W.T. Couch, (Chapel Hill: Univ. of North Carolina Press, 1934), 1–23; John C. Ransom, et al., eds., *I'll Take My Stand: The South and the Agrarian Tradition* (New York: Harper, 1930); Reed, *The Enduring South*; Edgar T. Thompson, "The South in Old and New Contexts," in

South in Continuity and Change, eds. John McKinney and Edgar T. Thompson, 451–80 (Durham, NC: Duke Univ. Press, 1965); Rupert B. Vance, *Human Factors in Cotton Culture* (Chapel Hill: Univ. of North Carolina Press, 1929); Woodward, *The Burden of Southern History*.

24. Miles Richardson, "Comments" on: "Anthropological Studies in the American South" by Carole E. Hill, *Current Anthropology* 18 (1977): 321.

25. Mencken, *A Mencken Chrestomathy*, 185–86.

26. Killian, *White Southerners*, x.

27. See Allison Davis, B. Gardner, and M. Gardner, *Deep South* (Chicago: Univ. of Chicago Press, 1941); John Dollard, *Class and Caste in a Southern Town* (New Haven: Yale Univ. Press, 1937); Gunnar Myrdal, *An American Dilemma: The Negro Problem and Modern Democracy* (New York: Harper & Row, 1944); Hortense Powdermaker, *After Freedom: A Cultural Study of the Deep South* (New York: Viking, 1939).

28. Jack Temple Kirby, *Media-Made Dixie* (Baton Rouge: Louisiana State Univ. Press, 1978).

29. Killian, *White Southerners*, 25.

30. As C. Vann Woodward admits, "'New South' is neither a place name as is 'New England,' nor does it precisely designate a period as does 'the Confederacy.' From the beginning it had the color of a slogan, a rallying cry." In order to avoid any confusion or misinterpretation, I employ the adjective "present" (see Woodward, *Origins of the New South*, ix).

31. Edgar G. Murphy, *Problems, and Political Issues in the Southern States* (New York: Macmillan, 1904), 23.

32. Cash, *The Mind of the South*, x.

33. Reed, *The Enduring South*, 4.

34. Reed, *One South*, 130.

35. "Peter Applebome's Conversations with John Shelton Reed," The *New York Times*, 24 January 1993: E7.

36. "The South Today," *TIME* Special Issue, 27 September 1976: 29.

37. Wright, *Old South, New South*, 269–70.

38. Rupert B. Vance, *The South's Place in the Nation* (New York: Public Affairs Committee, Inc., 1941), 4.

39. *Ibid.*

40. Rupert B. Vance, John E. Ivey, Jr., and Marjorie N. Bond, *Exploring the South* (Chapel Hill: Univ. of North Carolina Press, 1949), 72.

41. Cobb, *Industrialization and Southern Society*, 34–35.

42 Vance, et al., *Exploring the South*, 91–94.

43. Cobb, *Industrialization and Southern Society*, 35.

44. *Ibid.*

45. See Ransom, et al., *I'll Take My Stand*.

46. Woodward, *Origins of the New South*, 291.

47. *Ibid.*, 317.

48. *Ibid.*

49. *Ibid.*, 318-19.

50. Odum, *Southern Regions of the United States*, 210; see also Woodward, *Origins of the New South*, 291–320.

51. Woodward, *Origins of the New South*, 319–20.

52. Ransom et al., *I'll Take My Stand*.

53. Cobb, *The Selling of the South*, 5.

54. Ernest J. Hopkins, *Mississippi's BAWI Plan: Balance Agriculture with Industry* (Atlanta: Federal Reserve Bank of Atlanta, 1944); also see Charles P. Ronald, *The Improbable Era: The South Since World War II* (Lexington: Univ. Press of Kentucky, 1975), 11–29.

55. McGill, *The South and the Southerner*, 194.

56. Kim, *An Asian Anthropologist in the South*, 61.

57. Cobb, *The Selling of the South*, 6.

58. McGill, *The South and the Southerner*, 195.

59. Cobb, *The Selling of the South*, 6–7.

60. *Ibid.*, 7.

61. Wright, *Old South, New South*, 257.

62. Cobb, *The Selling of the South*.

63. The Tennessee Valley Authority (TVA) was created by an Act of Congress in May 1933 to develop the Tennessee River system and to aid the people of the region to put resources to work in overcoming problems of poverty and inadequate opportunity. The TVA is a corporate agency of the United States government charged with approximately 41,000 square miles of the Tennessee River Basin as its area of stewardship. See Ralph O. Fullerton and John B. Ray, eds., *Tennessee: Geographical Patterns and Regions* (Dubuque, IA: Kendall/Hunt, 1977, 61.

64. McGill, *The South and the Southerner*, 206. A partial credit for the increase of southern wages has to be given to the federal minimum wage. Since its enactment in 1938, the minimum wage has been upgraded periodically: $0.40 per hour by 1941, $0.75 in 1950, $1.00 in 1956, $1.25 in 1961, and $1.60 by 1970.

65. Cobb, *The Selling of the South*, 68.

66. Robert E. Corlew, *Tennessee: A Short History* (Knoxville: Univ. of Tennessee Press, 1981), 520.

67. George B. Tindall, *The Ethnic Southerners* (Baton Rouge: Louisiana State Univ. Press, 1976), 209.

68. Corlew, *Tennessee*, 520.

69. *Ibid.*, 521.

70. Cobb, *The Selling of the South*, 75–77.

71. *Ibid.*, 74.

72. McGill, *The South and the Southerner*, 207.

73. Currently, the states that have right-to-work laws either in statutes or by constitutional provisions are: Alabama, Arizona, Arkansas, Colorado, Florida, Georgia, Idaho, Iowa, Kan-sas, Louisiana, Mississippi, Montana, Nebras-ka, Nevada, New Hampshire, North Carolina, North Dakota, South Carolina, South Dakota, Tennessee, Texas, Utah, Virginia, and Wyoming.

74. Cobb, *The Selling of the South*, 91–92.

75. *Ibid.*, 98.

76. *Ibid.*, 89–90.

77. *Ibid.*, 90.

78. *Ibid.*, 78–79.

79. *Ibid.*, 79.

80. McGill, *The South and the Southerner*, 210.

81. Kim, *An Asian Anthropologist in the South*, 125.

82. The American Academy of Arts and Sciences was so impressed by the region's vibrant intellectual community that it designated the park as the location of its National Humanities Center. As "a think tank with an arrow," the center accepted its first group of scholars and associates in September 1978. (Cobb, *The Selling of the South*, 176.)

83. Cobb, *The Selling of the South*, 188.

84. See Alexander Gershenkron, *Economic Backwardness in Historical Perspective* (Cambridge: Harvard Univ. Press, 1962); *idem*, *Continuity in History and Other Essays* (Cambridge: Harvard Univ. Press, 1968); Marshall D. Sahlins and Elman R. Service, *Evolution and Culture* (Ann Arbor: Univ. of Michigan Press, 1960), 93–122; Leon Trotsky, *The History of the Russian Revolution* (Ann Arbor: University of Michigan Press, n.d.), 4–5; Kim, *The Culture of Korean Industry*, 6–7, 220.

85. Veblen, *Imperial Germany and the Industrial Revolution*, ch. 2–4.

86. Sahlins and Service, *Evolution and Culture*, 93–122.

87. Cobb, *The Selling of the South*, 87.

88. *Ibid.*, 162.

89. *Ibid.*, 161.

90. *Ibid.*, 154.

91. *Ibid.*, 177.

92. *Ibid.*, 169.

93. "Mississippi Hurt by Racial Strifer," The *New York Times*, 20 December 1964: 1, 33.

94. Cobb, *The Selling of the South*, 128.

95. *Ibid.*, 136.

96. *Ibid.*, 144.

97. *Ibid.*, 144.

98. *Ibid.*, 131.

99. *TIME*, 24 December 1990: 72–73.

100. *Ibid.*

101. Kevin P. Phillips, *The Emerging Republican Majority* (New Rochelle, NY: Arlington House, 1969), 437; See also Carl Abbott, "The American Sunbelt: Idea and Region," *Journal of the West* 18 (July 1979): 5–8.

102. Kirkpatrick Sale, *Power Shift: The Rise of the Southern Rim and Its Challenge to the Eastern Establishment* (New York: Random House, 1975), 9–14.

103. Roger W. Schmenner includes the states of Delaware, Florida, Georgia, Maryland, North Carolina, South Carolina, Virginia, and West Virginia in the South Atlantic division; Alabama, Kentucky, Mississippi, and Tennessee in the East South Central division; Arkansas, Louisiana, Oklahoma, and Texas in the West South Central; and Arizona, Colorado, Idaho, Montana, Nevada, New Mexico, Utah, and Wyoming in the Mountain division. See Roger W. Schmenner, "Geography and the Character and Performance of Factories," in *Industry Location and Public Policy*, eds. Henry W. Herzog, Jr., and Alan M. Schlottmann, 241–53 (Knoxville: Univ. of Tennessee Press, 1991), 242, 252.

104. Cobb, *The Selling of the South*, 187.

105. Gene Burd, "The Selling of the Sunbelt: Civic Boosterism in the Media," *Urban Affairs Annual Review* 14 (1977): 129–49; Larry L. King, "We Ain't Trash No More," *Esquire* 126 (November 1976): 89–90, 152–56; Reg Murphy, "The South as the New America," *Saturday Review*, 4 September 1976: 8–11; The *New York Times*, 11 February 1976: 1.

106. William Lee Miller, *Yankee from Georgia: The Emergence of Jimmy Carter* (New York: Times Books, 1978).

107. George Adcock, "Is International Status Taking the South by Surprise?," *South* 2 (July/August 1975), 34, 36; "Recruiting Industry Abroad," *South* 5 (April 1, 1978): 31.

CHAPTER 2
SOUTHERN INCENTIVES AND
JAPANESE INVESTMENT

1. Myrdal, *An American Dilemma*, 45.

2. Cobb, *The Selling of the South*, 190.

3. *Ibid.*, 191.

4. *Ibid.*; also see Adcock, "Is International Status Taking the South by Surprise?" 35.

5. Data from Tennessee Department of Economic and Community Development, November, 1994.

6. *Ibid.*

7. Alexander, *Friends*, 16.

8. Komiya and Wakasugi, "Japan's Foreign Direct Investment," 55.

9. The cost of investment in other areas, such as the East and Southeast Asia, has also been reduced, for most of the currencies in these areas were and still are by and large linked to the U.S. dollar.

10. Trevor, "The Overseas Strategies of Japanese Corporations," 95–96.

11. Komiya and Wakasugi, "Japan's Foreign Direct Investment," 56.

12. *Ibid.*, 52, table 3.

13. David Gelsanliter, *Jump Start: Japan Comes to the Heartland* (New York: Farrar, Straus & Giroux, 1990), 17–18.

14. *Ibid.*, 77–78.

15. Alexander, *Friends*, 16.

16. U.S. Department of Commerce, *Foreign Direct Investment in the United States:* tables B-6 and F-22.

17. An accurate counting of foreign manufacturing firms is indeed a difficult task, since one firm may be located in several states; thus various sources cite differing figures. According to the *Directory of Foreign Manufacturers in the United States*, published by Georgia State Univ. Business Press in 1990, the number of Japanese manufacturing firms in the United States was ranked fourth, following Germany, England, and Canada, out of fifty-four listed nations. The directory is confusing, for it separates England from the United Kingdom, and the Republic of Korea and South Korea are treated as if they were separate countries. See Jeffrey S. Arpan and David A. Ricks, *Directory of Foreign Manufacturers in the United States* (Atlanta, GA: Georgia State Univ. Business Press, 1990), xvii.

18. Alexander, *Friends*, 17.

19. *Ibid.*, 19.

20. Gelsanliter, *Jump Start*, 48.

21. Alexander, *Friends*, 150.

22. Gelsanliter reports that Tennessee spent about $20 million to recruit Nissan (Gelsanliter, *Jump Start*, 49). Others have estimated that the state spent $25 million (Ted Evanoff, "S.C. Auto Coup UPs Jobs Ante for South," The *Commercial Appeal*, 25 October 1992: 1, 16).

23. Gelsanliter, *Jump Start*, 50

24. Ted Evanoff, "S.C. Auto Coup UPS Jobs Ante for South," The *Commercial Appeal*, 25 October 1992: 1,16.

25. Robert B. Reich, "Who is Us?," *Harvard Business Review* (Jan.–Feb., 1990): 58.

26. Alexander, *Friends*, 150.

27. *Ibid.*, 151.

28. Alabama has its foreign offices in Hong Kong, Japan, Korea, and Switzerland; Arkansas, in Belgium, Japan, and Taiwan; Georgia, in Canada and Belgium; and North Carolina, in Germany, Japan, and Hong Kong.

29. Alexander, *Friends*, 150–51.

30. *Ibid.*, 74.

31. Herbert Barry, III, Irvine L. Child, and Margaret K. Bacon, "Relation of Child Training to Subsistence Economy," *American Anthropologist* 61 (1959): 51–63.

32. William G. Ouchi, *Theory Z: How American Business Can Meet the Japanese Challenge* (Reading, MA: Addison-Wesley, 1981), 11; John van Willigen and Richard Stoffle, "The Americanization of Shoyu: American Workers and a Japanese Employment System," in *Anthropology and International Business*, ed. H. Serrie. Studies in Third World Societies, Publication No. 28 (Williamsburg, VA: Dept. of Anthropology, College of William and Mary, 1986), 125–62.

33. Reed, *The Enduring South*, 45. Odum wrote that the "way of the South has been and is the way of the folk....The Culture of the South is the culture of folk." (Howard Odum, *The Way of the South* [New York: Macmillan, 1947], 61–62). The folk society (or *Gemeinschaft*), in its sociological incarnation, refers to the idea of "traditional" or "communal" society and its values. See Robert Redfield, "The Folk Society" *American Journal of Sociology*, 52 (1947): 293–308.

34. The school is in the city of Sweetwater (pop. 5,054 in 1990), fifty miles south of Knoxville, on the 144-acre campus of the former Tennessee Military Institute, a venerable academy purchased for $2.5 million by Meiji Gakuin High School. Currently, the school has twenty-six Japanese faculty members and enrolls 109 students from various states in the United States, Brazil, Mexico, Canada, and Germany, and about seventy students from Japan.

35. There are many studies on industrial location decisions. See J.P. Blair and R. Premus, "Major Factors in Industrial Location: A Review," *Economic Development Quarterly* 1 (1987): 72–85; F.J. Calzonetti and Robert T. Walker, "Factors Affecting Industrial Location Decisions: A Survey Approach," in *Industry Location and Public Policy*, eds. Henry W. Herzog, Jr., and Alan M. Schlottmann, (Knoxville: Univ. of Tennessee Press, 1971), 230; Ronald E. Carrier and William Schriver, "Plant Location Studies: An Appraisal," *Southwestern Social Science Quarterly* 47 (1969): 136–40; Richard A. Duvall, "Industry, State Rate Incentive, Assistance Programs," *Industrial Development* 37 (1986): 26–30; V. Fuchs, *Changes in the Location Manufacturing in the U.S. Since 1929* (New Haven: Yale Univ. Press, 1962); Jane Sneddon Little, "Location Decisions of Foreign Investors in the United States," *New England Economic Review* (July/August 1978): 43–63; William E. Morgan, *Taxes and the Location Industry* (Boulder: Univ. of Colorado Press, 1967); T.R. Plaut and J.E. Pluta, "Business Climate, Texas and Expenditures and State Industrial Growth in the U.S.," *Southern Economic Journal* 50 (1983): 99–119; Leonard F. Wheat, "The Determinants of 1963–77 Regional Manufacturing Growth: Why the South and West Grow," *Journal of Regional Science* 26 (1986): 635–60.

36. Douglas P. Woodward and Norman J. Glickman, "Regional and Local Determinants of Foreign Firm Location in the United States," in *Industry Location and Public Policy*, eds. Henry W. Herzog, Jr., and Alan M. Schlottman (Knoxville: Univ. of Tennessee Press), 209.

37. Jeffery Arpan, "The Impact of State Incentives on Foreign Investors' Site Selections," *Economic Review* 66 (1981): 36–42; Woodward and Glickman, "Regional and Local Determinants of Foreign Firm Location in the United States," 209, 215.

38. Wallace Wilkinson, the Democrat who succeeded Collins as governor, campaigned against the Toyota incentive package (see Gelsanliter, *Jump Start*, 143).

39. Richard Locker, "Kentucky's Tax Breaks Heat Up War for Industry," The *Commercial Appeal*, 13 December 1992: A1, A6.

40. *Ibid.*, A6

41. Woodward and Glickman, "Regional and Local Determinants of Foreign Firm Location in the United States," 190.

42. Corlew, *Tennessee,* 3. See also Lamar Alexander, *The Tennesseans: A People and Their Land* (Nashville: Thomas Nelson, 1981); *idem, Friends,* 25.

43. According to Fullerton and his associates, One of the most colorful aspects of the folk culture of this region is the speech of the people, which is not a dialect. Words popularized by Chaucer and Shakespeare have been passed down to the present. For example, the word "hit," for "it," Commonly used in this region, is an old Anglo Saxon form. Another aspect of the speech pattern is the compunction to reduce a long sentence into a short phrase, as in "He lives yonside," for "He lives on the other side of the mountain." (Fullerton and Ray., *Tennessee,* 45); See also John C. Campbell, *The Southern Highlander and His Homeland* (New York: Russell Sage Foundation, 1921), 50–71.

44. The fiddle was practically their only musical instrument. But after the Civil War, many younger men learned to play the banjo and the dulcimer (Fullerton and Ray, *Tennessee,* 45–46).

45. "Memphis was founded in 1819 by Andrew Jackson, James Winchester, and John Overton. Early settlers were mainly Scotch Highlanders, Scotch-Irish, and Germans from East and Middle Tennessee. The name 'Memphis' is of Egyptian origin and means 'Place of Good Abode.'" (Fullerton and Ray, *Tennessee,* 121).

46. Glenna Colclough, "Uneven Development and Racial Composition in the Deep South: 1970–1980," *Rural Sociology* 53 (1988): 73–86; Stuart A. Rosenfeld, Edward M. Bergman, and Sarah Rueben, *After the Factories: Changing Employment Patterns in the Rural South* (Research Triangle Park, NC: Southern Growth Policies Board, 1985); Michael Timberlake et al., "Race and Poverty in the Rural South: Racial Composition and Economic Development," Paper presented at the annual meeting of the American Sociological Association, August, 1989, San Francisco; Bruce B. Williams, *Black Workers in an Industrial Suburb: The Struggle Against Discrimination* (New Brunswick, NJ: Rutgers Univ. Press, 1987).

47. Rosenfeld, Bergman, and Rueben, *After the Factories,* 28.

48. Colclough, "Uneven Development and Racial Composition," 83.

49. Timberlake, et al., "Race and Poverty in the Rural South," 22.

50. Hamilton and Orru, "Organizational Structure of East Asian Companies," 39–47.

CHAPTER 3
MYTH AND REALITY OF JAPANESE INDUSTRY IN THE SOUTH

1. Trevor, "The Overseas Strategies of Japanese Corporations," 93.

2. Sarah Avery, "'Fine' Pioneers: Japanese school graduates its first students," The *Knoxville News-Sentinel,* 8 March 1992: 1, 13.

3. The state of Alabama hung the Confederate flag over the capital dome for thirty years until an Alabama court ruled in January 1993 against the practice. In a Univ. of North Carolina survey of thirteen southern states, 51 percent of the blacks surveyed said the flag reminds them of white supremacy and racial conflict, while 79 percent of whites said it reminds them of southern heritage and pride. South Carolina still displays the Confederate flag, and the state flags of Mississippi and Georgia include the Confederate emblem. "A Defeat for Dixie in Alabama," *U.S. News & World Report,* 18 January 1993: 14).

4. Kim, *An Asian Anthropologist in the South.*

5. Ann E. Kingsolver, "Tobacco, Textiles, and Toyota: Working for Multinational Corporations in Rural Kentucky," in *Anthropology and the Global Factory: Studies of the New Industrialization in the Late Twentieth Century,* eds. Frances Abrahamer Rothstein and Michael L. Blim, (New York: Bergin & Garvey, 1992), 201.

6. Gelsanliter, *Jump Start,* 119.

7. "Nissan is the only transplant [among Japanese auto-plants in the U.S.] in which status distinctions are more visible, e.g., a separate parking lot for top managers' cars and plush 'American-style' offices" (Richard Florida and Martin Kenney, "Transplanted Organizations: The Transfer of Japanese Industrial Organization to the U.S.," *American Sociological Review* 56 [1991]: 386).

8. Ferraro, *The Cultural Dimension of International Business,* 7.

9. Hays, "Expatriate Selection: Insuring Success and Avoiding Failure," 25–37; Tung, "Selection and Training of Personnel for Overseas Assignments," 68–78.

10. Christian Elenora Garza, "Studying

the Natives on the Shop Floor: How Anthropologists Are Helping Companies Improve Productivity," *Business Week*, 30 September 1991: 48–49; Claudia H. Deutsch, "Coping with Culture Polyglots: Anthropologists are Helping Companies Understand Workers and Customers," The *New York Times*, 24 February 1991: 25.

11. Kalervo Oberg, "Culture Shock: Adjustments to New Cultural Environments," *Practical Anthropology*, (July–August 1960): 177.

12. Ferraro, *The Cultural Dimension of International Business*, 140–41.

13. T.R. Reid, "Japanese Watching Out for Ugly Americans," The *Commercial Appeal*, 20 December 1992: A1, A11.

14. Koji Taira, "Japan, an Imminent Hegemon?" *The Annals of the American Academy of Political and Social Science* 513 (January 1991): 151–63, 158.

15. Kazuo Shibagaki, "Introduction," in *Japanese and European Management: Their International Adaptability*, eds. Kazuo Shibagaki, Malcolm Trevor, and Tetsuo Abo, (Tokyo: Univ. of Tokyo Press, 1989), ix.

16. Hiroshi Itagaki, "Application-Adaptation Problems in Japanese Automobile and Electronics Plants in the USA," in *Japanese and European Management: Their International Adaptability*, eds. Kazuo Shibagaki, Malcolm Trevor, and Tetsuo Abo, (Tokyo: Univ. of Tokyo Press, 1989), 130.

17. Tetsuo Abo, "The Emergence of Japanese Multinational Enterprises and the Theory of Foreign Direct Investment," in *Japanese and European Management: Their International Adaptability*, eds. Kazuo Shibagaki, Malcolm Trevor, and Tetsuo Abo, (Tokyo: Univ. of Tokyo Press, 1989), 16.

18. The center was established to promote mutual understanding of both American and Japanese cultures. Its activities include the organizing of Japanese women, mostly the spouses of the Japanese personnel working in Tennessee, to demonstrate Japanese arts and crafts in area schools. Among many other services, the center helped one Japanese family to find special training for a deaf child who had a special aptitude for art (see Alexander, *Friends*, 153).

19. Hideki Yoshihara, "The Bright and the Dark Sides of Japanese Management Overseas," in *Japanese and European Management: Their International Adaptability*, eds. Kazuo Shibagaki, Malcolm Trevor, and Tetsuo Abo, (Tokyo: Univ. of Tokyo Press, 1989), 27–28.

20. *Ibid.*, 28.

21. Trevor, "The Overseas Strategies of Japanese Corporations," 98.

22. Yoshihara, "The Bright and the Dark Sides of Japanese Management Overseas," 27.

23. *Ibid.*, 27–28.

24. Itagaki, "Application-Adaptation Problems in Japanese Automobile and Electronics Plants in the USA," 120.

25. Trevor, "The Overseas Strategies of Japanese Corporations," 98.

26. *Ibid.*, 100.

27. Yoshihara, "The Bright and the Dark Sides of Japanese Management Overseas," 25.

28. *Ibid.*

29. *Ibid.*, 26.

30. Yoshihara, "The Bright and the Dark Sides of Japanese Management Overseas," 23–24.

31. William McWhirter, "I Came, I Saw, I Blundered: For Bosses from Abroad, the U.S. is Tougher Than It Looks," *TIME*, 9 October 1989: 72, 77.

32. Trevor, "The Overseas Strategies of Japanese Corporations," 99; James R. Lincoln and Kerry McBride, "Japanese Organization in Contemporary Perspective," *Annual Review of Sociology* 13 (1987): 289–312.

33. Merry White, *The Japanese Overseas: Can They Go Home Again?* (Princeton: Princeton Univ. Press, 1992).

34. Mikio Sumiya, "Japan: Model Society of the Future?" *The Annals of the American Academy of Political and Social Science* 513 (January 1991): 148.

35. *Ibid.*

36. Thomas P. Rohlen, *Japan's High Schools* (Berkeley: Univ. of California Press, 1983), 104.

37. Sumiya, "Japan: Model Society of the Future?" 142.

38. White, *The Japanese Overseas*, 29–30.

39. *Ibid.*, 27.

40. Ferraro, *The Cultural Dimension of International Business*, 49.

41. Sandra Salmans, "Industry Learns to Speak the Same Language," *International Management*, April 1979: 45–47.

42. Edward T. Hall, *The Silent Language* (Garden City, NY: Doubleday, 1959).

CHAPTER 4
INDUSTRIAL RELATIONS OF
JAPANESE INDUSTRY

1. Trevor, "The Overseas Strategies of Japanese Corporations," 91.

2. S. Linstead and R. Grafton-Small distinguish between corporate culture and organizational culture: Corporate culture is attributed to management—who devises it and imposes it on the organizational through rites, rituals, and values; organizational culture is associated with workers as "organic," those who are not just passive consumers of corporate culture. Workers engage in a creative process of producing culture from mundane details of their work and through innumerable and infinitesimal transformations of the dominant culture, adapting it to their interests. (See S. Linstead and R. Grafton-Small, "On Reading Organizational Culture," *Organization Studies* 13 (1992): 331–55).

3. Solomon B. Levine and Makoto Ohtsu, "Transplanting Japanese Labor Relations," *The Annals of the American Academy of Political and Social Science* 513 (January 1991): 111.

4. *Ibid.*, 103.

5. Levine and Ohtsu elaborate:

Most Japanese themselves do not need to consider the divine treasures as anything more than out-of-reach stereotyped ideals.... One of the most important is that by far the huge majority—probably 75 percent—of the 45 million wage and salary earners in present-day Japan are employed in small-scale enterprises that do not often exhibit the divine treasures in any noticeable way. The treasures seem to belong only to the very large companies and to government bureaucracies....Lifetime employment and length-of-service wages and promotions indeed are found in Japan, but they should be seen more as exceptions than as the rule....[W]hile unionism extends to only 26 percent of the wage and salary work force, labor-management collective bargaining has an impact far beyond the borders of the individual enterprise" (*Ibid.*, 107).

6. "It should be noted that those principles have been incorporated into a 1985 fair-employment-opportunity law in Japan, so that in Japan itself affirmative action now has to be reconciled with established recruitment, training, tenure, compensation, and promotion practices" (*Ibid.*, 115).

7. *Ibid.*, 104.

8. *Ibid.*, 111 (original is in Makoto Ohtsu and Hem C. Jain, *Viability of the Japanese Industrial Relations System in the International Context: The Case of Canadian—Management Report*, Working Paper Series, no. 83–02 [Saskatoon, Canada: College of Commerce Univ. of Saskatchewan, 1983]).

9. Tamio Hattori, "Japanese Zaibatsu and Korean Chaebol," in *Korean Managerial Dynamics*, eds. Kae H. Chung and Hak Chong Lee, (New York: Praeger, 1989); see also Kim, *The Culture of Korean Industry*, 113–14.

10. Sumiya, "Japan: Model Society for the Future?," 149.

11. National and state figures were obtained from the Tennessee Department of Economic and Community Development.

12. Sumiya, "Japan: Model Society of the Future?," 144.

13. James C. Abegglen, *The Japanese Factory: Aspects of Its Social Organization* (Glencoe, IL: Free Press, 1958).

14. Koji Taira, "Characteristics of Japanese Labor Markets," *Economic Development and Cultural Change* 10 (1962): 150–68.

15. Cole, *Japanese Blue Collar*, 125.

16. Kim, *The Culture of Korean Industry*, 133.

17. Karen Lowry Miller, "Stress and Uncertainty: The Price of Restructuring," *Business Week*, 29 March 1993: 74.

18. *Ibid.*, 69.

19. Steven Butler, "Japan Struggles to Stand and Deliver," *U.S. News & World Report*, 12 April 1993: 49.

20. *Ibid.*

21. *Ibid.*, 48.

22. In Tennessee, for instance, the unemployment rate is still high at 6.2 percent, according to the 1990 census; the rates in some Tennessee counties are as high as 10 percent and more, and applicants always outnumber the available positions.

23. Levine and Ohtsu, "Transplanting Japanese Labor Relations," 106–107.

24. Cole, *Japanese Blue Collar*, 113.

25. An ethnography of the methods of recruiting Japanese workers right from school is in Thomas P. Rohlen, *For Harmony and Strength: Japanese White-Collar Organization in Anthropological Perspective* (Berkeley: Univ. of California Press, 1974), 67.

26. Levine and Ohtsu, "Transplanting Japanese Labor Relations," 115. Also see Bill Childs, "New United Motor: An American Success Story," *Labor Law Journal* (August 1989): 453–64.

27. Such societal restraint is also true in other East Asian countries, such as Korea. In Korean industrial communities, for instance, managers label the manufacturing workers who move from company to company as *ch'amsaejok*, "a flock of sparrows," flying over the fields in search of

better crops. In my survey of industrial workers, not managers, in a plant, the industrial workers themselves believed that "those who change jobs often have something wrong with them (56.7 percent), are unreliable (12.5 percent), or have no loyalty to the company (17.3 percent). Only 5.8 percent of the sampled workers believed that workers who change jobs often are capable and able workers" (Kim, *The Culture of Korean Industry*, 134).

28. Cole, *Japanese Blue Collar*, 75.

29. *Ibid.*, 76–77.

30. Sumiya states:

The leaders of these labor unions thought that their unions followed the model of Western labor unions and never imagined that their organizations were different from them....Members of individual Japanese unions consisted of employees of each enterprise or factory; that is, the union was organized in each enterprise or factory.... This has meant that the core of the Japanese labor movement is the individual union organized only by the employees of each separate company or factory. Collective bargaining is carried out by the individual union with the enterprise where union members are employed....[S]uch a union should be called an "enterprise union." This enterprise union is quite different from the union concept in Western countries, where the national union is central....In 1950, when we scholars explained that the organization of labor unions in Japan differed from that of the Western labor unions and that consequently they should be called "enterprise unions," unionists were shocked. (Sumiya, "Japan," 146).

31. Cole, Japanese Blue Collar, 1–15.

32. *Ibid.*

33. *Ibid.*, 146–47.

34. Levine and Ohtsu, "Transplanting Japanese Labor Relations," 112–13.

35. Alexander, *Friends*, 152–53.

36. Gelsanliter, *Jump Start*, 240.

37. Levine and Ohtsu, "Transplanting Japanese Labor Relations," 112.

38. Gelsanliter, *Jump Start*, 46–47.

39. *Ibid.*, 57.

40. Alexander, *Friends*, 152.

41. Gelsanliter, *Jump Start*, 57.

42. Gary M. Fink and Merl Reed, eds., *Essays in Southern Labor History: Selected Papers, Southern Labor History Conference, 1976* (Westport, CT: Greenwood, 1977); Gary M. Fink, Merl Reed, and Leslie Hough, eds., *South-*

ern Workers and Their Unions (Westport, CT: Greenwood Press, 1981); F. Ray Marshall, *Labor in the South* (Cambridge: Harvard Univ. Press, 1976).

43. Robert H. Zieger, "Introduction," in *Organized Labor in the Twentieth-Century South*, ed. Robert H. Zieger, (Knoxville: Univ. of Tennessee Press, 1991), 4–5.

44. Gilbert J. Gall, "Southern Industrial Workers and Anti-Union Sentiment," in *Organized Labor in the Twentieth-Century South*, ed. Robert H. Zieger, (Knoxville: Univ. of Tennessee Press, 1991), 239.

45. Gelsanliter, *Jump Start*, 80.

46. *Ibid.*, 112–13, 119, 198, 200

47. Everett M. Kassalow, "Japan as an Industrial Relations Model," *Journal of Industrial Relations* 258 (1983): 211.

48. Tennessee code annotated (*Whittaker v. Care-More, Inc.*, 621 S.W. 2nd 395 [Tenn. Ct. App. 1981]) states that "the 'employee-at-will' rule that all may dismiss their employees at will, be they many or few, for good cause, for no cause or even for cause morally wrong without being thereby guilty of a legal wrong is still viable in Tennessee, except where modified by statute.... An employer has a right to discharge an employee at any time for just cause. The fact the employer bears with the incompetency or irregularities of such employee for a time does not estop the employer from discharging the employee for such incompetency if it continues."

49. Catherine Breslin, "Working for the Japanese: Is the Yen Invasion Bringing New Opportunities for Women or Creating a Class of Office Geishas?," *Ms. Magazine*, February 1988: 27–29; "The Sumitomo Thirteen," *Ms. Magazine*, February 1988: 30–31.

50. Gelsanliter, *Jump Start*, 244.

51. *Ibid.*, 191.

52. *Ibid.*, 117; see also Itagaki, "Application-Adaptation Problems in Japanese Automobile and Electronics Plants in the USA," 127.

53. See Rohlen, *For Harmony and Strength*; Ouchi, *Theory Z*, 25–32.

54. Levine and Ohtsu, "Transplanting Japanese Labor Relations," 115.

55. Joseph Szczesny, "The Right Stuff: Does U.S. Industry Have It? With Teamwork and New Ideas, GM's Saturn Aims to Show That American Manufacturers Are Roaring Back," *TIME*, 29 October 1990: 74–84.

56. *Ibid.*, 74, 76.

57. According to *TIME*'s survey, a surprising number of foreign investors have failed

on U.S. turf. Among the many reasons cited for the failures are the investors' displays of superiority and their colonial attitudes (William McWhirter, "I Came, I Saw, I Blundered: For Bosses from Abroad, the U.S. is Tougher Than It Looks," *TIME*, 9 October 1989: 72–77).

58. Yoshihara, "The Bright and the Dark Sides of Japanese Management Overseas," 20–21; see also Levine and Ohtsu, "Transplanting Japanese Labor Relations," 115.

59. Imai, *Kaizen (Ky'zen)*, xxv.

60. James R. Healey, "U.S. Steel Learns from Experience," *USA Today*, 10 April 1992: 1B–2B.

61. The RIT/USA Today Quality Cup was created jointly by Rochester Institute of Technology and *USA Today* as an award for individuals and teams for accomplishing innovation and improvement in their work setting. A panel of experts, academicians, consultants, and quality professionals selected by the Rochester Institute of Technology choose the winner. The nomination process for the competition begins in the fall. For the 1992 competition, the total number of entries was 431.

62. James R. Healey, "U.S. Steel Learns from Experience," *USA Toady*, 10 April 1992: 2B.

63. Sumiya, "Japan: Model Society of the Future?," 141.

64. Ruth Benedict, *The Chrysanthemum and the Sword* (New York: Houghton Mifflin, 1946).

65. Ralph Linton, "One Hundred Percent American," *The American Mercury* 40 (1937): 427–29.

66. Levine and Ohtsu, "Transplanting Japanese Labor Relations," 114.

67. Stephen Butler, "Winning Chip Shots: America has surged ahead of Japan in the Global Semiconductor Wars," *U.S. News & World Report*, 1 March 1993: 53; cf. Ishihara Shintaro and Morita Akio, *"No" to Ieru Nihon* [The Japan That Can Say "No"] (Tokyo: Kobunsha, 1989).

CHAPTER 5

RESPONSE OF SOUTHERNERS TO THE JAPANESE CHALLENGES

1. Bill Powell and Bradley Martin, "What Japan Thinks of Us," *Newsweek*, 2 April 1990: 18–24.

2. Larry Moore, *Improving Workforce Basic Skills: The Foundation for Quality* (New York: Quality Resources, 1992), xiii.

3. *Ibid.*

4. Halberstam, *The Reckoning*, 727–28.

5. Saburo Okita, "Japan's Role in Asia-Pacific Cooperation," *The Annals of the American Academy of Political and Social Science* 513 (January 1991): 31.

6. *Ibid.*

7. Taira, "Japan, An Imminent Hegemon?," 157–58. It is reported that the flow of Japanese investment in U.S. real estate significantly decreased from $16.5 billion in 1988 to $13.1 billion in 1990, and it is estimated that annual investment in 1991 will range between $3 billion to $5 billion (see, Bill Montague, "Japanese Buy less U.S. Real Estate," *USA Today*, 21 January 1992: B1).

8. Janice Castro, "From Walkman to Showman," *TIME*, 9 October 1989: 70.

9. Taira, "Japan, An Imminent Hegemon?" 157; Martin Tolchin and Susan Tolchin, *Buying into America: How Foreign Money Is Changing the Face of Our Nation* (New York: Berkeley Books, 1989).

10. William McWhirter, "I Came, I Saw, I Blundered: For Bosses from Abroad, the U.S. is Tougher than It Looks," *TIME*, 9 October 1989: 72–77.

11. Alexander, *Friends*, 152; See also Jerry Buckley, "We Learned That Them may be Us," *U.S. News & World Report*, 9 May 1988: 50.

12. Gelsanliter, *Jump Start*, 143.

13. Kim, *An Asian Anthropologist in the South*, 128.

14. "A Wayne County judge sentenced his assailant [a former auto plant foreman at Chrysler who mistook a Chinese-American for a Japanese and bludgeoned him to death with a baseball bat] to only three years' probation and a fine of $3,790. It wasn't until two years later that a federal judge raised the sentence to twenty-five years in prison" (Gelsanliter, *Jump Start*, 143).

15. *Ibid.*, 190.

16. Alexander, *Friends*, 175.

17. Reich, "Who Is Us?," 63.

18. Robert B. Reich, *The Work of Nations: Preparing Ourselves for 21th-Century Capitalism* (New York: Knopf, 1991), 95.

19. Reich, "Who Is Us?," 54–55.

20. *Ibid.*, 55.

21. Leslie Cauley, "IBM to Cut 25,000 Jobs in '93," *USA Today*, 16 December 1992: 1, 4B.

22. Kevin McKenzie, "Sharp Starts Third Shelby Plant," The *Commercial Appeal*, 19 January 1992: C1, C14.

23. Laurel Campbell, "Nissan Rolling to Future on Smyrna Expansion," The *Commercial Appeal*, 12 January 1992:1, 14–15.

24. Reich, "Who Is Us?," 59.

25. *Ibid.*, 58

26. Alexander, *Friends*, 151.

27. Jerry Buckley, "We Learned That Them May Be Us," *U.S. News & World Report*, 9 May 1988: 48.

28. Alexander, *Friends*, 152.

29. Yoshihara, "The Bright and the Dark Sides of Japanese Management Overseas," 23.

30. Sara Collins, Don L. Boroughs, David Hage, Kenneth T. Walsh, Warren Cohen, and Katherine T. Beddingfield, "How the States Stack Up," *U.S. News & World Report*, 14 September 1992: 62–66.

31. *Ibid.*, 63.

32. Alexander, *Friends*, 18.

33. Stratford P. Sherman, "Japan's Influence on American Life," *Fortune*, 17 June 1991: 115–24.

34. *Ibid.*, 118

35. William McWhirter, "I Came, I Saw, I Blundered: For Bosses from Abroad, the U.S. is Tougher Than It Looks," *TIME*, 9 October 1989, 72.

36. Yoshihara, "The Bright and the Dark Sides of Japanese Management Overseas," 23–24.

37. Robert B. Reich, and Eric D. Mankin, "Joint Ventures with Japan Give Away Our Future," *Harvard Business Review* (March–April 1986): 78–79.

38. Catherine Breslin, "Working for the Japanese: Is the Yen Invasion Bringing New Opportunities for Women or Creating a Class of Office Geishas?" *Ms. Magazine*, February 1988: 28.

39. Laurel Campbell, "Investment, Enthusiasm Bond Nissan, Tennesseans," The *Commercial Appeal*, 12 January 1992: A15.

40. Gelsanliter, *Jump Start*, 106–7.

41. *Ibid.*, 190.

42. The wages paid by GM's Saturn are better than those of Nissan, although both plants are located in almost identical small towns in Tennessee. In 1992, Nissan's base pay ranged from $11.60 to $15.59 an hour, while Saturn's wages ranged from $15.57 to $17.91 an hour. Nissan, however, guarantees employees a bonus of $1.55 per hour worked. That averages about $3,224 in a typical year. Bonuses are paid the day before Thanksgiving and just before the two-week plant shutdown in June. Three years ago, Nissan added a "success sharing" bonus that is based on quality-control and cost-control calculations, and amounts to a percentage of the regular bonus. This extra bonus in November 1991 ranged from 10 percent to a high of 16.8 percent (see Laurel Campbell, "Investment Enthusiasm Bond Nissan, Tennesseans," The *Commercial Appeal*, 12 January 1992: A14).

43. Jerry Buckley, "We Learned That Them May Be Us," *U.S. News & World Report*, 9 May 1988: 50.

44. Kingsolver, "Tobacco, Textile, and Toyota," 191–205.

45. Thomas F. O'Boyle, "Toyota Plant Remolds Small U.S. Town," *Asian Wall Street Journal*, 28 November 1991: 11.

46. Laura Campbell, "Investment, Enthusiasm Bond Nissan, Tennesseans," The *Commercial Appeal*, 12 January 1992: A14. According to the 1990 Census, the unemployment rate in Rutherford County, Tennessee, which includes Smyrna, was 4.7 percent, while the state of Tennessee average was 6.4 percent (see U.S. Bureau of the Census, *1990 Census of Population and Housing: Summary Social, Economic, and Housing Characteristics Tennessee* (Washington, DC: U.S. Department of Commerce, 1992), 45–71.

47. John Greenwald, "Surprise! Detroit is Winning Back Market Share from the Japanese, and Making Money to Boot," *TIME*, 26 July 1993: 51.

48. Michael E. Porter, "The Competitive Advantage of Nations," *Harvard Business Review* (March-April 1990): 74. See also *idem, The Competitive Advantage of Nations* (New York: Free Press, 1990).

49. *Ibid.*, 75.

50. *Annual Statistical Report* (Chicago: National Association of Suggestion Systems, 1991), vii.

51. *Ibid.*

CHAPTER 6
THE ETHNOGRAPHER'S VIEW OF JAPANESE INDUSTRY IN THE SOUTH

1. Beginning in 1994, visitors are allowed to taste the whiskey on the premises of the distillery.

2. Edward S. Mason, et al., *The Economic and Social Modernization of the Republic of Korea* (Cambridge: Council on East Asian Studies, Harvard Univ., 1980), 16.

3. Robert O'Brian, "Selective Dispersion as a Factor in the Solution of the Nisei Problem," *Social Forces* 23 (1944): 140–47.

4. It was reported that Nissan in Tennessee has made generous contributions to a number of local and state projects:

It contributed $250,000 to health, civic, and cultural projects in the state, $35,000 for a new county ambulance, and $10,000 to a new $1 million recreational complex in Rutherford County. It has also contributed cherry trees to an art museum in Nashville; cosponsored, with Middle Tennessee State Univ. and the Murfreesboro Little Theater, an Artists Residency program for Rutherford and surrounding counties; and cosponsored with the Japan Center of Tennessee an art and flower show at a city museum. Finally, it sponsored an automaker new car show in Nashville, a first in the area. (Robert Perrucci, *Japanese Auto Transplants in the Heartland: Corporatism and Community* [New York: de Gruyter, 1994], 143).

5. Perrucci has documented detailed accounts about the roles of regional and local newspapers (*Ibid.*, 77–103).

6. Christian Berggren has written of the disadvantages of Japanese industrial organizations such as the spread and intensity of work, the expansion of work time, potential physical and mental health risks, and the hegemonic nature of the factory regime. See Christian Berggren, *Alternatives to Lean Production* (Ithaca, NY, Industrial and Labor Relations Press, 1992).

7. Perrucci, *Japanese Auto Transplants in the Heartland*, 108.

8. Gelsanliter, *Jump Start*, 66.

9. Perrucci, *Japanese Auto Transplants in the Heartland*, 115.

10. Indirect quotation, *Ibid.*, 118.

11. *Ibid.*, 123.

12. Danny Katayama, "What Price Growth?" The *Jackson Sun,* 11 September 1994: 11A.

13. *Ibid.,* 155. See the original in James G. Houghland,"Community-Industry Accommodation: The Case of Toyota in Central Kentucky," paper presented at the annual meeting of the North Central Sociological Association, Toledo, Ohio, 1993).

14. Johnson, *The Japanese Through American Eyes*, 142.

15. Stratford P. Sherman, "Japan's Influence on American Life," *Fortune*, 17 June 1991: 116.

16. David Friedman, *The Misunderstood Miracle: Industrial Development and Political Change in Japan* (Ithaca, NY: Cornell Univ. Press, 1988); Womack, Jones, and Roos, *The Machine That Changed the World*.

17. Micheline Maynard, "GM Plan Tops Survey for Quality," *USA Today*, 5 June 1992: 1B.

18. *Ibid.*, 12.

19. Michael V. Angrosino, "The Culture Concept and the Mission of the Roman Catholic Church," *American Anthropologist* 96 (1994): 824–32. See also Susan Wright, ed., *Anthropology of Organizations* (London: Routledge, 1994).

20. Wright, *Anthropology of Organizations*, 2; See also Terrence E. Deal and Allan A. Kennedy, *Corporate Cultures* (Reading, MA: Addison-Wesley, 1982).

21. Indeed, cultural determinism can lead to "a gross distortion of what actually happened" (Cole, *Japanese Blue Collar*, 11).

22. Geertz, *The Interpretation of Cultures*, 21.

23. Miles Richardson, "Anthropologist—The Myth Teller," *American Ethnologist* 2 (1975): 530.

BIBLIOGRAPHY

Daily, weekly, and monthly newspapers and magazines are not included. Following the customary practice of East Asians and contrary to American usage, I give the family names of people first in the bibliography list without placing a comma before their personal names when their publications are in their native language.

Abegglen, James C. 1958. *The Japanese Factory: Aspects of Its Social Organization*. Glencoe, IL: Free Press..

Abbott, Carl. 1979. "American Sunbelt: Idea and Region." *Journal of the West* 18 (July): 5–8.

Abo, Tetsuo. 1989. "The Emergence of Japanese Multinational Enterprises and the Theory of Foreign Direct Investment." In *Japanese and European Management: Their International Adaptability*. Ed. by Kazuo Shibagaki, Malcolm Trevor, and Tetsuo Abo, 3–17. Tokyo: Univ. of Tokyo Press.

Adcock, George. 1975. "Is International Status Taking the South by Surprise?" *South* 2 (July/August): 31–41

Aguayo, Rafael. 1990. *Dr. Deming: The American Who Taught the Japanese about Quality*. Secaucus, NJ: Carol Publishing.

Alexander, Lamar. 1981. *The Tennesseans: A People and Their Land*. Nashville: Thomas Nelson.

———. 1986. *Friends: Japanese and Tennesseans*. New York: Kodansha International.

Almond, Gabriel A. 1967. *The American People and Foreign Policy*. New York: Praeger.

Angrosino, Michael V. 1994. "The Culture Concept and the Mission of the Roman Catholic Church." *American Anthropologist* 96: 824–32.

Annual Statistical Report. 1991. Chicago: National Association of Suggestion Systems.

Arpan, Jeffery. 1981. "The Impact of State Incentives on Foreign Investors' Site Selections." *Economic Review* 66: 36–42.

Arpan, Jeffery S., and David A. Ricks. 1975. *Directory of Foreign Manufacturers in the United States*. Atlanta. Georgia State Univ. Business Press.

———. 1990. *Directory of Foreign Manufacturers in the United States*. Atlanta. Georgia State Univ. Business Press.

Baba, Marietta L. 1986. *Business and Industrial Anthropology: An Overview*. NAPA Bulletin, no. 2. Washington, DC: American Anthropological Association.

Baker, Christopher. 1981. "Economic Reorganization and the Slump in South and South-East Asia." *Contemporary Studies in Society and History* 23: 325–49.

Barry, Herbert, III, Irvine L. Child, and Margaret K. Bacon. 1959. "Relation of Child Training to Subsistence Economy." *American Anthropologist* 61: 51–63.

Befu, Harumi. 1971. *Japan: An Anthroppological Introduction*. New York: Thomas Y. Crowell.

Benedict, Ruth. 1946. *The Chrysanthemum and the Sword*. New York: Houghton Mifflin.

Berggren, Christian. 1992. *Alternatives to Lean Production*. Ithaca, NY: Industrial and Labor Relations Press.

Bertelson, David. 1967. *The Lazy South*. New York: Oxford Univ. Press.

Billington, Monroe L., ed. 1969. *The South. A Central Theme?* New York: Holt, Rinehart and Winston.

Blair, J.P., and R. Premus. 1987. "Major Factors in Industrial Location. A Review." *Economic Development Quarterly* 1: 72–85.

Booth, David. 1984. "Marxism and Development Sociology: Interpreting the Impasse." *World Development* 13: 761–87.

Burd, Gene. 1977. "The Selling of the Sunbelt: Civic Boosterism in the Media." *Urban Affairs Annual Review* 14. 129–49.

Bureau of the Census. *1990 Census of Summary Population and Housing Characteristics*. Washington, DC: U.S. Department of Commerce.

Bureau of Economic Analysis. 1991. *Foreign Direct Investment in the United States: Operations of U.S. Affiliates of Foreign Companies*. Preliminary 1989 Estimates. Washington, DC: U.S. Department of Commerce.

Calzonetti, F.J., and Robert T. Walker. 1991. "Factors Affecting Industrial Location Decisions: A Survey Approach." In *Industry Location and Public Policy*, Henry W. Herzog, Jr., and Alan M. Schlottmann, eds., 221–40. Knoxville: Univ. of Tennessee Press.

Campbell, John C.. 1921. *The Southern Highlander and His Homeland*. New York: Russell Sage Foundation.

Carrier, Ronald E., and William Schriver. 1969. "Plant Location Studies: An Appraisal." *Southwestern Social Science Quarterly* 47. 136–40.

Carter, Hodding. 1950. *Southern Legacy*. Baton Rouge. Louisiana State Univ. Press.

Cash, W.T. 1941. *The Mind of the South*. New York: Knopf.

Childs, Bill. 1989. "New United Motor: An American Success Story." *Labor Law Journal*, (August): 453–64.

Cobb, James C. 1982. *The Selling of the South: The Southern Crusade for Industrial Development, 1936–1980*. Baton Rouge: Louisiana State Univ. Press.

———. 1984. *Industrialization and Southern Society, 1877–1984*. Lexington, KY: Univ. Press of Kentucky.

Colclough, Glenna. 1988. "Uneven Development and Racial Composition in the Deep South, 1970–1980." *Rural Sociology* 53. 73–86.

Cole, Robert E. 1971. *Japanese Blue Collar. The Changing Tradition*. Berkeley: Univ. of California Press.

———. 1989. *Strategies for Learning. Small-Group Activities in American, Japanese, and Swedish Industry*. Berkeley: Univ. of California Press.

Corlew, Robert E. 1981. *Tennessee: A Short History*. Knoxville: Univ. of Tennessee Press.

Couch, W.T., ed. 1935. *Culture in the South*. Chapel Hill. Univ. of North Carolina Press.

Cusumano, Michael A. 1985. *The Japanese Automobile Industry: Technology and Management at Nissan and Toyota*. Cambridge: The Council on East Asian Studies, Harvard Univ.

Davis, Allison, B. Gardner, and M. Gardner. 1941. *Deep South*. Chicago: Univ. of Chicago Press.

Deal, Terrence E., and Allan A. Kennedy. 1982. *Corporate Cultures*. Reading, MA: Addison–Wesley.

Dolan, Ronald E., and Robert L. Worden, eds. 1992. *Japan: A Country Study*. Area Handbook Series. Washington, DC: Federal Research Division, Library of Congress.

Dollard, John. 1937. *Class and Caste in a Southern Town*. New Haven: Yale Univ. Press.

Dore, Ronald. 1987. *Taking Japan Seriously: A Confucian Perspective on Leading Economic Issues*. Stanford: Stanford Univ. Press.

Duvall, Richard A.. 1986. "Industry, State Rate Incentive, Assistance Programs." *Industrial Development* 37: 26–30.

Egerton, John. 1974. *Americanization of Dixie: The Southernization of America*. New York: Harper.

Evans–Pritchard, E.E. 1962. *Social Anthropology and Other Essays*. New York: Free Press.

Fallows, James. 1989. *More Like Us: Making America Great Again*. Boston: Houghton Mifflin.

Fernandez, James W. 1982. *Bwiti: An Ethnography of the Religious Imagination in Africa*. Princeton: Princeton Univ. Press.

Ferraro, Gary P. 1994. *The Cultural Dimension of International Business*. 2d ed. Englewood Cliffs, NJ: Prentice–Hall.

Fink, Gary M., and Merl Reed, eds. 1977. *Essays in Southern Labor History: Selected Papers, Southern Labor History Conference, 1976*. Westport, Conn.:Greenwood.

Fink, Gary M., Merl Reed, and Leslie Hough, eds. 1981. *Southern Workers and Their Union*. Westport, CT: Greenwood.

Florida, Richard, and Martin Kenney. 1991. "Transplanted Organizations: The Transfer of Japanese Industrial Organization to the U.S." *American Sociological Review* 56: 381–98.

Friedman, David. 1988. *The Misunderstood Miracle: Industrial Development and Political Change in Japan*. Ithaca, NY: Cornell Univ. Press.

Friedman, George, and Meredith LeBard. 1991. *The Coming War with Japan*. New York: St. Martin's.

Fuchs, V. 1962. *Changes in the Location Manufacturing in the U.S. Since 1929*. New Haven: Yale Univ. Press.

Fullerton, Ralph O. and John B. Ray, eds. 1977.

Tennessee: Geographical Patterns and Regions. Dubuque, IA: Kendall/Hunt.

Gabor, Andrea. 1990. *The Man Who Discovered Quality: How W. Edwards Deming Brought the Quality Revolution to America: The Stories of Ford, Xerox, and GM.* New York: Times Books.

Gall, Gilbert J. 1991. "Southern Industrial Workers and Anti–Union Sentiment." In *Organized Labor in the Twentieth–Century South*, edited by Robert H. Ziger, Knoxville: Univ. of Tennessee Press.

Garvin, D.A. 1988. *Managing Quality. The Strategic and Competitive Edge.* New York: Free Press.

Geertz, Clifford. 1973. *The Interpretation of Cultures: Selected Essays.* New York: Basic Books.

Gelsanliter, David. 1990. *Jump Start: Japan Comes to the Heartland.* New York: Farrar, Straus & Giroux.

Gershenkron, Alexander. 1962. *Economic Backwardness in Historical Perspective.* Cambridge: Harvard Univ. Press.

———. 1968. *Continuity in History and Other Essays.* Cambridge: Harvard Univ. Press.

Hackney, Shelton. 1969. "Southern Violence." *American Historical Review* 74: 906–925.

Halberstam, David. 1986. *The Reckoning.* New York: William Morrow.

Hall, Edward T. 1959. *The Silent Language.* Garden City, NY: Doubleday.

Hamilton, Gary G., and Narco Orru. 1989. "Organizational Structure of East Asian Companies." In *Korean Managerial Dynamics*, ed. Kae H. Chung and Hak Chong Lee, 39–47. New York: Praeger.

Hattori, Tamio. 1989. "Japanese Zaibatsu and Korean Chaebol." In *Korean Managerial Dynamics*, ed. by Kae H. Chung and Hak Chong Lee, 79–95. New York: Praeger.

Hays, R.D. 1974. "Expatriate Selection: Insuring Success and Avoiding Failure." *Journal of International Business Studies* 5: 25–37.

Heberle, Rudolf. 1943. "Regionalism: Some Critical Observations." *Social Forces* 21: 280–86.

Hess, Alfred O. 1965. *The Southerner and World Affairs.* Baton Rouge: Louisiana State Univ. Press.

Hill, Carole E. 1977. "Anthropological Studies in the American South: Review and Directions." *Current Anthropology* 18. 309–26.

Holzberg, Carol S., and Maureen J. Giovan-nini. 1981. "Anthropology and Industry: Reappraisal and New Directions." *Annual Review of Anthropology* 10: 317–60.

Hopkins, Ernest J. 1944. *Mississippi's BAWI Plan: Balance Agriculture with Industry.* Atlanta: Federal Reserve Bank of Atlanta.

Houghland, James G. 1993. "Community–Industry Accommodation: The Case of Toyota in Central Kentucky." Paper presented at the annual meeting of the North Central Sociological Association, Toledo, Ohio.

Hsu, Francis L.K. 1970. *Americans and Chinese: Purpose and Fulfillment in Great Civilizations.* Garden City, NY: The Natural History Press.

———. 1977. "Intercultural Understanding: Genuine and Spurious." *Anthropology & Education Quarterly* 8: 202–209.

———. 1983. *Rugged Individualism Reconsidered: Essays in Psychological Anthropology.* Knoxville: Univ. of Tennessee Press.

Hunter, David E., and Phillip Whitten, eds. 1976. *Encyclopedia of Anthropology.* New York: Harper & Row.

Imai, Masaaki. 1986. *Kaizen (Ky'zen): The Key to Japan's Competitive Success.* New York: McGraw Hill.

Ishihara Shintaro and Morita Akio. 1989. *"No" to Ieru Nihon* [The Japan that can say no]. Tokyo: Kobunsha.

Itagaki, Hiroshi. 1989. "Application-Adaption Problems in Japanese Automobile and Electronic Plants in the USA." In *Japanese and European Management: Their International Adaptability*, ed. by Kazuno Shibagaki, Malcolm Trevor, and Tetsuo Abo, 118–31. Tokyo: Univ. of Tokyo Press.

Jackall, Robert. 1988. *Moral Mazes: The World of Corporate Managers.* New York: Oxford Univ. Press.

Janelli, Roger L., and Dawnhee Yim. 1993. *Making Capitalism: The Social and Cultural Construction of a South Korean Conglomerate.* Stanford: Stanford Univ. Press.

Johnson, Sheila K. 1988. *The Japanese Through American Eyes.* Stanford: Stanford Univ. Press.

Kassalow, Everett M. 1983. "Japan as an Industrial Relations Model." *Journal of Industrial Relations* 258: 201–219.

Key, Valdimer O. 1949. *Southern Politics in State and Nation.* New York: Knopf.

Keyes, Charles F. 1983. "Peasant Strategies in Asian Societies. Moral and Rational Economic Approaches—A Symposium. *"Journal of Asian Studies* 42. 753–68.

Killian, Lewis M. 1970. *White Southerners.* New York: Random House.

Kim, Choong Soon. 1972. "Life Patterns of Pulpwood Workers in a South Georgia Community." Ph.D. diss., Univ. of Georgia.

———. 1977. *An Asian Anthropologist in the South: Field Experiences with Blacks, Indians, and Whites.* Knoxville: Univ. of Tennessee Press.

———. 1987. "Can an Anthropologist Go Home Again?" *American Anthropologist* 89: 943–45.

———. 1988. *Faithful Endurance: An Ethnography of Korean Family Dispersal.* Tucson. Univ. of Arizona Press.

———. 1990. "The Role of Non–Western Anthropologist Reconsidered: Illusion versus Reality." *Current Anthropology* 31: 196–201.

———. 1992. *The Culture of Korean Industry: An Ethnography of Poongsan Corporation.* Tucson. Univ. of Arizona Press.

Kim, Choong Soon, and Wilfrid C. Bailey. 1971. *Community Factors in Productivity of Pulpwood Harvesting Operations.* Atlanta: American Pulpwood Association Harvesting Research Project.

King, Larry L. 1976. "We Ain't Trash No More." *Esquire* 126 (November): 89–90, 152–56.

Kingsolver, Ann E. 1992. "Tobacco, Textiles, and Toyota: Working for Multinational Corporations in Rural Kentucky." In *Anthropology and the Global Factory: Studies of the New Industrialization in the Late Twentieth Century,* ed. Frances Abrahamer Rothstein and Michael L. Blim, 191–205. New York: Bergin & Garvey.

Kirby, Jack Temple. 1978. *Media–Made Dixie.* Baton Rouge: Louisiana State Univ. Press.

Komiya, Ryutaro, and Ryuhei Wakasugi. 1991. "Japan's Foreign Direct Investment." *The Annals of the American Academy of Political and Social Science* 513 (January): 48–60.

Lee, Changsoo and George DeVos. 1981. *Koreans in Japan: Ethnic Conflict and Accommodation.* Berkeley: Univ. of California Press.

Levine, Solomon B., and Makoto Ohtsu. 1991. "Transplanting Japanese Labor Relations." *The Annals of the American Academy of Political and Social Science* 513 (January): 102–116.

Lincoln, James R., and Kerry McBride. 1987. "Japanese Organization in Contemporary

Perspective." *Annual Review of Sociology* 13: 289–312.

Linstead, S., and R. Grafton–Small. 1992. "On Reading Organizational Culture." *Organization Studies* 13: 331–55.

Linton, Ralph. 1937. "One Hundred Per Cent American." *The American Mercury* 40: 427–29.

Little, Jane Sneddon. 1978. "Location Decisions of Foreign Investors in the United States." *New England Economic Review.* (July/August): 43–63.

McGee, Harold Franklin, Jr. 1977. "Comments" on: "Anthropological Studies in the American South" by Carole E. Hill. *Current Anthropology* 18: 318–19.

McGehee, Larry T. 1989. "Anthropologists Can Weep." *Fulton Daily Leader,* 20 February 1989: 2.

McGill, Ralph. 1964. *The South and the Southerner.* Boston: Little, Brown.

McLaughlin, Glenn E., and Stefan Robock. 1949. *Why Industry Moves South: A Study of Factors Influencing the Recent Location of Manufacturing Plants in the South.* NPA Committee of the South Report III. Kingsport, TN: Kingsport.

Marshall, F. Ray. 1976. *Labor in the South.* Cambridge: Harvard Univ. Press.

Maruyama, Magoroh. 1969. Epistemology of Social Science Research: Explorations Inculture Researchers. *Dialectica* 23. 229–80.

Mason, Edward S., Mahn Je Kim, Dwight H. Perkins, Kwang Suk Kim, and David C. Cole, 1980. *The Economic and Social Modernization of the Republic of Korea.* Cambridge: Council on East Asian Studies, Harvard Univ.

Mencken, H.L. 1949. *A Mencken Chrestomathy.* New York: Knopf.

Miller, William Lee. 1978. *Yankee from Georgia: The Emergence of Jimmy Carter.* New York: Times Books.

Ministry of Education, Science, and Culture. 1982. *Education in Japan. A Graphic Presentation.* Tokyo: The Ministry.

———. 1983. *Course of Study for Elementary Schools in Japan.* Tokyo: Monbusho.

Moore, Larry. 1992. *Improving Workforce Basic Skills: The Foundation for Quality.* New York: Quality Resources.

Morgan, William E. 1967. *Taxes and the Location Industry.* Boulder: Univ. of Colorado Press.

Murphy, Edgar G. 1904. *Problems, and Political Issues in the Southern States.* New York: Macmillan.

Murphy, Reg. 1976. "The South as the New America." *Saturday Review*, 4 September 1976. 8–11.

Myrdal, Gunnar. 1944. *An American Dilemma: The Negro Problem and Modern Democracy*. New York: Harper & Row.

Nicholls, William H. 1960. *Southern Tradition and Regional Progress*. Chapel Hill: Univ. of North Carolina Press.

Oberg, Kalervo. 1960. "Culture Shock: Adjustments to New Cultural Environments." *Practical Anthropology* (July–August): 177–82.

O'Brian, Robert. 1944. "Selective Dispersion as a Fact in the Solution of the Nisei Problem." *Social Forces* 23: 140–47.

Odum, Howard W. 1936. *Southern Regions of the United States*. Chapel Hill: Univ. of North Carolina Press.

———. 1947. *The Way of the South*. New York: Macmillan.

Ohtsu, Makoto, and Hem C. Jain. 1983. *Viability of the Japanese Industrial Relations System in the International Context: The Case of Canadian-Management Report*. Working Paper Series, no. 83–02. Saskatoon, Canada: College of Commerce, Univ. of Saskatchewan.

Okimoto, Daniel I., and Thomas P. Rohlen, eds. 1988. *Inside the Japanese System: Readings on Contemporary Society and Political Economy*. Stanford: Stanford Univ. Press.

Okita, Saburo. 1991. "Japan's Role in Asia–Pacific Cooperation." *The Annals of the American Academy of Political and Social Science* 513 (January): 25–37.

Ouchi, William G. 1981. *Theory Z: How American Business Can Meet the Japanese Challenge*. Reading, MA: Addison-Wesley.

Peacock, James L. 1986. *The Anthropological Lens: Harsh Light, Soft Focus*. New York: Cambridge Univ. Press.

Perrucci, Robert. 1994. *Japanese Auto Transplants in the Heartland: Corporatism and Community*. New York: de Gruyter.

Phillips, Kevin P. 1969. *The Emerging Republican Majority*. New Rochelle, NY: Arlington House.

Phillips, Ulrich B. 1928. "The Central Theme of Southern History." *American Historical Review* 34: 30–43.

———. 1929. *Life and Labor in the Old South*. Boston: Little, Brown.

Plaut, T.R., and J.E. Pluta. 1983. "Business Climate, Taxes and Expenditures and State Industrial Growth in the U.S." *Southern Economic Journal* 50. 99–119.

Porter, Michael E. 1990. "The Competitive Advantage of Nations." *Harvard Business Review* (March–April): 73–93.

———. 1990. *The Competitive Advantage of Nations*. New York: Free Press.

Powdermaker, Hotense. 1939. *After Freedom: A Cultural Study of the Deep South*. New York: Viking.

Ramsdell, Charles. 1934. "The Southern Heritage." In *Culture in the South*, ed. W.T. Couch, 1–23. Chapel Hill: Univ. of North Carolina Press.

Ransom, John C., et al. 1930. *I'll Take My Stand: The South and the Agrarian Tradition*. New York: Harper.

Redfield, Robert. 1947. "The Folk Society." *American Journal of Sociology* 52. 293–308.

Reed, John Shelton. 1972. *The Enduring South: Subcultural Persistence in Mass Society*. Chapel Hill: Univ. of North Carolina Press.

———. 1982. *One South: An Ethnic Approach to Regional Culture*. Baton Rouge: Louisiana State Univ. Press.

———. 1986. *Southern Folk, Plain & Fancy*. Athens: Univ. of Georgia Press.

Reich, Robert B. 1990. "Who Is Us?" *Harvard Business Review* (January–February): 53–64.

———. 1991. *The Work of Nations: Preparing Our-selves for 21st–Century Capitalism*. New York: Knopf.

Reich, Robert B., and Eric D. Mankin. 1986. "Joint Ventures with Japan Give Away Our Future." *Harvard Business Review* (March–April): 78–86.

Richardson, Miles. 1975. "Anthropologist—The Myth Teller." *American Ethnologist* 2: 517–33.

———. 1977. "Comments" on: "Anthropological Studies in the American South" by Carole E. Hill. *Current Anthropology* 18: 321.

Rohlen, Thomas P. 1974. *For Harmony and Strength: Japanese White–Collar Organization in Anthropological Perspective*. Berkeley. Univ. of California Press.

———. 1983. *Japan's High Schools*. Berkeley: Univ. of California Press.

Ronald, Charles P. 1975. *The Improbable Era: The South Since World War II*. Lexington: Univ. Press of Kentucky.

Rosenfeld, Stuart A., Edward M. Bergman, and Sarah Rueben. 1985. *After the Factories: Changing Employment Patterns in the Rural South*. Research Triangle Park, NC: Southern Growth Policies Board.

Sahlins, Marshall D., and Elman R. Service.

1960. *Evolution and Culture*. Ann Arbor: Univ. of Michigan Press.

Sale, Kirkpatrick. 1975. *Power Shift: The Rise of the Southern Rim and Its Challenge to the Eastern Establishment*. New York: Random House.

Salmans, Sandra. 1979. "Industry Learns to Speak the Same Language." *International Management* (April): 45–7.

Schmenner, Roger W. 1991. "Geography and the Character and Performance of Factories." In *Industry Location and Public Policy*, edited by Henry W. Herzog, Jr. and Alan M. Schlottmann, 241–53. Knoxville: Univ. of Tennessee Press.

Schor, Juliet B. 1991. *The Overworked American: The Unexpected Decline of Leisure*. New York: Basic Books.

Shibagaki, Kazuo. 1989. "Introduction." In *Japanese and European Management: Their International Adaptability*, ed. Kazuo Shibagaki, Malcolm Trevor, and Tetsuo Abo, ix–xii. Tokyo: Univ. of Tokyo Press.

Shinohara, Miyohei. 1991. "Japan as a World Economic Power." *The Annals of the American Academy of Political and Social Science* 51 (January): 12–24.

Sumiya, Mikio. 1991. "Japan: Model Society for the Future?" *The Annals of the American Academy of Political and Social Science* 513 (January): 139–50.

Taira, Koji. 1962. "Characteristics of Japanese Labor Markets." *Economic Development and Cultural Change* 10: 150–68.

———. 1991. "Japan, an Imminent Hegemon?" *The Annals of the American Academy of Political and Social Science* 513(January): 151–63.

Tate, Allen, ed. 1947. *A Southern Vanguard*. New York: Prentice–Hall.

The World Book Encyclopedia. 1975. Chicago: Field Enterprises Educational Corporation, vol. 5.

Thompson, Edgar T. 1965. "The South in Old and New Contexts." In *South in Continuity and Change*, ed. John McKinney and Edgar T. Thompson, 451–80. Durham, NC: Duke Univ. Press.

Timberlake, Michael, Darryl Tukufu, and Bonnie Thornton Dill. 1989. "Race and Poverty in the Rural South: Racial Composition and Economic Development." Paper presented at the annual meeting of the American Sociological Association, August 1989, San Francisco.

Tindall, George B. 1967. *The Emergence of the New South, 1913–1945*. Baton Rouge: Louisiana State Univ. Press.

———. 1976. *The Ethnic Southerners*. Baton Rouge: Louisiana State Univ. Press.

Tolchin, Martin, and Susan Tolchin. 1989. *Buying into America: How Foreign Money is Changing the Face of Our Nation*. New York: Berkeley.

Trevor, Malcolm. 1991. "The Overseas Strategies of Japanese Corporations." *The Annals of the American Academy of Political and Social Science* 513 (January): 90–101.

Trotsky, Leon. n.d. *The History of the Russian Revolution*. Ann Arbor: Univ. of Michigan Press.

Tung, Rosalie L. 1981. "Selection and Training of Personnel for Overseas Assignments." *Columbia Journal of World Business* (Spring): 68–78.

Tylor, Edward. 1958. *Primitive Culture*. Vol. 1. New York: Harper & Row. (Originally published London: J. Murray 1871.)

U.S. Bureau of the Census. 1992. *1990 Census of Population and Housing: Summary Population and Housing Characteristics Tennessee*. Washington, DC: U.S. Department of Commerce.

———. 1992. *1990 Census of Population and Housing: Summary Social, Economic, and Housing Characteristics Tennessee*. Washington, DC: U.S. Department of Commerce.

U.S. Commission on Civil Rights. 1992. *Civil Rights Issues Facing Asian Americans in the 1990s*. Washington, DC: The U.S. Commission on Civil Rights.

U.S. Department of Commerce. 1994. *Foreign Direct Investment in the United States: Operations of U.S. Affiliates of Foreign Companies*. Revised 1991 Estimates. Washington, DC: U.S. Department of Commerce.

U.S. Department of Education. 1987. *Japanese Education Today*. Washington, DC: U.S. Government Printing Office.

Vance, Rupert B. 1929. *Human Factors in Cotton Culture*. Chapel Hill: Univ. of North Carolina Press.

———. 1941. *The South's Place in the Nation*. New York: Public Affairs Committee.

Vance, Rupert, John E. Ivey, Jr., and Marjorie N. Bond. 1949. *Exploring the South*. Chapel Hill: Univ. of North Carolina Press.

Veblen, Thorstein. 1915. *Imperial Germany and the Industrial Revolution*. New York: Macmillan.

Vogel, Ezra F. 1979. *Japan as Number One:*

Lessons for America. New York: Harper Colophon.

Wax, Rosalie H. 1971. *Doing Fieldwork: Warnings and Advice.* Chicago: Univ. of Chicago Press.

Webster's New World Dictionary of American English. 1988. 3rd ed. New York: Simon & Schuster.

Wellin, Edward. 1978. "Review" of: *An Asian Anthropologist in the South* by Choong Soon Kim. *Rural Sociology* 43: 312–14.

Welty, Paul Thomas. 1984. *The Asians: Their Evolving Heritage.* New York: Harper & Row.

Wheat, Leonard F. 1986. "The Determinants of 1963–77 Regional Manufacturing Growth: Why the South and West Grow." *Journal of Regional Science* 26. 635–60.

White, Merry. 1992. *The Japanese Overseas: Can They Go Home Again?* Princeton: Princeton Univ. Press.

Williams, Bruce B. 1987. *Black Workers in an Industrial Suburb: The Struggle Against Discrimination.* New Brunswick, NJ: Rutgers Univ. Press.

Willigen, van John, and Richard Stoffle. 1986. "The Americanization of Shoyu. American Workers and a Japanese Employment System." In *Anthropology and International Business,* ed. H. Serrie, 125–62. *Studies in Third World Societies,* publication no. 28. Williamsburg, VA: Dep. of Anthropology, College of William and Mary.

Womack, James P., Daniel T. Jones, and Daniel Roos. 1990. *The Machine That Changed the World.* New York: Rawson Assoc.

Wong, Eugene Franklin. 1978. *On Visual Media Racism: Asians in the American Motion Pictures.* New York: Arno.

Woodward, C. Vann. 1951. *Origins of the New South, 1877–1913.* Baton Rouge: Louisiana State Univ. Press.

———. 1957. *The Strange Career of Jim Crow.* New York: Oxford Univ. Press.

———. 1960. *The Burden of Southern History.* Baton Rouge: Louisiana State Univ. Press.

Woodward, Douglas P., and Norman J. Glickman. 1991. "Regional and Local Determinants of Foreign Firm Location in the United States." In *Industry Location and Public Policy,* ed. Henry W. Herzog, Jr., and Alan M. Schlottman, 190–216. Knoxville: Univ. of Tennessee Press.

World Almanac. 1992. *The World Almanac and Book of Facts.* New York: World Almanac.

World Book Encyclopedia, vol. 5. 1975. Chicago: Field Enterprises.

Wright, Gavin. 1986. *Old South, New South: Revolutions in the Southern Economy Since the Civil War.* New York: Basic Books.

Wright, Susan, ed. 1994. *Anthropology of Organizations.* London: Routledge.

Yi Ŏ–yŏng. 1986. *Ch'ŭkso Chihyang–ŭi Ilbon–in* [Japanese ethos toward miniaturization]. Seoul: Kirin–wŏn.

Yoshida, Mitsukuni, Ikko Tanaka, and Tsune Sesoko. 1982. *The Compact Culture: The Ethos of Japanese Life.* Hiroshima: Toyo Kogyo.

Yoshihara, Hideki. 1989. "The Bright and the Dark Sides of Japanese Management Overseas." In *Japanese and European Management: Their International Adaptability,* edited by Kazuo Shibagaki, Malcolm Trevor, and Tetsuo Abo, 18–30. Tokyo: Univ. of Tokyo Press.

Zieger, Robert H. 1991. "Introduction." In *Organized Labor in the Twentieth–Century South,* ed. Robert H. Zieger, 2–12. Knoxville: Univ. of Tennessee Press.

ABOUT THE AUTHOR

Professor Choong Soon Kim holds his B.A. and M.A. from Yonsei University, Seoul, Korea, his M.A. from Emory University, and a Ph.D. from the University of Georgia. He is University Faculty Scholar and Professor of Anthropology at the University of Tennessee at Martin, where he has taught since 1971. From 1981 to 1991, he was chairman of the Department of Sociology and Anthropology. He was Senior Fulbright Researcher at Seoul National University, Seoul, Korea (spring 1989); Visiting Professor at Hirosaki University in Japan (fall 1990); and a Rockefeller Foundation's Scholar-in-Residence at the Bellagio Study Center, Bellagio, northern Italy (spring 1993). He taught business and industrial anthropology at Yonsei University, Seoul, Korea, as Senior Fulbright Scholar (1993–94).

In addition to publishing in various scholarly journals, monographs, and volumes, he is the author of several books, including *The Culture of Korean Industry* (1992), *Faithful Endurance: An Ethnography of Korean Family Dispersal* (1988), and *An Asian Anthropologist in the South: Field Experiences with Blacks, Indians, and Whites* (1977, 1991 2nd printing).

INDEX